One Hundred Summers

ONE HUNDRED SUMMERS

A Family Story

VANESSA BRANSON

MENSCH PUBLISHING

Mensch Publishing
51 Northchurch Road, London N1 4EE, United Kingdom

First published in Great Britain 2020

A catalogue record for this book is available from the British Library

ISBN: HB: 978-1-9129-1414-2; eBook: 978-1-9129-1415-9
Export TPB: 978-1-9129-1416-6

2 4 6 8 10 9 7 5 3 1

Typeset by Newgen KnowledgeWorks Pvt. Ltd., Chennai, India
Printed and bound in Great Britain by CPI Group (UK) Ltd, Croydon CR0 4YY

For Noah, Florence, Louis and Ivo

'If you don't do it, you haven't done it.'

Eve Branson

CONTENTS

CONTENTS

FAMILY TREE (SIMPLIFIED)

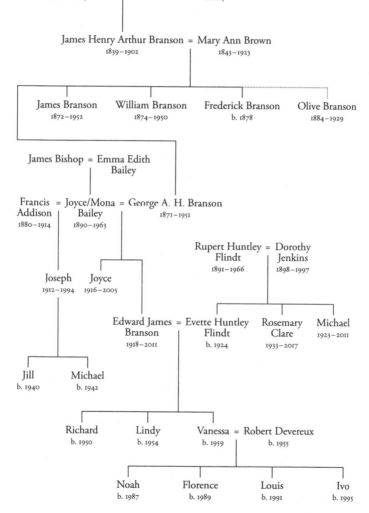

Harry Wilkins Branson = Eliza Cornelia Wilson Wellington Reddy
c. 1800–1863   b. 1817

James Henry Arthur Branson = Mary Ann Brown
1839–1902   1843–1923

James Branson
1872–1952

William Branson
1874–1950

Frederick Branson
b. 1878

Olive Branson
1884–1929

James Bishop = Emma Edith Bailey

Francis Addison
1880–1914
= Joyce/Mona Bailey
1890–1963
= George A. H. Branson
1871–1951

Rupert Huntley Flindt
1891–1966
= Dorothy Jenkins
1898–1997

Joseph
1912–1994

Joyce
1916–2005

Edward James Branson
1918–2011
= Evette Huntley Flindt
b. 1924

Rosemary Clare
1933–2017

Michael
1923–2011

Jill
b. 1940

Michael
b. 1942

Richard
b. 1950

Lindy
b. 1954

Vanessa
b. 1959
= Robert Devereux
b. 1955

Noah
b. 1987

Florence
b. 1989

Louis
b. 1991

Ivo
b. 1995

PROLOGUE

Sri Lanka, 20 January 2017

I'm sitting with my great friend Navin – a keen historian, linguist, thespian and wit – next to a monumental stone Buddha in the Sri Lankan hills. We're contemplating how we got to this point, and where on earth we're going.

Those of us lucky enough to be born in the decades after the Second World War sailed towards the new millennium with innocent, wide-eyed enthusiasm, taking it for granted that the waters ahead would be calm. Improvements in health, human rights and education, together with the decline in conflict and inequality, gave us cause for optimism. We placed our faith in the rule of law, and in diplomacy. Walls were tumbling and bridges were being built. It's true that the dark clouds of climate change were rumbling in the distance, but the storm hadn't yet broken.

But now we're not so sure.

'You've got to laugh,' said Navin, breaking the silence.

'Yes,' I said, shrugging my shoulders and raising my palms to the air in surrender. 'It's frightening though, as if everything our parents and grandparents fought for is being undermined.'

I was already grappling with my own unresolved past and now, approaching my sixties and with the world so unsure of which direction it was taking, I was wondering how on earth to deal with the coming years. We could hear the rumble of bulldozers as they began their day's work, ripping up the rich jungle nearby and transforming it into neat palm oil plantations. Then the words of that wise old Buddha broke into my thoughts.

'To understand where you're going to, you first have to understand where you've come from.'

'I can't just sit here and do nothing, Navin,' I said, opening my laptop. 'I need some sort of anchor, some certainties to grab hold of. I'm going to do some digging into my past.' Navin was silent as I continued, warming to my theme. 'I'm going to delve back, maybe by a century, to see how my family coped, while history tossed them on the wild seas of fortune.'

'Wow, good luck,' he chortled, before opening his own laptop.

'I'll give it a year,' I whisper, somewhat startled by my conviction. 'I like the symmetry of spending one year covering three generations over one hundred years.' I've said it now. There's no going back. My fingers hover over the keys. But where to begin?

'I wonder what your father would have made of the world today?' Navin asks.

I smile as I recall Dad's slow, deep, twinkly, oh-so-English voice. The thought that so much of him is me and that his essence is spiralled through every inch of my being comforts me as I try to channel a little of his ease. I close my eyes and feel his warm chuckle enter my soul.

Part One

1918–1959

1

Sloe Gin

Sussex, 2011

My father was one of the happiest people I've ever known. Not laugh-out-loud happy (although he would often weep with laughter); more a purring, contented sort. His diet consisted of standard English fare: plenty of eggs, white sauces, cheese and sausages, and a slug of Gordon's gin each evening, poured into a cut-glass tumbler as the pips for the six o'clock news rang out from the wireless. Regardless of this, and despite the stresses of work and living with my restless mother Eve, my father discovered the secret to deep contentment.

Nearing the end of his long life, Dad would drive to my Sussex farm to join me for a walk. Achieving this simple task was a complicated affair that involved ingenuity and effort on his behalf and a certain amount of patience on mine. On reflection, although these few walks were just a couple of hours, carved out of odd weekends here and there, they were of monumental significance in my life. They were the only occasions that my father and I spent time together, alone and at peace.

The battered silver BMW that he still proudly drove, aged ninety-two, would crunch up the drive, towing a trailer on which his mobility scooter teetered precariously. It tickled me to note that, for someone who'd rarely been in a grocery store in his life, his scooter was called a 'Happy Shopper'. We would then carefully position two scaffolding planks from the back of the trailer a wheel-width apart and my father, armed with walking sticks and virtually blind, would shuffle up the planks, position himself behind the controls of his beast, turn on the ignition and reverse towards the planks, often after a false start or two as he tried to line the wheels up with the planks. Watching him reverse gingerly down, with a wheel first an inch over one edge and then the other was, quite frankly, terrifying.

'Oh lordy,' he'd whoop, once he was safely on the ground. 'All's well that ends well!'

'Well done, Dad – you've made it. How lovely to see you.' I'd bend down and kiss his cheek while patting his bulky shoulders. 'Any excitements?' I'd ask.

'Darling, I have to tell you, this morning I bagged that old father fox – he'd been wreaking havoc with our chickens. There's nothing quite like the Happy Shopper when it comes to silently creeping up on foxes, armed with my twelve-bore.'

Leaving the front drive, we'd head off around the fields, his electric buggy setting the pace. We were often silent as we settled into each other's moods. I found it hard not to feel moved by the sight of this once-powerful man who was now barely my height, his spine having concertinaed into an agonising rub of bone on bone. He would cheerily explain his widening girth as the consequence of his torso being squeezed outwards as he shrank. The truth had more to do with the fact that, since the war and subsequent rationing, he could not allow a morsel of leftover food to go unfinished. We called him 'the family dustbin', as he would happily exchange his plate for ours with a grin. 'Pity to let this go to waste.'

Over the years, Dad had had numerous melanomas removed from his face and head and as a result always wore a battered old Tilley Hat that he lined with tin foil, having read somewhere that it would radiate the sun's harmful rays away from his bald head. Invariably he wore one of the flamboyant short-sleeved shirts he'd collected on his travels over the years, with khaki shorts and, over the bandages covering his ulcerated shins and swollen ankles, a pair of flesh-coloured surgical stockings to keep the dreaded thrombosis at bay.

I was always excited to show him new developments on the farm and to talk through the ideas we had for the future, such as how I was planting avenues of oak saplings with a view that, in years to come, these walks would be transformed by the dappled shade of mighty trees.

'Well, Nessie, this is just wonderful,' he said. And then, with a gleeful chuckle, 'I've never had the land to plant trees myself, but then I suppose I planted you and you've planted them for me, so I can take a little bit of the credit!'

I'd mown a grassy path around the perimeter of the fields that was wide enough for the two of us to make our steady progress.

'How're you feeling, Daddy? Any new ailments?' I'd nervously ask.

I shouldn't have worried as he would inevitably reply, 'Ah darling, I can't complain. If I start to tell you what hurts I wouldn't stop, and we don't want to waste a good walk, do we?'

'Do you ever get bored at home?' I asked.

He smiled and paused for a second. 'You know, Ness, in this day and age it's criminal for the elderly to admit to boredom. At the flick of a switch I can have the entire Berlin Philharmonic playing in my sitting room on Radio 3, or I can be transported to Mao's China with the History Channel, or I can take part in the migration of the wildebeest on the Nature Channel.' I also knew that he could make *The Times* last the entire day and always had the radio tuned to Radio 4 for company.

After ten minutes or so he'd say, 'Shall we stop a minute and take in this beautiful morning?' His watery eyes could notice far more detail than mine. He loved to point out things of interest, like the cornflowers dancing as the bumblebees bounced from one bloom to another, or a seething mass of cinnabar caterpillars, with their distinctive black and yellow woolly jumpers, on the stem of the ragwort plant.

He would carefully remove his dark glasses and place them in his shirt pocket. Like all elderly people with diminishing eyesight, everything he did was considered and painfully slow. His shaking hands reached for the battered pair of binoculars that always hung around his neck, and he raised them to his eyes. The binoculars would wobble up and down at an alarming rate, but still he would thrill at spotting something unusual.

'Oh, do look, Ness, there's a family of roe deer. Ah, the mum has seen us and is being protective of her young. She's standing stock-still and not taking her eyes off us. Do take a look – the young one is such a dear little thing.'

We would discuss the best mix for English country hedges. 'Always include plenty of blackthorn,' he insisted.

He then told me his grandmother's recipe for sloe gin. 'Take three gallons of gin,' he started. 'Imagine three gallons of gin! I make mine in four large Kilner jars now. Some say to wait for the first frost before picking, but I'm not sure. Pick enough plump sloes to fill half the jar. I prick each berry with a safety pin. Some people freeze them to burst the skins and allow the flavour out. Come to think of it,' he added, 'that must be the reason that some people wait until the first frost, but you're risking the birds getting to them first if you wait too long. Then you pour in enough sugar to cover the sloes and cover the lot with gin. The secret is to add a few drops of almond essence to each bottle. Delicious!'

Dad used to store his batches of sloe gin in the boot of his car until the following season. 'Isn't life wonderful,' he chuckled. 'While I'm driving up front, the gin is stirring behind.'

Walking down the avenue of Scots pines, we talk about my friend Shelagh and the fifty-four trees we have planted, one for each year of her life, and are silent for a moment as I recall her bravery in the face of her illness and remember her laugh. We notice one of the trees leaning at an alarming angle. 'She'll get younger as each tree topples,' says Dad.

Around the corner is my friend Annabel's mulberry tree, planted by Poppy and Wilf, her two young children, to remember their mother. Dad and I pause here, too. The trees grow so fast – can it really be that long since she died?

Walking with someone close to you is magical, but walking in nature with someone you love is nothing short of a miracle. Being side by side removes the need for eye contact and allows for far more intimacy than in the usual exchanges you'd have over a table. It was here, walking around the fields in late spring, with the gulls catching the sea air, that we discussed my father's belief in heaven.

'You know, darling, the closer I get to meeting my maker, the less I believe in him.' We talked about his relationship with Mum and her unpredictable ways, and we discussed how I should feel after his death. 'I've had a good innings. An extraordinary life – it would be an indulgence to grieve for me.'

Oh Daddy, I thought, I'll try.

Our circuit complete, we'd drink a long glass of his homemade elderflower cordial. The reverse journey up the planks was always a little more straightforward, after which he'd tuck himself into the car seat, his crumbling spine supported by foam padding, his hands level with his head as they rested on the steering wheel.

I'd bend down towards him, say goodbye and gently kiss his soft jowls. He in turn would look me in the eye with tender love, raising his hand to stroke my cheek, as if tickling a spaniel behind its ear. He'd close the car door, buckle up and then slowly set off down the drive.

I'd stand and wave, big arms-up, whole-body waves to express my pleasure in seeing him and to stop my throat constricting and turning into ridiculous tears, all too well aware that each walk is more precious than the last.

2

MYSTERIES SOLVED

Sussex, February 2017

To travel back a century is a small historical hop, but it's a giant leap into the dark for me as I look for clues in the muffled world of family myth and memory. Mum's grasp of the truth is tenuous now: so many stories have been embroidered in the retelling and her memories are no longer clear. I begin to root around her cupboards for memoir treasure, whether a fading photograph or an object slipped into a top drawer as a keepsake, but it's impossible to make any sense from these oddments.

Then I remember Michael Addison, a distant cousin twenty years my senior. As a child, he spent many weekends with our grandparents and their siblings. He welcomes the idea of delving back, his clear memory able to flesh out stories with not only names but also juicy personality quirks of generations past. A retired judge, he's a reliable witness – his photographic memory and attention to detail clear the fog and give me a framework in which to piece a number of clues together. I can touch the Victorians now, at only one remove. The past is so near that I can almost smell it.

* * *

It's the spring of 1918. The Representation of the People Act has just been passed, giving some women the right to vote, and German forces are making their devastating attack along the Western Front. But all is calm in the Surrey nursing home where my father Edward James Branson emerges into the world. As beautiful as this scene is, we won't dwell here for long; we need to go back a further thirty years, when the nineteenth century was drawing to its close in a country where the classes 'knew how to behave' and women 'knew their place'.

We're in the Scottish Highlands, on the banks of Loch Lochy in Inverness-shire in 1890. This was the year that my grandmother, Joyce Mona Bailey, was born, delivered by a doctor who'd been summoned from Fort William, fourteen miles away. The good doctor had urged his horse to go as fast as it could and just managed to enter the master bedroom of Invergloy House as the baby took her first breath.

The only memory I have of my grandmother is when I last saw her. I was four years old when I was led to her bedside in 1964, to say goodbye as she lay dying. A uniformed nurse stood next to a tall mahogany dresser and sunlight streamed through a gap in the curtains. The grandfather clock ticked loudly on the landing. My eyes were level with Granny Branson's enormous bed and it took me a moment to realise there was someone in it, her emaciated legs barely making a bump under the blanket. She was propped up in her powder pink crochet jacket, and everything else was white: her hair, the sheets, her skin. I distinctly remember her lifting her trembling hand to stroke my cheek and smiling down at me. I'm afraid the moment was just too terrifying, and rather than say my prepared piece, I buried my head in my mother's skirts.

Invergloy House was built in an era when labour was cheap and stones were plentiful. The house was so remote that if all the family were out for the day, they would lower the flag on the front lawn by the water's edge, saving the postman the long drive around the loch to deliver the post. Intriguingly, the house was to burn down in mysterious circumstances in 1947 – a fate it shared with a number of other large houses whose owners could no longer afford to run them.

We take so much of our family history for granted, but when you begin putting the jigsaw together, some pieces refuse to slot neatly in. I wondered where the funds to set up an educational trust for us children came from; my father certainly never earned enough. What were the origins of my great-grandparents' wealth, and why didn't all the names connect?

It wasn't until my brother Richard was invited to take part in the American version of *Who Do You Think You Are?* that we learned of the Dickensian story behind the family's first bit of good fortune. It transpired that my great-grandfather James, Granny Branson's father, had been born a poor gardener's son and the youngest of four children. When his mother died, though his biological father was still very much alive, he was adopted by his father's employer, an unmarried and celebrated surgeon. Ten years later, when the surgeon died, both James and his father were pallbearers at the old man's funeral and afterwards James learned that, in return for changing his surname to that of his benefactor, Bailey, and bearing the family crest, he would inherit £18,000, the equivalent of over £2 million today. This was enough money to set himself up as a gentleman, find himself a society wife and build himself a mansion, Invergloy House.

Granny Joyce had three beloved brothers – Ron, Charles and Harold – and an equally adored sister, Dora. When looking through the sepia photographs of their youth I find it extraordinary to think that I touched that era personally, if a little reluctantly. My childhood memory of visiting Uncle Ron and his ancient wife Doff still haunts me. A doddering maid would serve us thick, slithery slices of hot, all-too-tongue-like ox tongue. I'd agonise over my plate, attempting to slip bits of tongue under the damask tablecloth towards Ron's pack of snuffling Pekinese dogs.

Throughout the 1890s and into the twentieth century, the girls were educated at home by a governess. It's fascinating to trace family characteristics back a generation or two and see so clearly where the seeds of our own interests were originally sown. Having never experienced the rough and tumble that comes with going to school, the shy, gentle Joyce failed to develop the thick skin required to survive outside her closed society. Freedom from a strict curriculum allowed her to follow her interests in botany and entomology, and she retained a deep knowledge of the natural world around her. Her other passion was photography: she was happiest when viewing the world through a camera lens. The sisters spent many days together in their timeless landscape – Joyce with her camera and butterfly net and Dora with her sketchbook and watercolour paints.

As with many other Edwardian boys from the landed classes, the brothers became adept at fly fishing, deer stalking and grouse shooting. With so few neighbours to play with, the young Bailey family forged close bonds with each other. Joyce's photographs capture the pleasure they all took in each other's company and their sense of fun.

Invergloy House was remote, but local suppliers were up to the challenge of catering for their Highland customers. Uncle Ron told us that buying a new suit would entail a number of visits from the tailor in Fort William, who would ride his bicycle out for three consecutive weeks for the fittings, returning on the fourth week with the finished suit and a bill for £2.

'Necessity is the mother of invention' might have been the Bailey family motto. Most injuries were dealt with at home, with plucky Emma Edith, Joyce's mother, regularly sewing up the children's open wounds with fishing gut, after one of the all-too-frequent accidents that resulted from their adventurous lives.

Joyce's life in Invergloy, so idyllic as a child, became increasingly lonely and isolated when she was a teenager, as her three brothers left home in quick succession. Harold, who was much older, had gone off to fight in the Boer War, while the other two went to London to seek their fortunes. The grand houses in the area would have held an annual ball, but these were few and far between, so the opportunities for the young Bailey girls to find romance were rare.

One weekend in January 1910, Ron travelled home to Scotland from London on the sleeper train. Accompanying him was his new friend, old Harrovian Francis (Frank) Addison. Frank was still adjusting to his new circumstance: his father, who had been a senior partner in the law firm Linklaters, had recently died, leaving him a healthy legacy of £20,000. The family still lived in a grand house in one of the elegant terraces built by Robert Adam overlooking Regent's Park.

The boys were full of expectation as the pony and trap pulled up to collect them for the four-mile homeward journey from Spean Bridge, along the banks of Loch Lochy. I wonder how Ron had described his sisters to Frank. I wonder if he'd had romance in mind, or if he simply wanted to bring his friend home for the weekend, to share a spot of shooting and stalking. I also wonder whether Frank had been honest with Ron about his recent diagnosis, or if youthful optimism meant that having a terminal disease was the last thing he wanted to dwell on.

The weekend was clearly a success. The family made plenty of fuss over Ron's new friend, keeping the fires burning with fragrant pine logs and providing lavish Scottish fare. Both girls giggled and flirted coyly, escorting the boys on their hunting trips and showing off their photos and paintings. Frank was bewitched and was soon writing letters of overwhelming tenderness to the shy and innocent Joyce. Less than a month later, she visited her brother in London with every intention of meeting Frank once more and by the following October, the young couple were engaged.

Joyce clearly knew that Frank was dying. Knowing the story now, I was fascinated when my cousin Michael showed me the young couple's wedding portrait. Joyce looks serene with a hint of an enigmatic smile and a sly angle to her head that emphasises the elongated chin that made her fall just short of beautiful. Handsome Frank looks equally content but he also looks utterly exhausted, his eyes lost in blackened sockets and his skeletal body shrouded in a morning suit that is two sizes too large. On Joyce's right stands her cousin and maid of honour, Mildred Higgs. Mildred's family owned Scaitcliffe, the boys' preparatory school that was one day to provide miserable memories for my brother Richard. On Frank's left is his old friend and Joyce's dear brother Ron, his head leaning towards Frank. His lopsided smile seems a touch tentative for one known for his mischievous delight in life.

A year before the wedding, Frank had been diagnosed with diabetes. The technique to manufacture purified insulin was to be developed in 1922, just a decade later, but for Frank there was no cure.

The Bailey family, including Joyce, must have been aware that this marriage was destined for tragedy, but I like to believe that their young love overwhelmed all sense. This was certainly a love match but, when weighing up the pros and cons of committing to Frank and his health, Joyce would have also taken into account the promise of a future of financial security, in an era when women didn't have the vote and were dependent on their husbands for support. And what's more, Frank offered her a swift escape route from her crushingly dull existence at Invergloy.

Her sister Dora's story, on the other hand, fulfilled Joyce's worst fears. The girls' mother didn't leave her side and prevented her poor daughter from meeting up with other young people. As the years passed her confidence trickled away; Dora was to remain her mother's companion for decades, and a spinster for her whole life.

Frank and Joyce moved into the five-bedroomed, Georgian Tilhill House, just off the picturesque village green in Tilford in Surrey. Joseph, their son, was born in July 1912. Frank had intended to commute to London to work but soon realised that this was unfeasible. Type 1 diabetes is a disease that affects the immune system. The first indication that something is wrong is an unquenchable thirst, followed by a continual hunger – but however much you eat, you are unable to sustain a healthy body weight. Your breath becomes foul and your moods become unpredictable.

At the time of his wedding, Frank was experiencing extreme fatigue. When little Joe was born a year later, his father's eyesight was poor and his kidneys were failing, along with his good humour. Frank stayed at home, devoting his time to his son and his wife. Joyce remained gracious throughout Frank's illness, nursing him until his painful death. The couple's short love story was encapsulated by Frank's funeral in the spring of 1914. Ron, his loyal friend and brother-in-law, gave the elegy. Frank's mother, recently widowed herself, sat weeping throughout. Joyce sat with baby Joe on her lap, quietly staring at the coffin that contained the body of her young husband. It was a tragic scene that would soon be repeated with alarming frequency all over Europe.

Whether the build-up to the Great War, the conflict that was to become the most devastating conflict known to humankind, had impacted on this family, which was suffering its own personal drama in Tilford, I'm not sure. We can only surmise that my young, widowed grandmother allowed little of the outside world to unsettle her tenuous hold on stability, which she needed to cling to for the sake of her fatherless toddler. With barely any support from Frank's grieving family, and with her parents hundreds of miles away in Scotland, Joyce had to garner all her own resources. Her practical and disciplined upbringing in Invergloy gave her the strength to continue; thanks to this resilience, a new chapter in her life was about to begin – with, some would say, unseemly haste.

Years after her death, a neat pile of twenty letters, tied up with ribbon, was discovered in a secret compartment behind her writing desk. Feeling unable to destroy the letters herself, the grieving Joyce had written a note in her careful script: 'Could anyone who finds these letters please burn them.' It amazes me that the bundle had passed through various family members' hands and no one had opened it; I'm afraid that when I saw the note I couldn't resist. I poured myself a cup of tea, guiltily untied the pink ribbon and read the letters slowly. Forgive me, dear Grandmother – I'm going to include one here, for these letters are too tender to remain hidden from view.

20 Harley House, Regent's Park NW
18 October 1910

Little Woman,

I am quite silly tonight, silly with happiness; how I am, not having left you an hour ago, already sitting down to write to you! I have often laughed at this particular form of foolishness in others, and now I am being guilty of it myself; you can laugh at me as much as you like but I am going to be silly tonight, and I don't care a bit! Don't you imagine though for one minute, young woman, that I am going to write to you every day, like most people do when they get engaged; not a bit of it, once a month is about all you need expect from now! But tonight I am off my head, not responsible for my actions, and all because I know now for certain that you love me; you must be very careful of giving me your love Joyce, when you see what an evil effect it has on me! I can't resist the joy of writing my first love letter to you now, however foolish you may think

16

me; I have longed and longed for this moment, and now I won't be ashamed of it.

Do you know, little woman, that once or twice, when my heart was nearly breaking and everything seemed black, I have sat down and written to you just as I wanted to; simply poured my heart out on paper to you to try and get some little relief; you never got any of those letters, as I always tore them up directly after they were written, and I am not quite sure that they did me much good, but I had to do something to appease the longing: don't think that my brain is going, after reading this confession, I don't really think it is. I loved you so, little woman, and I was so helpless, and could not say a word.

Oh Joyce, my darling, nothing matters to me now; now that I know for certain that you love me; I want to live badly, oh so badly, to try and show you how much I love you, but whether I live and get quite well, or whether I die soon, it does not matter to me now; I think I can stand anything as long as I have your love; and if ever that is denied me, well, then there won't be anything left for me to live for.

My darling, I love you; be quite, quite certain of that, whatever may have happened before, and whatever may happen in the future, never doubt that I love you more than anything else on this earth.

Frank

3

Museum of Curiosities

Our story moves swiftly on, for one of the guests at Frank's funeral was my grandfather, George Branson.

George was born on 11 July 1871 in Great Yarmouth, Norfolk. His father, James Branson, was a barrister and would later become a judge, a senior acting magistrate, in Kolkata in India. George's mother, Mary Ann Branson, *née* Brown, was born in India to an English father and Indian mother, a marriage that colonial prejudice of the era would have regarded as fairly controversial. Family albums show joyful pictures of George, his three brothers, their sister and one adopted sister, Olive (the daughter of an uncle who lived in India) acting the fool, cross-dressing, playing games, sailing and travelling. The family was clearly a happy one.

The Branson line was not particularly illustrious. My father once said that the only family claim to fame was that one of our ancestors was the first 'Marian Martyr', the protestants who were burnt at the stake in Smithfield Market, in the reign of Queen Mary. As children we were proud to know that the ill-fated Captain Robert Scott who died with his team while attempting to be the first to reach the South Pole, was my great-grandfather James Branson's first cousin. Scott became a hero in Britain, a symbol of grit and determination for the country's youth as they marched off to war.

Open the cupboard on any family's past and dislodge a fact or two, and incredible stories begin to tumble out. There is something reassuring in knowing that your past is littered with unusual personalities. The historian Susannah Stapleton contacted me recently; she's writing a book about my great cousin Olive, my grandfather's adopted sister, a fine artist who gained notoriety by coming to an untimely end. 'I remember feeling very pleased with myself,' Dad once told me about the moment that he was summoned to his prep school headmaster's office to be told the distressing news. 'Although I'd barely met Olive, as quick as a flash I brought my hands to my eyes and began wailing and was given the rest of the day off lessons.'

In fact, her death was quite the cause célèbre in its day, but it wasn't until Susannah filled me in on the details that I realised how grizzly her end had been. Olive was forty-four when her body was found submerged in a water tank near her house in Provence. She had been shot between the eyes. It was never ascertained whether it had been murder or suicide, or indeed whether it was the shooting or the drowning that killed her. All evidence pointed towards her twenty-six-year-old French lover, but when he was tried for her murder he was found not guilty, perhaps an inevitable verdict when a jury consists of local townspeople and the defendant is the owner of the town's only bar.

Susannah also sent me a press cutting from *The Standard* dated 11 February 1912, which features both a picture of Captain Scott's departure for his final expedition and a story relating to cousin Olive's stepmother, Grace Branson. Grace, who had married Olive's father, was a militant suffragette who was twice arrested for smashing windows alongside Sylvia Pankhurst. On 11 April 1913 she gave this restrained description of their time together while on hunger strike in Holloway Prison:

> Twice a day they fed me with the tube down the throat.
> I resisted every time. I clutched and held on to the bed
> with my legs and arms. They put me flat on the bed. Then
> they held me down, each of the wardresses holding a leg
> or an arm. There was one very strong big one who held
> my head between her two hands. When she was there
> I couldn't move at all. There were always two doctors,
> one of them took the gag and owing to the gap in my
> teeth he was able to get it in. The gag fixed, they began
> to insert the tube. I resisted it with my tongue as long as
> I could.

My grandfather George had three remarkable brothers, Bill, Jim and Fred, who would go on to play an enriching role in my father's formative years. Bill, Jim and Fred went to Bedford Grammar School, where their contemporaries included Harold Abrahams, the Olympic sprinter featured in the film *Chariots of Fire*, and John de Vars Hazard, who disappeared while taking part in Mallory and Irvine's 1924 British Mount Everest Expedition. There was also their cousin Lionel Branson, who joined the Magic Circle and became known for debunking spiritualism as a mere conjuring trick, disappointing many who believed they were in contact with their loved ones who had been killed in the war.

George went on to study Classics at Trinity College Cambridge. He was clearly in possession of a profound intellect: after being articled to a firm of solicitors called Markby, Stewart & Co, he swiftly became a member of the Inner Temple, was called to the Bar and joined the Northern Circuit. Writing books on the London Stock Exchange helped make his name as a barrister before he became junior counsel to the Treasury in 1912.

Joyce and George married with little ceremony in 1915. A lavish gathering was not only inappropriate so soon after Frank's death but also unseemly during the war. Still struggling with grief and wishing to start this new chapter on a fresh page, Joyce asked George to call her by her middle name; from then on, she was known as Mona. George, at forty-three, was exempt from service but, worryingly for Mona, her brother, 2nd Lt Ron Bailey, was fighting at the front with the Royal Engineers. He was mentioned in despatches from General Allenby in 1917, for gallant service in the field; the letter was signed by Winston Churchill, who was then Secretary of State for War.

1916 was a busy year. George was junior counsel for the prosecution in the trial of Roger Casement, perhaps the most notorious trial during the First World War. Casement's story had all the elements to capture the imagination of the nation. He had joined the British Colonial Service as a young man and was appointed British consul to the Congo in 1891. By all reports he was a charismatic, beautiful man. Having witnessed colonial atrocities inflicted against indigenous people, he had grown to distrust imperialism and became a poet and humanitarian activist who was knighted for his investigation of human rights abuses in Peru. After retiring from the Colonial Service in 1913, he became involved in Irish Republicanism and, with German support, planned an armed rebellion against British rule in Ireland. It was a messy affair. Casement soon suspected that the Germans were toying with his plan. Weakened by malaria, he was arrested in Tralee Bay in County Kerry, and tried for high treason.

His defence was that, realising that German support was not forthcoming, he had landed in Ireland to call off the operation. The prosecution never had a watertight case, as the uprising hadn't been planned on British soil. Many pleaded for clemency, including George Bernard Shaw, Arthur Conan Doyle and William Butler Yeats. Prior to the start of the trial, extracts from Casement's diaries were maliciously leaked, several of which depicted lurid homosexual scenes with native boys (later known as *The Black Diaries*). Whoever leaked the offending passages had hoped to influence the trial against Casement; decades later, it has been suggested that the diaries were fabricated for this purpose, but at the time there was no doubt of their authenticity.

George worked assiduously on building the case against Casement, though ensured that the diaries were not used as evidence by the prosecution. After the trial, George received a letter from Casement's Irish defence barrister, Alexander Martin Sullivan, thanking him for his good conduct during the case. Casement was found guilty and hanged in Pentonville Prison on 3 August 1916. The case sealed George Branson's reputation as a hard-working barrister with a fine legal mind.

That same year, the Bransons bought Wharfenden House in Frimley Green, Surrey, an imposing if ungainly Edwardian house. They were to own it until 1952, and until 1919 they also owned a house at 59 Gordon Square in London. A daughter named Joyce, perhaps to remind Mona of her past life, was born in 1916.

Mona's photos from the summer of 1918 give no clue to the tumultuous state of the world. The war was drawing to a close and the horror that it had unleashed was slowly being revealed. Rumours were emerging of the Armenian genocide, where more than one and half million people had been systematically murdered by the Ottoman Empire. The shattering realisation was dawning that millions of young men had been carelessly sacrificed by the decisions of incompetent generals using outdated methods of warfare. The country was walking a fine line between retaining national pride and supporting the returning troops, while also coming to terms with what had been going on during the war, now that public information was no longer subject to government propaganda.

1918 also saw the outbreak of the Spanish Flu epidemic, which in that year is said to have killed between fifty and a hundred million people – millions more than were killed in the war itself. The flu killed many of the physically debilitated and run-down soldiers who had survived the slaughter in the trenches and was most deadly for men of fighting age – the majority of children and the elderly survived the illness. No corner of the world was spared. To maintain morale during the war, the censors minimised early reports of the illness. The name 'Spanish Flu' derived from the fact that Spain, being a neutral country, had no censors and reported the reality of the catastrophe, leading to the erroneous impression that the epidemic had originated there.

On 10 March 1918, as the enormity of the epidemic was being realised, my father, Edward James Branson, was born at 5.30 a.m. in Orchard House Nursing Home in Byfleet, weighing a healthy 8 lbs 14 oz. Born as one overwhelming conflict was coming to a close, he would be the perfect age to head off into battle when the next conflict began twenty-one years later, in September 1939.

There are numerous photographs of the bonny Branson babies dressed in home-knitted bloomers on windswept beaches as they busily built sandcastles. There is a photo of my father in Scotland during his first summer, his fat cheeks rosy from the West Coast sun. Pictures of his sister Joyce show her to be as robust as a baby as she would become as an adult; at only two years old her thick dark hair was already well past her shoulders. The photos of Joseph, Joyce's son by Frank, show a more delicate, fair-skinned child occasionally raising a wry smile for the camera. Years later, Dad recalled that his father would always put Joe first, to compensate for any feelings of unfairness the child may have felt when he became aware that George wasn't his biological father.

When little Joe heard the news that his father was to become a 'Sir', he ran around the house shouting, 'Daddy's been made a saint!' Becoming a high court judge in 1919 bought George a great deal of privilege and a decent salary, in addition to an automatic knighthood.

The family were well served by a team of staff, including a chauffeur called Parton. To this day, whenever I enter a lift I can hear my chuckling father telling the story of how, as a small boy, he went to a drinks party with his parents in a smart London mansion block. His mother Mona, who rarely drank beyond a thimble of sherry, must have nervously gulped down one glass of champagne too many. On leaving, when the family entered the lift, my slightly squiffy grandmother turned to the attendant and said in a tone of great authority, 'Home, Parton, please!'

Wharfenden, with its ten-acre lake and mature woodland, was quite a home to grow up in. The house had eight bedrooms for the family, with a staff courtyard leading away from the kitchen at the back. At the front of the house, French windows opened from every reception room onto an expansive lawn. The staid Victorian and Edwardian furniture was enriched by objects inherited from various ancestors, including my great-grandfather's pair of muskets, their stocks inlaid with intricate silverwork. On the mantelpiece above the fireplace there were delicately carved ivory balls, made for ceremonial decoration for elephants, as well as tigers' teeth and Tibetan prayer wheels. The house was cluttered with artefacts and natural objects, which provided an endless source of intrigue. Every one held a magical story, whether of a great battle or massacre, or of ritual and mystery.

The lawn, which was laid out with badminton and croquet sets, led down to the water, with its abundance of fascinating life to explore. There were trout to tickle and fish, and perch, pike, crayfish, newts, water boatmen and dragonflies to catch, either to study and return to the wild, to immerse in chloroform and label, to eat, or simply to marvel at. In spring, billowing clouds of frogspawn and threads of toadspawn appeared and were collected into jars and observed as the eggs grew fat, developed legs and leapt out of their containers to freedom.

Bats loved flying over the water at dusk and catching the rising mosquitoes. They shared their meal with the faithful swallows, which returned summer after summer following their mighty migration from South Africa, taking it in turns to swoop down to scoop up a beak of water, like fighter planes coming into attack.

Young Ted, as my father soon became known, would spend as much time as he could outside, investigating the wildlife in the lake, swimming in it or skating on it. The family built rafts and swings, camped out and cooked freshly caught trout and crayfish on open fires.

As a child, I loved it when my father, Joe and Joyce reminisced about their childhood days without end. They spoke with such affection as they told stories of teasing their long-suffering, gullible mother, of hapless gardeners and of being spoilt by cooks. Their father, though a formal and distant man, was clearly loved by the three children. Photographs of him in his red robes and horsehair wig show a man comfortable in his role; he carried himself as a stern man of judgment, but his eyes betrayed a softer side.

In reality, Nanny did a great deal of the childcare. A young Irish girl of simple education, she was instructed to bind little Ted's sticking-out ears in 'Mother Hubbard's Ear Protectors' each night, a contraption that went over his head and tied under his chin. On the night of every full moon, Nanny would pop my startled father, complete with ear protectors, in a gigantic wicker laundry basket – 'to stop the banshees gettin' to ya,' she would explain. What effect this had on his state of mind is unclear, but he readily used the trauma as an excuse not to give up pipe smoking until he was in his sixties.

The family all adored their dogs, but Dad felt his Jack Russell terrier, Bonny, was an extension of his soul, that she could read his mind and understand his mood. He loved his pony too and felt completely at one with her, becoming a fearless young horseman. He also became a crack shot. On his eighth birthday, Ted was given an air rifle and shot a sparrow from the scullery window.

In his excitement, he leapt from the window but caught his foot on the ledge and fell headfirst into the coal cellar, giving himself a nasty gash on the forehead. Fifty years later, I was with him when he scratched his head, 'Well, I'll be blowed,' he said. 'Isn't the body a wonderful thing?' and a tiny piece of coal appeared under his fingernail.

In the days before Google, when Ted's grandchildren were young and had endless questions about how the world works, the cry would go up: 'Ask Granddaddy! Granddaddy knows everything!' His curiosity as to physics, astronomy, nature and history gave him a deep well of knowledge. He rarely offered information unprompted, but when asked he shared it with enthusiasm.

Dad revelled in the wonder of nature, or in interesting objects of any kind. He relished anything that had a good anecdote attached to it. For example, he might hand you a button from a First World War uniform and ask you to guess why it was special. Gleeful at your bafflement as you fiddled with it, he would unscrew the brass ring at the back of the button, clockwise to fool the enemy, hooting with pleasure as he revealed the tiny compass hidden inside. Or he would show you the mechanism that fired the antique muskets, with their bowls designed to contain a pinch of gunpowder that would fire when a spark was created by the strike of the flint. 'If the powder only flared, but didn't fire the ball,' he'd cheerfully explain, 'it was called a "flash in the pan."'

When we despair today at how the internet reduces our children's attention span, we can only contrast their lives to my father's and weep. One summer holiday when he was about twelve years old, Ted became obsessed by pike and was curious to understand how fast they grew and whether they moved from lake to lake. The pike is the largest and most vicious of freshwater fish, but he invented a trap and caught every pike in the lake – ringing and weighing them before returning them to the water. He repeated the exercise the following year, noting down their sizes and numbers.

The support he must have received to follow his passions was considerable. One summer's morning, the thirteen-year-old budding geologist spotted an item in the morning newspaper. There'd been a large rockfall at Lyme Regis, on Dorset's Jurassic Coast. Keen to be one of the first fossil hunters at the site, Ted managed to persuade Uncle Ron to drive him across the country to investigate. I wonder if it was his powers of persuasion, his enthusiasm or his engaging company that convinced his uncle to satisfy his nephew's demands? Whatever charm Dad possessed, it clearly worked. They arrived at the enormous pile of newly broken cliff face as light was fading, his keen eyes spotted a hint of grey jutting from the local yellow sandstone, and he started chipping away with his hammer and chisel there and then. Afraid that someone would come and claim his fossil, he chipped and hammered all through the night. As the sun began to rise over the headland, the excited boy finally managed to free a perfectly formed giant ammonite from the sedimentary rock. His magnificent prize measured fifty centimetres in diameter and, at its fattest, was thirty centimetres thick. In his enthusiasm, the little chap managed to haul the heavy fossil along the beach, up the cliff path and back to the car single-handedly, waking his crumpled and long-suffering uncle with whoops of victory.

Anything that caught Ted's interest, he collected. He soon had enough exhibits to open a 'Museum of Curiosities' in a stable in the courtyard behind the house. He lined boxes with cotton wool from his mother's dressing table and after placing the objects inside, he stuck a thin window of glass on top and wrote the description on a label in his schoolboy script.

Young Ted's museum proudly displayed his hoard of ancient pottery, Bronze Age fishhooks, numerous fossilised shark teeth and Stone Age flint arrowheads. He collected eggs, seeds, crystals and bones; nothing of interest was left uninvestigated, and all the adults around him enjoyed adding to his collection, too. His museum of curiosities contained a private world of fascination; every exhibit had a story to tell. My father would never lose his uncanny knack for finding objects of interest. Days of our summer holidays in Menorca were spent rooting around caves for treasure; we'd inevitably find a Roman coin or Neolithic bone or two.

Another great influence on young Ted's life was Uncle Bill, brother of Sir George. Bill was a doctor and a 'confirmed bachelor'. When I asked my cousin Michael, who'd known him well, whether he thought his great-uncle was gay, he replied, 'No, I don't think so. Anyway, it was illegal back then.' He added, 'To imagine Uncle Bill doing anything between the sheets is unthinkable!'

With no children of his own, Bill was happy to share his knowledge and explore the natural world with his curious young nephew. He generously gave Ted a microscope, enabling the keen amateur biologist to investigate the intricate veins of a daddy longlegs' wings or the organisms that squirm around in a pinprick of Stilton cheese with thrilling clarity. He taught Ted to make his own slides, placing a thin layer of whatever he wanted to investigate onto a rectangle of glass before sticking a square of thin, brittle glass on top. This beautiful brass instrument came in a mahogany box, with tiny drawers containing the slides and five felt pockets, where the different-strength lenses were housed. How I loved playing with it as a child, pushing the slides labelled with my father's childish handwriting under the lens and catching the light in the mirror below.

Uncle Bill moved into Wharfenden in 1932 and lived with the family until his death in 1958. It was a happy arrangement for all parties, for Bill wasn't only enriching company but also contributed £500 per year to the family coffers, having landed himself a cushy job as chief medical officer for an insurance company. Without emergencies to deal with or illnesses to cure, he simply had medical assessments to make and a healthy salary to pocket. He devoted so much time to the Branson family and was always entertaining with his stock of medical anecdotes and cheery intrigue. Bill also kept Sir George happy by allowing himself to be trounced at billiards on a nightly basis. Furthermore, having a doctor in the house was a handy bonus as His Honour, a notorious hypochondriac, needed constant reassurance that his various ailments were not life-threatening.

As a young boy, my father remembered overhearing his mother saying to the family dentist, 'I just don't understand what's the matter with Ted. He knows every planet in the universe and can name every insect, plant and bird in the garden, but when it comes to schoolwork, he's hopeless.' It was the first time my father learned that he was considered in some way handicapped or different. His mother's experience of being home-schooled meant she had a more empathetic approach to his academic shortcomings, but Sir George came from a long line of distinguished lawyers and was less forgiving. As a consequence, my father suffered terribly at his boarding prep school; his response was, whenever possible, to seek out knowledge from those with a natural passion for their subjects rather than exam-focused teachers.

Grandfather George's other brother, Uncle Jim, was a slight embarrassment to the family. After receiving a knock to the head when falling from his horse, he decided that his tenants were more worthy of their cottages then he was and readily gave his small Hampshire estate over to them. A hundred years ahead of his time, Uncle Jim became an ardent vegan and foraged for food in the parks around his flat in the unfashionable south London borough of Balham. He would often cycle the forty miles to Wharfenden to stay with the family for the weekend, carrying his 'nosebag', into which he would put anything edible he found in the hedgerows as he pedalled along Surrey's country lanes, before insisting on eating nothing else for the length of his stay.

Evening meals were formal but animated affairs. Everyone would dress for dinner, and drinks were served by the butler at 8 p.m. sharp. Candlelight danced off the crystal wine glasses and decanters of red wine that had been left to happily breathe on the sideboard, having been selected by my grandfather from the cellar earlier that day. Monogrammed linen napkins were laundered for every meal. At the age of twelve, children progressed from eating with Nanny in the nursery and joined the adults in the dining room. Meals were long, and the men drank with enthusiasm. As Dad recalled longingly, 'There was always a cheeseboard, followed by a pudding.'

It was the 1920s and the world was evolving. The German, Russian, Austro-Hungarian and Ottoman Empires ceased to exist and national borders were redrawn. During the Paris Peace Conference of 1919, the 'Big Four' – Britain, France, the United States and Italy – imposed the terms and the League of Nations was formed, with the aim of preventing any repetition of such a conflict. Many believe that the harsh treatment of Germany, rather than creating a lasting peace after 'the war to end all wars', sowed the seeds for economic depression, renewed nationalism and deep-rooted feelings of humiliation that would lead directly to the Second World War.

Talk around the dinner table would have focused on the rapidly changing roles of women at work and in political life. The family would have despaired about the Great Depression, worried about the state of Europe and discussed Sir George's current case. Sir George, aware of his grammar school roots, tended to overcompensate by being something of a snob. The family were not sufficiently aristocratic to be eccentric in their taste and they were too 'establishment' to take risks. Their interest in the arts focused on Bill's appreciation of poetry (there is a book of his own poetry in the British Library), Cousin Olive's painting and Mona's love of Gilbert and Sullivan. The only books my father kept from his childhood were a copy of Hilaire Belloc's *Cautionary Tales*, all of which he'd learned by heart, a book of Edward Lear's collected limericks and J. M. Barrie's *Peter Pan*.

Ted adored Uncle Jim and would spend hours listening to his tales. A few years later, during the Second World War, a sergeant major marched into the crowded mess hall at his barracks during dinner. 'Has this fellow James Branson got anything to do with you, Branson?' the notorious bully bellowed. Everyone in the room turned to stare at Dad. The sergeant major was brandishing a copy of *Picture Post*, a popular magazine of the era.

Ted, aware that the family considered Jim to be a sandwich short of a picnic and not confident as to the content of the article, stuttered a cautious, 'Why do you ask, Sir?'

'By God, the man's a hero!' came the reply as he hurled the magazine towards Ted. 'You should be damned proud of him.' There, before him, was an entire page of pictures of Uncle Jim gathering lawn cuttings and teaching Allied troops how to survive in the wild by eating grass, twigs and berries. 'My motto,' reads the caption under a photograph of Uncle Jim, spooning foliage into his open mouth, 'is a Branson never says "can't"'. He goes on to claim, 'I'm as fit as a flea at harvest.'

'Well done, Branson,' the sergeant major said, as he marched from the mess hall. The room erupted into cheers.

Try as he might, Ted found passing the entrance exam to Eton impossible. His brother Joe had sailed into the school a few years earlier and would come home for the holidays with groups of confident friends. My father would never express disappointment, but failing to make the grade must have had a crushing effect on him at the time.

Instead of Eton, Ted was sent to Bootham School in York, a Quaker school that states on its website today that it 'encourages its students to be creative thinkers, peacemakers and humanitarians,' adding that 'each person has the capacity for goodness and a responsibility to recognise that goodness in others.' The Bootham culture was more forgiving and better suited than Eton would have been to my father's non-competitive, diffident though trusting personality.

Ted was reserved at school and, although his quick wit made him popular with his peers, he disliked the attention of those in authority. He developed a lifelong horror of speaking in public as he had a tendency to roll his r's – not easy if your surname name happens to be Branson. As an adult, he talked little of his schooldays. His sister Joyce told us there would usually be much walking up and down the platform to hide his tears as the family saw him off on the train to York at the beginning of each term.

Towards the end of his time at school, Sir George suggested that Ted go to a careers adviser. After asking him to fill out various forms and answer a plethora of questions, taking note of the young man's knowledge and interest in natural and ancient history, geology and physics, the adviser recommended that Ted should become an archaeologist. Horrified by the prospect of one of his sons not following the family tradition of going to the Bar, Sir George refused to pay the career adviser's bill.

The entire family would occasionally accompany Sir George when he travelled the country on circuit, which was unheard of at the time. Having been at Trinity College, he would stay in the master's lodge while sitting at the Cambridge Assizes. Mona took matters even further: not content with having the children simply see their father at work, she insisted that they act as marshals in the court and bizarrely that she sit on the bench beside her husband.

On reflection, my grandfather's cosy relationship with the master of Trinity must have helped my father win a place to read law in this most hallowed of academic institutions. It was here that Ted developed his immense sense of fun, his love of puns and the pleasure he took in a good party. I know only three things about his Cambridge life: that he was captain of the Cambridge swimming team, that he kept a Great Dane called Appin in his rooms at Trinity, and he told me the third only a few years ago, prompted by the noise of a champagne cork popping. He laughed out loud as he remembered a fellow undergraduate shouting to him across a crowded room, 'Branson,' he said, 'bring me a fuckin' firkin!'

4

TED'S WAR

As I dig deeper, the past feels increasingly tantalising. The leather-bound photo albums, so recently populated with unidentifiable figures, are now teeming with flesh-and-blood personalities. Piecing together entire lives, with their stories of dashed expectations, sweet romance and untimely death is beginning to feel voyeuristic, as if I'm a puppet-master in a Victorian tale of the unexpected. But learning how these relatives were born, how they fared in wars, dealt with adversity, prospered and, finally, how they died is fascinating, and I'm relishing every minute.

In the summer of 1937, Hitler was threatening peace in Europe but Sir George, who had just retired, was optimistic enough to take Mona, Joyce, Ted and Uncle Bill on a cruise to South Africa. The family had rented out Wharfenden and moved to Suffolk, taking a long lease on Bradfield Hall, a Georgian mansion in the grounds of Euston Hall, the Duke of Grafton's estate. The grounds, landscaped by Capability Brown, were elegant and the main house, designed by William Kent, was outrageously grand. Dad told us that the duke's wine cellars were so extensive that he'd built a small underground railway to transport the wine from its racks to the dumb waiter that would carry the cases up to the butler's pantry. Sir George was thrilled with the move. His friend the duke was a generous host, inviting the family to join in his magnificent shoots, fish on his lake and dine in the main house.

The pension of a high court judge was a good one and Mona had come to the marriage with some income, so Sir George and Lady Branson were able to live well; Uncle Bill's financial contribution was the cherry on the cake. Between them, they retained eight staff. In his will, Bill left money not only to Parton but to another chauffeur called Dewdney. However, regardless of their apparent financial comfort, according to cousin Michael money was 'always a niggle'. The Branson children were conscious of tension around household expenses and were themselves kept on a tight financial rein.

The cruise, followed by a safari, was to last nine weeks. With four first-class cabins booked on the MV *Dunbar Castle*, it was to be Sir George's last hurrah before he settled down to retirement in Suffolk. Ted was nineteen and, as he said himself, 'quite a deb's delight.' He couldn't believe his luck, being one of the few eligible bachelors on the boat among a positive bevy of young beauties. En route to their first stop at Port Elizabeth, Ted's eye was caught by a girl who was travelling with her formidable mother. The couple managed to snatch loving dances here and there, and even exchanged the odd kiss. As the relationship progressed they decided that for secrecy's sake they shouldn't talk to each other in public. On the night before they disembarked, the eager girl sneaked into Ted's cabin. Unbeknown to the lovers, the girl's mother noticed that she was missing and sounded the alarm. Presuming she'd fallen overboard, the Captain ordered the ship to turn around and sail north once more.

The girl sneaked back to her cabin early in the morning. Ted awoke feeling very pleased with himself and looked through his porthole, expecting to see Port Elizabeth's harbour but there was no land in sight. As he entered the breakfast room to join his parents he learned the reason that the ship had had to turn around. The captain came to their table to apologise for the eight-hour delay in getting to port. He caught the eye of Ted, who was blushing to the roots of his blond hair but said nothing. Ted was terrified and tried to reassure himself that there was no reason that he should be implicated in the fiasco, until the girl sidled up beside him and muttered under her breath words that would haunt him for many a year to come. 'Mother knows,' she said. 'Mother knows.'

On the return voyage, fate was to play its tricks once more with a chance encounter that was to impact not just on my father's generation, but on mine too. Ted became friendly with two 'gorgeous girls', South African sisters called Wendy and Jacqueline Payne. Wendy was not only beautiful, she was outspoken, funny, athletic and adventurous. Ted, infatuated by their playful teasing, turned on his usually foolproof charm, but it was in vain. Sir George and Lady Branson were also quite taken with the girls and invited them to stay with them for the weekend on their return to England.

News of the sisters' invitation spread fast, and Ted's brother Joe made an effort to get home that weekend too, arriving late on the Friday night after the rest of the party had turned in. The story goes that Wendy had recently seen a fortune teller, who told her that the man she was going to marry would have a number plate that added up to thirteen. Waking up on the Saturday morning, she looked out of the window, and blow me down, the number plate on Joe's Morris Eight added up to nuptial heaven. Before she'd even laid eyes on him, Wendy decided that, come what may, here was the man she would marry.

Their marriage turned out to be a happy and fruitful one: they had two children, Jill and Michael, my secret source. Visiting the Addisons as a child was awe-inspiring. Wendy, who never lost her strong South African accent, kept a menagerie of animals, including an aggressive African grey parrot named Papageno, who would sit on her shoulder and threaten to nip us with his terrifying beak while screeching, in an Afrikaans accent, 'Who's my beautiful boy, then?'

Before Ted went up to Cambridge, the family travelled to Mougins in France. 'It cost £14 for fourteen days and fourteen nights,' Dad told me. 'We would spend most of the morning climbing up a mountain with our skis tied to our backs, have a picnic lunch at the summit, then strap on our skis and whizz down again. There were no safety features or special bindings on the skis. The return train to London was chock-full of people with broken legs or twisted knees, being wheeled around in outsized bath chairs.'

Ted volunteered for service on 2 September 1939, reporting to the recruiting office in Chancery Lane, and war was declared the next day. He told the recruiting officer that he was a good horseman and became a trooper at the Redford Barracks outside Edinburgh. On his way up north, with a certain glee, he alarmed a number of fellow travellers; for in his determination to win a bet with his brother Joe of who would be the first to finish knitting a jumper, Ted sat in full uniform, needles clicking away, for the entire journey.

Returning to Trinity was unthinkable now. Before being commissioned, he was sent on a liaison officer course that included becoming proficient at riding cross country on a motorbike, a skill he would retain for the rest of his life. He was also sent to the Army School of Equitation at Weedon as an officer cadet. NCOs had to call officers 'Sir', but they could use any epithet before ending a sentence with that term of respect. Ted remembered having some problems with his spurs on his first day of training, and the sergeant major shouting at him, 'Keep your knees together on the saddle, Mr Branson. You look like a willing whore, Sir.'

The prospect of going to war on horseback thrilled Ted and he embraced his new family in the Staffordshire Yeomanry, the Queen's Own Royal Regiment. I was always under the impression that he took his own polo ponies to training camp, but cousin Michael soon put me straight. If he didn't go to war on Tishy and Nobby, he must have seconded a couple of horses from a patriotic neighbour. It's hard to believe that horses were used by the British Army until 1943; cavalry played a vital role in mountain combat, as horses could cover terrain that was inaccessible to tanks. Ted's uniform was made up at his father's tailor, and he had two pairs of leather knee-high riding boots made by the shoemaker Peal & Co.

Ted's brother Joe joined the Queen's Royal West Surrey Regiment, but before he went off to fight he hit a stone in the road during a motorcycle journey in the blackout, and flew over the handlebars, fracturing his skull. Medically discharged from active service, he reluctantly spent the rest of the war in the UK as an adjutant in the Queen's Regiment. The gods were on his side, though: most of his regiment were killed in action during the war. His accident had almost certainly saved his life.

Dad's diary for January 1940 displays a combination of excitement and dread. His youthful enthusiasm bursts from each page, with the exception of his frustration at 'Church parade again and an awful sermon. "God could stop the war by raising a little finger" we are told, "but he is testing us". Silly little man, how does he know what's what? Why we are compelled to go to church to listen to such a fool I can't think.'

Later he writes, 'I rather wish I was going off to Finland with Bill [who had volunteered for the Friends' Ambulance corps]. It seems so much better to be able to save life than doing our best to destroy it. However it is obvious that we can't all be ambulance men – someone must use force. Bill says no, and I say as a counter that he wouldn't talk to a tiger savaging a friend.' And later, 'The poor old *Dunbar Castle* has been struck by a mine, I have many happy memories of our nine weeks on her. Not many lives were lost.'

Dad told me that those going to fight had no idea how long they would be out of the country. As it happened, after sailing for

North Africa in 1940, he didn't set foot on English soil for over five years. He found saying goodbye to his fox terrier Patsy more agonising than saying goodbye to his parents, even though the elderly judge was convinced he was going to die of a heart attack at any moment. On his last weekend in Suffolk before being posted abroad, Ted worked out a secret code by which he could let his parents know where he was in his letters home, without drawing the censor's attention.

'Let's imagine that this wall of shelves, in the cellar, is a map of Europe and Africa,' he told them. 'If I'm posted to, say, Palestine, I'll ask you to look out for my skates on the middle shelf on the right and if I'm posted to France, I'll ask you to find them on a shelf towards the left.' They spent some time perfecting the code, and it was a great success; throughout the years that Dad spent at war, his parents knew of his exact whereabouts.

Ted's war was a jumble of anecdotes, japes and adventures. A story of racing tanks across the desert on his horse, and winning; another of tripping on some marble steps in Algiers, scattering a mass of papers containing the plans of the 7th Armoured Division's upcoming attack. As he protected himself in his fall, he realised, to his horror, that the well-meaning crowd around him was gathering up the top-secret papers as they caught the wind.

Ted told of digs with the eminent archaeologist Dr George Reisner, the then seventy-two-year-old Harvard professor of Egyptology. Whenever he had leave, Ted joined this droll elderly man on his excavations around the pyramids at Giza; delighted that he could fulfil his true passion, he revelled in the doctor's knowledge and humour. Ted's fellow officers would tease him about his love of archaeology and when they asked him how he was spending his leave, he would happily reply, 'I'm infra dig with Reisner. Do you care to join me?'

I was keen that Dad should be present to hear his tribute speech rather than wait for his funeral, so when planning his ninetieth birthday I invited our family friend Stephen Navin (who would sit beside the Buddha with me a decade later) to do the honours. Navin embraced the task with enthusiasm, interviewing Dad at great length and capturing this magical story about his desert excavations:

> The extraordinary thing about Dr Reisner was that he
> was both dumb and blind, but Ted was convinced that
> his instinct for archaeology provided him with senses that
> compensated where nature had failed. Ted would ride
> out to the desert to look for shards of pottery and bring
> them back to the doctor who would feel them carefully,
> place them in order on the table in front of him, go to his
> typewriter and proceed to tell Ted the route that he had
> taken across the necropolis, by the pieces of pottery which
> he was able to date through his fingertips.
>
> Reisner had a loyal and devoted secretary – Miss
> Perkins. She was in her forties as Ted describes it and used
> to light Reisner's pipe for him because he couldn't see the
> smoke. Miss Perkins also took to smoking a pipe. The
> Americans were particularly concerned to ensure that no
> harm came to the doctor, as he had done very valuable
> excavating but had not yet had time to write it up. There
> was concern that the Germans might blow him up and they
> therefore insisted that he sleep at the site of his excavation.
> A young Arab would guard the outside chamber, Miss
> Perkins would sleep inside and Reisner would sleep in the
> sanctum sanctorum. I have this image of Ted, Miss Perkins
> and Reisner sitting on a rug, enjoying a post-prandial pipe
> beneath the Sphinx in the cool Egyptian evening, before
> Reisner and Miss Perkins retired to their tomb and Ted
> mounted his horse and cantered back across the desert to
> his base.

Ted was full of happy tales of pretty nurses caring for his every need after he fell from his horse, or of the time when, while attached to the 2nd Armoured Division, he suffered a nasty bout of jaundice and was hospitalised in Cairo. While in hospital, his headquarters was overrun by Field Marshal Rommel. 'This was very inconvenient,' he told me, 'as it meant that I and another junior officer, who had not been captured, suddenly found ourselves liable for the entire regimental mess bill, amounting to £800. To put this into perspective,' he laughed, 'my monthly pay was only £4.'

For all his bonhomie, it became apparent to me as I researched the progress of the Staffordshire Yeomanry, that Ted's war years were terrifying, sad, and tough. His regiment joined up with the Americans, forming the famous 'Desert Rats' and fighting the Battle of El Alamein. The only correspondence I can find from him during the war is a letter to his father. The envelope is addressed to 'The Rt Hon. Sir George Branson, Bradfield Hall, Bury St Edmunds, Suffolk'. It has been stamped, passed by the censor dated 19 January 1943 and was received on12 January 1944. In it is a scrap of paper, on which the young soldier has written the following:

Capt. E. Branson. HQ II Corps CMF.

My dear Dad,

When I changed my HQ yesterday, General Lucas gave me this copy of a letter he sent my General, for (as he put it) my personal file. I think he thought I might have a father I should like to send it to, so I'm doing so.

My love, Ted

The address on the typed letter is headed *HEADQUARTERS VI CORPS. APO 306*, and the letter reads as follows:

Dear General McCreery

Capt. Edward Branson, Staffordshire Yeomanry, has been on duty as Liaison Officer with the VI Corps since the initial landing. During this period of time he has been most active and enthusiastic in furnishing me and the members of my staff with accurate and timely information. In addition, his contributions to our daily conferences have been extremely valuable in acquainting the entire corps staff with the successes and problems which have confronted our British Allies.

Captain Branson has shown himself to be an accomplished and cultured gentleman and has been popular with all of our officers and myself. I hate to lose him.

With hearty wishes for your continued success, I am
Sincerely Yours
John P. Lucas
Major General, US Army

My father's final fighting years were spent in Italy. He took part in the Battle of Anzio, which began with an Allied amphibious landing known as Operation Shingle. When Dad mentioned the Battle of Anzio, I imagined it as being like a film – a few heroic days, with some near-misses before victory was achieved. In reality, they were pounded by heavy shells for over one hundred days, between January and April 1944. He was the liaison officer with the 36th Texas Division at the Salerno landings and told us that the Americans considered him very brave, as he remained standing during German artillery bombardments while they dived for cover at the sound of the 88 mm shells passing overhead. It was a clever party trick, for he knew that by the time you can hear an 88 mm shell you are completely safe, as it has already passed overhead.

The Allies went on to capture Rome on 4 June 1944. It's no wonder that those involved had no appetite to talk about the experience afterwards. The war in Europe was declared over on 8 May 1945, when Germany finally surrendered, following Hitler's suicide in a Berlin bunker. After the war, Ted was posted to Berlin to administer the dispersal of refugees and displaced persons.

During one of our late-summer walks, my father told me about a German girl he'd become attached to during his time in Berlin. I believe it was the first time he truly fell in love. How emotionally complicated their relationship must have been, as tales of Nazi brutality and the Final Solution unfolded. Perhaps members of her family had been killed by the Allies or were now struggling on meagre rations. My young father's wartime experiences were so fresh in his mind. I asked him what she was called, and his eyes twinkled at the memory. 'Oh, I don't know, Nessie,' he said. 'I think we should put that time behind us now, don't you?'

'Don't you understand, Dad?' I persevered. 'In this day and age, we can Google her name and then probably make contact.' I found the idea of a ninety-three-year-old lady receiving an email from a man she'd met nearly seventy years previously, telling her that he'd never forgotten her in all those years, too tender for words. 'Oh no, darling, we shouldn't do that,' Dad said. 'It would upset your mother.'

While foraging for clues in my parents' cellar, I came across a shoebox of cuttings and photos that Dad had kept. It was touching to see what he'd chosen to set aside. Apart from a number of his liaison officer maps and notebooks, there were many folders of black and white photographs. Dad had inherited his mother's passion for photography. Here were beautiful images of the Pyramids, majestic in the desert, fellow officers on horseback, Arabs wearing flowing robes, camels and oases. Wading through these wallets of unidentified people and places, I found one that was stamped with the logo of a Berlin photo lab. Inside were eight small pictures, four taken by Dad and four by his sweetheart. They are both staring at the camera with love in their eyes, Dad loose-limbed and athletic and she with a fresh-faced calm.

Dad had hinted at the reality of his war but I hadn't enquired too deeply, for fear of disturbing the veneer of cheer with which he'd managed to gloss over his darker memories. Only twice did I notice him drop this façade. Once was at Alton crematorium after his sister Joyce's funeral. We'd been standing side by side as her coffin slid behind the curtains. 'Daddy, how did you manage not to shed a tear?' I whispered, holding his hand as we walked past the next group of mourners.

'Ah, darling,' he replied. 'You know, I lost most of my friends in the war. I gave up crying at funerals a long time ago.' The second time, just before he died, I was fortunate enough to talk to him about his real wartime experiences: how during the Battle of El

Alamein he had taken up smoking a pipe to keep the flies away – there were clouds of them laying their eggs on all the rotting bodies. 'It really was a pretty ghastly time,' he admitted.

Ted returned to England, twenty-seven years old and one of the youngest majors in the British Army. He travelled straight to Suffolk, knocked at the front door and was greeted by the butler who calmly said, 'Good evening, Master Ted.'

'Good evening, Dobson. It's good to see you again.' Before another word was uttered, there was a commotion in the kitchen. On hearing her master's voice, Patsy, Ted's faithful fox terrier, came careering down the corridor, skidding on the parquet floor, and leapt into her master's arms.

After the war, Ted learned that, as a veteran whose BA course was cut short by the war, if he sent £10 to Trinity he would automatically qualify for a Master's degree. Within a few months, at the insistence of his father and though he had no real academic experience or interest in pursuing a career as a barrister, he was sent off to law school in London.

5

Deepest Darkest Devon

Necker, British Virgin Islands, July 2017

I'm sharing a room with Mum and she is, at ninety-three, as delicate as a robin. I have no idea how her thin legs and wonky hips support her, but she still scuttles around, emptying her neat suitcases that were packed back in Sussex by one of her two nurses.

We all found her memory slippages alarming at first, but they now form part of her personality. When corrected, she laughs them off with murmurs of, 'Oh yes, silly me. I should leave other people to think for me now!' A week before our trip, I visited her at her home in West Wittering and found her leafing through her diary.

'Now let me see,' she said. 'On Monday I'm seeing my old friend Maggie McGee. I'm not sure what for – take a look for me, Nessie. Is it for her birthday?' She checked her diary entry again before handing it to me and bursting into giggles. 'Oh no, I've got that wrong,' she said. 'It's for her funeral!'

Mum has become adept at hiding her erratic memory loss by remaining curious about other people's lives and hoping that no one will ask her about hers. Her lights go on and off according to her level of anxiety (usually zero), her energy (usually bountiful) and her whisky levels (more often than not, topped up).

Her coiffed hair has been flattened by the journey, and she looks like an impish version of Jean Seberg in *Breathless*. Around her neck she wears a mother-of-pearl crucifix on one chain and a gold hand of Fatima on another. She lies on her bed, staring out at the swaying palms towards the glistening Caribbean beyond and running her fingers back and forth over her temple, something she does when she wants to think. I finish unpacking for her, hanging her delicate gowns on padded hangers. She has always adored clothes and, as an act of defiance against her old age, regularly adds to her wardrobe. Three swimsuits, a pair of skinny white jeans, four or five chiffon dresses, T-shirts, gold sandals, and satin slips with matching bras and panties. I continue to unpack, amazed at what she has managed to fit in her two small cases. Next come her wash bag and make-up, her jewellery and curlers, her book of French grammar, her Kindle, her mobile phone and, finally, her diary.

Mum has always written. To her, capturing the passing days in her diaries is an urgent task. She tells everyone she meets that they should write their experiences down. 'Trust me,' she says, 'you will forget.' Looking at her now, I have a hunch that she is right.

'Shall we be little devils and have a drink, Vanessa?' she asks.

'No, Mummy,' I reply. 'I'll get you a cup of tea for now. We've almost finished unpacking and then you can have your whisky.'

'You old spoilsport,' she laughs and we settle down into the rhythm of easy companions, knowing we have an entire week of holiday stretching before us. 'Tell me, Nessie,' she says suddenly. 'Have you got a special man in your life?'

'No, Mummy,' I say. 'I haven't given up hope of finding someone special again but, for now, I'm quite content as I am.' My answer is fundamentally true. Obviously having a partner would be the ideal but surrounding myself with interesting, challenging people is a happy compensation. That is unless I'm made to feel humiliated by my mother, of course. I should lie. If Mum asks my sister Lindy if she has a boyfriend, she says, 'Yes, his name is Net Flix,' and Mum approves.

'I don't believe a woman is a real woman unless she has a man,' Mum continues. I grit my teeth – we've been through this routine many times before. My voice goes a little sing-songy as I reply, 'You may well be right, Mummy, but at my age it's not so easy to find a man who is worth making the necessary compromises for. And anyway,' I finish, 'I'm not sure I find older men that attractive.'

She floats off into her own thoughts. 'Of course *I've* got a man,' she says, reassuring herself. 'Well, I think I have. I have got a man, haven't I, Nessie? I really can't remember.'

'Yes, Mummy, you have a special friend,' I say.

She looks at me and smiles. 'Now tell me, Nessie, have you got a special man in your life?'

'Let's go and get you that whisky,' I say, and we make our way into the cavernous main room of the great house on the hill.

Mum is happy as she washes down a dementia pill with a good slug of whisky. We sit quietly watching the clouds form abstract paintings, as the sun sets on the horizon. All is quiet. The babies are being put to bed by their exhausted parents, the young are showering in various outbuildings and I can't help feeling I'm exactly where I should be, witnessing the last of the old generation and the birth of the new.

Mum breaks into my thoughts. 'What are you reading at the moment, Nessie?' she asks.

'A book called *The Bright Hour*, about a woman dying of terminal cancer,' I reply.

'Oh dear,' she says. 'It must be terrible for people knowing that they're going to die soon.'

I nod and smile. 'Mummy, you really are an extraordinary lady. How about another whisky? You've certainly earned it.'

* * *

Our family tale now takes us back to Scotland and this time to Edinburgh, for the birth of my mother's mother, Dorothy Constance Jenkins, on Sunday 19 June 1898. Her father, the Reverend Charles James Jenkins, barely had time to congratulate his wife, Mary Eve, before dashing off for the 7 a.m. matins service. By all accounts he took his vocation as rector of St James the Less Episcopal Church very seriously indeed. He hailed from seven generations of clergy, including two bishops, and had a powerful legacy to uphold. Dorothy, or Young Dock as she soon became known, her older sister Eve and little brothers Charles and Jack, were always aware that Reverend Jenkins put his parishioners first, while his family came a firm second.

The Jenkins clan lived in a dour but comfortable Victorian vicarage, next to the church in Inverleith Row. There wasn't money to spare for luxuries, but there were plenty of opportunities to excel. My great-grandmother's belief in the importance of a sound education, self-discipline, hard work and a focus on the job at hand served her children well and provided the foundation for their matter-of-fact practicality. All four went on to thrive. Eve and Dock were educated at St Brandon's Clergy Daughters' School in Bristol, while Charles and Jack won full scholarships to Fettes College, Edinburgh's most prestigious public school. Mercifully, both boys were too young to be enlisted to fight in the First World War.

Dock resisted church life from an early age. She didn't believe in metaphor or transcendence and had little truck with spirituality, but she approached her responsibility towards the poor of the parish with enthusiasm. Helping her mother support the unfortunate, who would knock at the kitchen door of the vicarage asking for help, was a formative experience for her. For these wretched souls, the alternative to seeking help from the parish was entering the dreaded workhouse. Year after year she witnessed babies being born to undernourished women. As an impressionable girl, she also saw the effects of domestic abuse on wives who were entirely dependent on their alcoholic husbands. The insight she gained while helping with the congregation of St James provided a lesson she was to remember for the rest of her life.

Dock was sixteen when the First World War broke out. This frightening period was made even more challenging when her father died of a heart attack in 1917. Her mother then took on the job of secretary to the Bishop of Edinburgh, a job she retained until she retired at the age of eighty. Dock received a fine education at Lansdowne House School in Murrayfield and went on from there to St Brandon's. She fitted into school life in every respect, being bright and gifted at sport. She took up gymnastics and cricket, captained the squash team, became a keen ice-skater, a fine golfer and tennis player, and also swam for her school. She was fearless and loved performing for an audience; her family enjoyed telling the story of how, finding the top diving board at the Drumsheugh Baths not challenging enough, she climbed into the rafters before diving from there – the only girl ever to have done so.

Young Dock was a tomboy and fiercely competitive. The role of girls at the time was to emulate their mothers in being ladylike and decorative. The long skirts and enormous hats of the day were not conducive to thrashing your brothers at tennis, but this didn't stop Dock from taking them on at every opportunity. Sadly, as she neared her eighteenth birthday, she had to leave St Brandon's; the journey there was considered too hazardous as the war developed. To leave school without any academic qualifications must have been unbearable for my clever, energetic grandmother, and she wasn't alone – few women at the time went on to higher education.

For Dock and many women of her era, the war was a liberating godsend. The restrictions of middle-class Edwardian life lifted and not only *could* they work; they were expected to. Women were needed to support the war effort at home and to fill the holes left by a generation of workers who had been called up to fight. Dock first trained as a nurse and then as a mechanic in the Royal Army Service Corps, becoming the only woman driver in the north of Scotland – a tough assignment, as the lorries had no windscreens and had to be started by hand. She enjoyed the admiring looks she received as she fired up the truck's engine, turning the crankshaft while wearing a long coat pulled tight at the waist with a brown leather belt.

In September 1918, as the war was coming to a close, Dock was sent to pick up a quietly spoken major from the Lowland Brigade. As she drove him back to his headquarters in Edinburgh, she caught his eye in the rear-view mirror. He responded to her charm and cheery banter with a smile, but then looked out of the window in silence. He was unlike the other officers returning from the front, who were keen to flirt.

'Who is this handsome, mysterious officer sitting behind me?' she thought, as they bumped along the rough roads. She stole more surreptitious glances in the rear-view mirror, wondering how to get him talking – just the sort of challenge she couldn't resist. 'Do you play golf?' she asked.

In 1911 Rupert Huntley Flindt had signed up as a volunteer to the London Rifle Brigade, a territorial regiment. Following the declaration of war on 4 November 1914, when he was twenty-three years old, he happily abandoned his City job and embarked for France with the 1st Battalion. Soldiers who became part of the British Expeditionary Force at this stage of the war later became known as Old Contemptibles, an assignation which derived from the Kaiser's reference to 'Britain's contemptible little army'.

Rupert's unit was first in action in Flanders, near the town of Ploegsteert (which soon became known to the British as

'Plugstreet'), just as the First Battle of Ypres was ending in May 1915. In February he had been commissioned as a 2nd Lieutenant and during the month-long battle he earned a 'mention in dispatches'. He also experienced a dreaded mustard-gas attack and was wounded by a mortar bomb.

While on home ground recovering from his injuries – I've found no record of them, but Mum told me he had 'lumps all over his head that still contained shrapnel' and that his lungs never fully recovered from breathing the mustard gas – he attended staff college and became a staff captain. In the breezy language of the time, he wrote that he 'spent a further spell at the Front' with the New Zealand Division, and at the end of the war he was a brigade major with the Lowland Brigade in Scotland. This was where fate played its part and he ended up being driven to Edinburgh by the striking young Dorothy Jenkins.

Soldiers on the front line had spent months knee-deep in mud, living on meagre rations in trepidation of being sent over the top, to run over barbed wire and into machine gun fire, with nothing more to protect them than a tin helmet. Those who survived the war had experienced pure hell and witnessed most of their friends being bayoneted, blown up, gassed or shot. Their ragged nerves were worn out, too, by constant aerial bombardment. A million young souls survived these scenes of devastation only to be condemned to a future haunted by scenes too agonising to refer to and frozen in a state of brittle dignity.

It's not surprising that Rupert was attracted to Dock. He would have found her no-nonsense approach to life comforting and her healthy presence and clear opinions on right and wrong reassuring. In her memoir, *Testament of Youth*, Vera Brittain wrote, 'The difference between the First and Second World Wars was that in the Second World War some of my friends came back.' What a complicated world for our two young lovers to meet in.

After marrying in Edinburgh in March 1922, the gentle major and his 'little treasure' set up home in Hadley Wood in Hertfordshire, now one of north London's sprawling suburbs but then a thriving market town. Rupert took up his old post as a City trader in the family firm and soon became a partner in the company. Hadley Wood was convenient for the City, its neat station being on the direct line to Kings Cross. He and the other commuters, all dressed in black coats, pinstripe trousers and bowler hats, and carrying tightly furled umbrellas, took the train to London at the same time every morning and home again at the same time each evening.

Their first child, Michael, was born in the spring of 1923, quickly followed by my mother, Eve, on 12 July 1924. Michael and Evette were born into a happy home. Dock was confident and predictably took motherhood in her stride. The years of helping her mother with her younger brothers and caring for struggling parishioners had given her an understanding of just how robust a newborn baby is, and she enjoyed showing off her proficiency. But Rupert's enigmatic silences were beginning to affect her sense of well-being and the more she encouraged him to share in the joy of their adorable children, the more taciturn he became.

One evening, Rupert returned to Hadley Wood on his usual train, walked into the house, threw his hat and umbrella to one side and announced that he was never going to work in the City again. 'I want to do something clean,' he said.

For an articulate man, this didn't give his wife much of a clue as to his true feelings, but the vision Dock had of her future life was instantly shattered. She'd imagined evenings spent dancing to brass bands at the Ritz and the Criterion and had dreamed of building a network of glamorous, successful London types. Now, all of a sudden, Rupert insisted that he wanted to live in what Dock, with gritted teeth and a fixed smile, would forever refer to as 'Deepest Darkest Devon.'

Nowadays we would recognise that Rupert was having a comprehensive nervous breakdown, but Dock was confused and angry and I don't believe she ever forgave him. Neither Dock nor Rupert had the language to connect with each other's points of view. At that time only those with fine, upstanding characters were respected, and this meant exposing no weakness or doubt. Those who returned from the front were supposed to consider themselves fortunate; the Great War hadn't been won by sensitive flowers.

Rupert had calculated that he could buy the family a decent house with some land. If he sensibly invested their savings, supplemented their income by growing their own vegetables and selling their eggs, bacon, honey and apples, he could just about support the family, though they would have to stop at two children.

Dorothy dragged her feet as they moved into what, to many people, would be considered the idyllic smallholding of Higher Leigh near Kingsbridge in South Devon (it is now a luxury bed and breakfast). The house was remote and down a winding, high-banked lane, equidistant from Kingsbridge, Loddiswell and Churchstow. On its seven acres, Rupert planted a great variety of English apple trees: Beauty of Bath, Lord Lambourne, Lady Sudeley, Bramley, Cox's Orange Pippin, Cox's Pomona, Ellison's Orange, Laxton's Superb and Devonshire Quarrenden. He also bred rare breeds of chickens and grew soft fruits and flowers. Over half a century later, I occasionally bite into a rosy, home-grown apple and am transported by the taste straight back to that blissful shaded orchard of my childhood summers.

Life in Devon was indeed 'clean'. Rupert tended to his bees and trees, played golf twice a week and spent a great deal of time sculpting rather good figurines of naked women draped in flowing fabrics, lying back on plinths. Mum later kept a few of them, and they ended up in our old barn where we kept the billiard table. I would play with them as a child, accidentally lopping off the odd hand or head. None have survived.

The Huntley Flindts managed to maintain the middle-class lifestyle expected at the time and had both a maid and a car. Rupert, always careful with money, had set up trusts to educate the two children privately. They were members of the country and golf club and their sense of civic duty impelled them to volunteer in community initiatives. Dock managed to keep her frustrations below the surface as she volunteered for the local Red Cross and entered numerous golf and tennis tournaments.

Dock tried to be a loving mother and succeeded in many ways, though she was not always conventional. She was a dreadful cook and rarely baked, but she was decades ahead of her time in extolling the virtues of raw food. 'A salad can't really call itself a salad unless it contains at least ten different ingredients,' she said. Her motto was 'pale foods are for pale people,' and she rightly claimed that you should eat unprocessed foods whenever possible. Brown rice, brown sugar and brown flour and wholemeal bread – 'not just brown bread,' she insisted, 'you need to eat the wheatgerm.' She thought that too much salt caused heart attacks and recommended that everyone eat very little meat. The children were told to chew each mouthful of their breakfast, a homemade muesli, twenty times. 'Much of the digestive process takes place in your mouth,' she told them, before giving them a tablespoon of cod liver oil and sending them off to school.

Dock was keen to keep the children's feet on the ground. She didn't agree with the 'deception' of telling them about Father Christmas or the tooth fairy, and could never understand the role of magic or make-believe. Nor did the family ever have a pet of any kind. 'I've never understood why people like dogs,' she once told me. 'You can see their bottoms!'

Years later, my husband Robert and I went to visit Granny Dock in her immaculate flat in New Milton in Hampshire, excited to tell her the news that we were expecting our first baby. We were sitting down by her electric fire, sipping tea from delicate bone china cups. She was obviously thrilled – both for us and that she could boast to her bridge club friends that grandchild number eleven was on the way.

Understanding that I had joined some inner sanctum of sisterhood, she went quiet for a minute or two and then said, 'Did I ever tell you about the time I had the abortion?' Robert and I sat rigid, our faces stuck in awkward smiles, wondering how much she was going to tell us. As I took a sip of tea, Granny continued, slowly at first. 'There I was, stuck in that godforsaken backwater. Your grandfather was perfectly happy keeping himself busy with his garden and parish council work. At first, when I told him I thought I was pregnant, he was angry, blaming me for being careless. I realise now he was desperate – his well-ordered vision of an early retirement and of pottering about in the country was going up in smoke. There was no way we could afford another child. In truth, I too realised that having a third child would anchor me to Devon forever.'

Years of sadness and pent-up frustration began to show in her voice. 'I agreed that I had to have an abortion,' she whispered. 'I remember it as if it were yesterday. I remember taking the train up to Blackheath and wandering up and down the lanes, trying to find the address I'd been given. I remember eventually finding the house and standing outside for ages, trying to pluck up the courage to knock.'

Rob and I avoiding catching each other's eye. She didn't need us to speak – she had to finish her story. 'The woman answered the door. She didn't really say anything other than ask if I had the cash ready. She then took me to a room behind the kitchen, and without further ado asked me to take my pants off and lie on the table. I lay there with my eyes closed, wishing I was anywhere but there. Then she got out a knitting needle and started jabbing. She jabbed and twisted, and then just kept jabbing and jabbing . . .'

'Oh, my darling Granny. How ghastly. I'm so sorry for you,' was my inadequate response. Shame at my lack of courage to say more made my hair on my neck prickle. Robert said nothing, his teacup frozen halfway to his mouth.

Thankfully Dock didn't suffer from septicaemia, the life-threatening result that was common following such a brutal termination. The operation was never mentioned, and life in Devon continued as before.

Dock and Rupert worshipped Eve. She was growing up to have her mother's impish humour, an interest in sport and a love of dancing. She would walk the two miles to church hand-in-hand with her father, trying to keep up with his massive strides. These walks were often their only one-on-one time, and while she hummed tunes and pointed out things of interest, he would use the time to impart as many Christian values to her as he could. He also taught her the importance of careful financial management.

'Little Chimp,' he would say, 'what are you going to do with your sixpence pocket money this week?'

'Two pennies for the poor, two pennies in my piggy bank and two pennies for me,' they would chant together.

Sensitive, artistic Rupert also used these walks to impart his love of the imagination to his daughter, teaching her a poem he'd written as a counterpoint to her mother's matter-of-fact approach to parenting.

'To All Very Young People'

Live on in our land of make believe,
A land so enchantingly true:
For the years go fast and childhood's past
Ere you capture what is your due.
Fairy and fantasy, let's pretend –
Such adventures and thrills in store.
Come get your coat, pull gumboots on,
Slip out by the garden door.
Hand in hand – no, you go first,
But be careful where you tread:
Down the path to the woods beyond.
What's that by the old woodshed?
Dragons or Indians; let them come,
We'll fight them soon as seen.
Or in gentler moments, but properly dressed,
We'd welcome the Fairy Queen.
The smells in our woods are especially nice,
At times when we're free to roam.
Oh! Which way back? Come! Let's be quick
To mother and tea and home.
Play on in your land of make believe,
For the happiest years will fly,
And your pirates and fairy friends of today
Will return to the sea and sky.

Eve couldn't have been more different from her brother Michael, who had inherited their father's sensitive disposition and was a gentle giant with a tendency towards depression. Playing the violin and reading were his passions, whereas Eve was always the centre of a gaggle of giggling girls, encouraging them to take part in the shows she wrote and performed – incidentally, shows that she would then charge her family sixpence each to watch.

Unlike her brother, Eve seemed not to have a care in the world. Their physiques were very different, too – she never grew beyond a petite five foot four inches. Their only mutual interest was tennis. They played endless early morning games at the club, Eve making up for her lack of stature with a devious net game that won her many doubles matches, until she gave up playing aged eighty-eight.

In 1933, Dock realised she was pregnant yet again. The idea of taking the train back to Blackheath was too traumatic, and Clare was born nearly a decade after Eve and Michael. Their unhappy mother was now condemned to life in the country.

6

MOTHER COURAGE

In 1936, Michael was sent to Bryanston, the progressive boarding school. He arranged to come home as seldom as possible, and when he did, he reacted to the domestic tensions by locking himself in his bedroom with a book. Eve developed an acute sensitivity to negativity of any sort and reacted by becoming the joker of the family. As none of the Devon schools offered an outlet for her drama and dance interests, Dock, determined to fulfil her daughter's ambition of a life on the stage, sent her fourteen-year-old daughter to Heatherton House, a boarding school in London that took promising young dancers. Eve was never to live at home again.

As Ted was knitting his way towards life in the army, Rupert was recalled to Woolwich as garrison adjutant. On Sundays he'd take Eve to a tea dance at the Grosvenor House Hotel on Park Lane and tried to temper her ambitions by pouring practical sense onto her dreams of becoming an actress. He also hoped that by restricting her allowance, he would tempt her back to Devon once she had finished her studies.

Eve left school when she was seventeen, her last two terms having been spent in Shamley Green, the sleepy village in Surrey that Heatherton House had moved to because of safety concerns. She was too young to join up for military service, but eager to start working. Wartime London was an exciting place for an adventure-hungry young girl – everything was so vital, and everyone was friendly and supportive. Eve moved into a 'ladies club' at Lancaster Gate with around forty other girls, who all shared an enormous dormitory with only dividing curtains affording some privacy. Each girl had to take a two-hour duty shift, standing on the roof as a fire watcher. Those hours spent in the cold London air, watching the powerful searchlights crisscross the black sky, the silence punctuated by the odd cry of a fox or the singing of a drunk stumbling home, were manna from heaven for Eve's fertile imagination. With her senses heightened by the need for vigilance and the ever-present fear of an imminent 'doodlebug' explosion, she would spend her watch inventing grisly dramas taking place beneath the roofs around her.

The only qualification Eve gained on leaving school was her Royal Academy of Dance Diploma. The reason for her lack of academic success wasn't simply the dismal formal schooling she received at the dance academy. Passing exams simply wasn't in her DNA, for like Ted, she too was dyslexic. She had an agile, inquisitive mind but was unable to process information from the classroom blackboard and put it on paper. In many ways, this gene has been the making of our family – being unable to gain academic qualifications has meant that none of us has been conventionally employable, and explains our entrepreneurial drive.

Eve's school had an agency that placed its young alumni in various stage shows. With her impish energy and ability at mime and dance, Eve was cast in most of the roles she auditioned for. Being involved in big West End productions, with all the camaraderie, glamour and drama that it involved, was Eve's dream come true. She was in her element. But all was not so happy at Higher Leigh, where Eve's younger sister Clare was leading a solitary life, with the family maid her only companion. When I talked to Clare about her childhood, she could only recall one happy memory – lying on her back under the cider barrel with her mouth wide open, catching the drips as they seeped through the old wooden tap. With no brother and sister at home – Michael was training to be a doctor at St Thomas's Hospital Medical School – she craved love and warmth from her mother but Dock, now virtually a single parent with Rupert posted to London for weeks on end, had taken a job as a secretary at a local boys' prep school.

Clare's parents, thinking that she would be happier living with other children, sent her, aged just six, to boarding school, but the little girl was miserable there. On more than one occasion, Dock received a call from the headmistress telling her that Clare had run away. Dock would then search the Devon lanes until she spotted a diminutive figure plodding determinedly homeward. She'd scoop up her daughter and drive her back up the long gravel drive before depositing her, kicking and screaming, in the strong arms of matron and fleeing for home.

Last year, while clearing out Aunt Clare's desk after her death, I found a bundle of letters written in childish script, tucked away at the back of her filing cabinet.

Darling Daddy

PLEASE PLEASE come down and take me out this
Sunday, the 17th. PLEASE PLEASE, if you cannot come
could you tell Eve to come and take me out instead?

PLEASE come its very urgent, send a postcard please
saying when you will arrive and when you will go. I shall
die if you don't come. Tons of love. Clare

The image of a miserable little girl making a bid for freedom
still breaks my heart. Talking to my much-loved but tough and
eccentric eighty-five-year-old aunt, I tried to sympathise, saying
that I understood how it felt to be brought up in a family as an
'afterthought'.

'Ha!' she spluttered. 'It's OK for you. I wasn't just the
afterthought – I was the mistake.'

I paused for a while, unsure of what to say in the face of this
awful truth. 'Did you think Granny was unkind or cruel in any
way?' I ventured.

'No, she was never cruel,' Clare replied. 'She just wasn't at all
maternal.'

During the school holidays, Clare and her mother spent their
days at Thurlestone Golf Club. Clare would skip around the
players as they sat having their tea in the sun, while waiting for
her mother to return from her round. Thurlestone was to become
the venue of a life-changing encounter for Clare, for it was here,
at the age of fourteen, that she was to meet Douglas Bader, the
real-life hero of *Reach for the Sky* and the love of her life. He was
in his late thirties when they met, but it was the beginning of an
extraordinary relationship that lasted until his death in 1982. To
this day we speculate about its nature, but the sparkle in her eyes
whenever his name was mentioned certainly hinted at intimacy.

Born in 1910, Bader was a keen sportsman who went on
to be a famous flying ace during the Second World War. It has
been suggested that his swaggering confidence and daredevil
personality were amplified by his wartime experiences and that
his fame encouraged an innate sense of superiority and a tendency

to bully those less capable than himself. However, his eccentricity gave Clare a new confidence and freedom.

I learned a wonderful story about Douglas that may have related to Clare's invitation to him to give a talk at her secondary boarding school, Cranborne Chase. Bader was not one to temper his language, and when he was invited to give a talk at a smart girls' school, he began, 'So there were two of the fuckers behind me, three fuckers to my right, another fucker on the left . . .'

At this point the headmistress blanched and interjected: 'Ladies, the Fokker was a German aircraft.'

'That may be, madam,' Bader replied, 'but these fuckers were in Messerschmitts.'

Meanwhile in London, Eve was falling in love with a young fighter pilot called John Roper, whom she had met through a friend at the theatre. When he was on leave, they would go dancing at the Milroy Nightclub or the 400 Club. The intensity of wartime relationships was summed up in the way they spent their evenings: full of gaiety and laughter on meeting and then, as the evenings drew to a close and they grew aware of the danger their partners would imminently face, the dances would become slower and slower until they were dancing what they called the 'goodnight shuffle', doing nothing more than clinging to each other and taking the odd step. Mum describes kissing John goodnight one evening, then never hearing from him again.

Barely a family was left untouched by the war, and with each ghastly blow came the resolve of rising to the spirit of the age. It was the 'stiff upper lip', the 'what doesn't kill you makes you stronger' sort of spirit – layer upon layer of emotional pain buried under platitudes to encourage you to get back in the saddle.

Eve worked with Morecambe and Wise, who were in 1942 just beginning to form their unique double act. She remembers going to the pub with them after every show and listening as they cut their teeth, performing for their stage mates. Her final foray on the West End stage was in Sir Alan Herbert's production, *Bless the Bride*.

While London was under threat, dressing up for the stage night after night began to feel unfulfilling to Eve. Being surrounded by so much excitement satisfied her passion for drama, but her life needed purpose. Being too young to sign up to one of the services, she looked for other sources of adventure. It was at this time that someone told her that the Air Training Corps were looking for people to train cadets to fly gliders. I can't begin to understand how she thought she would be qualified for such a job – not least because the position was only open to men. But yet again, her charm shone through and she managed to convince the recruiting officer that she was capable of taking on such a role. She had turned up to the interview at the glider training centre in Heston in Middlesex wearing baggy khaki trousers, a roll-neck sweater and with her hair tucked into a cap. She may not have been disguised as a man, but she was certainly playing down her femininity. When asked if she had any experience, she explained that she had none at all but would love to learn and help out in any way she could.

The officer in charge agreed to take her on as an 'instructor under instruction', as long as she kept on dressing as a boy; as he explained, headquarters certainly wouldn't sanction employing a woman in such a dangerous sport.

Stories of my mother's days at Heston echoed through our own childhood. Whenever she was encouraging us to leap off cliffs into freezing seas or to climb to the top of trees, her own bravery in the face or fear would encourage us to push on. She loved working with the young boys, teaching them how a glider catches the thermals and showing them the simple instruments that kept the craft stable. She was in her element chanting the mantras of strict safety drills and giving the cadets the confidence to climb into the tiny solo cockpit, lifting their spirits as she strapped them in.

'Don't worry Charlie,' she would sing. 'You know you can do it!' She would then give the boy a hearty slap on his shoulder and a kiss on the forehead before the glider was winched three hundred feet into the air and cast adrift into the clouds. With the trace of her kiss on his skin and her encouraging words still ringing in his ears, he would happily swirl over the fields, coming down with a bumpy landing ten minutes later. And there Eve would be, whooping with joy as he struggled out of the bucket seat, his arms raised in triumph. He would give her a hug in gratitude, for Eve had shown him that he could turn fear, full-body-stress fear, into pure, adrenalin-pumping excitement.

Then it was her turn. All the cadets and officers had turned out to watch this 'maiden voyage'. Amid good-natured banter and proud salutes from her fellow instructors, the young tomboy settled into the cockpit. She gave a cheery wave to the crowd and off she went, winched higher and higher, but at the critical point she forgot the vital instruction that she had drilled into her young cadets: never release the nose from the winch cable while the glider is pointing skyward. She released the glider and it promptly stalled and began spiralling towards the ground. She remembers feeling dizzy and sick, as complete terror caused her to momentarily freeze. At the last moment, self-preservation clicked in and she managed to pull the joystick back just in time to bring the glider to a haphazard landing. Her audience ran to her as she emerged from the cockpit, shaking. She began to take off her flying helmet, but her excitable students chanted, 'Again! Again!'

The idea of going back up into the clouds made her palms sweat. 'Come on, Evie, my girl,' she muttered to herself as she forced a smile, 'you can do it.' With a victorious twirl of her helmet and to a roar from the crowd, she twanged her goggles back over her eyes, snapped on her seatbelt and was winched skyward again. Up and up she flew, counting to a hundred to settle her nerves. This time she calmly waited for the glider to straighten up before she pulled the release lever, its head down. She gave the cheering cadets a fly-past, blew them a kiss and followed through with a near-perfect landing. She never went up in a glider again.

In 1943, when Eve was nineteen, she applied to become a member of the Women's Royal Naval Service. Every girl dreamed of becoming a Wren, and she was no exception – the lure of the sea, the boats, the outdoors and the saucy uniform were too much to resist. With virtually no preparation for the interview, Eve puffed up her chest and walked into the recruitment office to ask for a job. Once again, her audacity paid off, and they offered this uneducated, dyslexic girl a job as a visual signaller on the spot.

Visual signallers, sometimes known as 'bunting tossers' or 'flashers', were instructed to communicate in Morse code, either with hand-held Aldis lamps or a larger, fixed ten-inch lamp. Semaphore flags were used for signalling in daylight. After four months of training, eight young Wrens were posted to the Black Isle, a peninsula on the bitterly cold east coast of Scotland. Much of the Allied fleet was based there and the girls felt responsible for the safety of every ship.

After the majority of the ships left Scotland for the south, their next posting was at Yarmouth, on the Isle of Wight. The island was in virtual lockdown, with civilians unable to enter or leave without special permission. This created a true feeling of community and although rationing was strict, with no meat, eggs or fish available, the girls were well looked after. Not a day went by when the friendly publican or a neighbour didn't take pity on them and slip them a freshly laid egg or other treat of some sort.

Mum gives a slightly guilty grin when she describes her year in Yarmouth as being 'one of the best of her life,' but I can easily imagine it to be true. She and her seven colleagues had by this time become real friends, and they were all billeted together above a chemist shop at the end of their signalling pier. Yarmouth is still a charming village, with its colourful cottages surrounding the harbour, and the young Wrens felt safe in this tight-knit community, yet proud to be playing their part in the war effort. Mum loved to walk to the end of the pier, dressed in her navy duffle coat, to her wooden signalling hut, with its wood-burning stove and where a steaming mug of cocoa awaited her. The fact that the island was swarming with fit young servicemen didn't go unnoticed, either.

Eve's dreadful spelling didn't have much effect on the outcome of the war, but it led to some good laughs. On one occasion she was happily flashing an instruction to a Motor Torpedo Boat. 'B-I-R-T-H-H-E-R-E' she signalled, to which the captain's response was, 'W-H-A-T-A-R-E-Y-O-U-G-O-I-N-G-T-O-D-O-A-B-O-U-T-I-T?'

Another time, a sailor tied his dinghy to her jetty and walked into her hut. 'Little Wren,' he said. 'It seems you're having trouble with your Morse code. I'll teach you a secret and I guarantee that you'll never forget it.' Thereupon this kind man proceeded to write the alphabet out in capitals, before demonstrating the dots and dashes and marking each letter accordingly. This way, she was able to visualise each letter according to its Morse code equivalent. In five minutes he had taught her what navy school had been attempting to do for months, and she has remembered Morse code to this day.

There was romance on the pier, too. Mum remembers looking through her telescope and spotting a good-looking lieutenant commander, dressed in a white naval sweater and standing on the deck of a motor torpedo boat. Without giving it too much thought, she flashed him an unintelligible message. His response was to question what on earth the message was about. She then sent another message back, slowly and clearly. 'Would you come alongside?'

He immediately brought his boat alongside the pier and was surprised to be offered a mug of cocoa. The next day, Eve was thrilled to receive a parcel wrapped in brown paper, hand-delivered by a sailor who stood waiting for a reply. As she untied the string, her heart lifted; there was the woolly jumper that had caught her eye the night before. So began another moving wartime relationship, of private moments grabbed during shore leave, silent seaside walks, intense conversations and final urgent kisses, before she waved her loved one off as he steamed away into the unknown.

When Germany finally surrendered on 8 May 1945, the young Wren was homeless and broke. Her old friend Brenda, a dancer with the Ballet Rambert, was going on a tour of Germany to entertain the British troops there, and suggested that Eve join them. The idea was preposterous: after years away from the world of classical dance, the prospect of her doing a respectable *plié* was dubious, let alone dancing in a full ballet show. The tour was to be sponsored by the Entertainments National Services Association, and the charming naivety of the time is highlighted in the thought that sending a ballet company to keep up the troops' morale with performances of *Swan Lake* was regarded as a good idea.

Eve made an appointment for an audition with Madame Rambert herself. Mim, as she was known to all who worked with her, must have had a sense of humour, for she roared with laughter as Eve appeared from the wings dressed in her uniform of bell-bottoms and a sailor's hat and proceeded to dance and mime her way through a prepared piece about life in the navy. Mim hired her. 'At least you'll keep the troops amused,' she said, 'but please don't expect to have a job with us on your return.'

'Adventure out of adversity' was Eve's mantra during the next two months. She had no sense of entitlement and never expected the weather to be perfect, her accommodation to be comfortable or the food to be wholesome. In truth, the harsher the conditions, the better the story. This attitude lifted the spirits of other dancers in the troupe, who laughed and joked their way through the devastation that was Germany in November 1945.

I can't imagine what the wretched, starving, humiliated Germans made of this group of young dancers. The girls walked among the rubble as the vanquished population picked away at their pitiful cities. They were spat upon by children and hugged by the elderly, who looked them directly in the eye, a plea for understanding. It was bitterly cold. Compassion was the only emotion that rang true during those two months, alongside the pleasure of being adored by an audience of four hundred men every night.

Eve's imagination could have been getting a little fanciful when she included the following story in her memoir, *Mum's the Word*. 'I have one lovely memory from those days,' she writes. 'Just outside Berlin, a young, handsome British general invited me to go riding with him and lent me a thoroughbred Army horse. We went galloping through the forest, playing hide-and-seek as we wove in and out through the trees. It was thrilling, but perhaps a bit risky for a working ballet dancer!'

I don't believe for a minute that Mum has ever been on a horse in her life, but reading this story tells me so much about her all the same. Reading this extract, I wonder if it ever crossed her mind that she might have passed her future husband as she visited the army stables, for he too was posted in Berlin at this time.

Post-war Britain was a dreary place. Once the end-of-fighting euphoria was over, a depressing reality struck home. Emergency laws were passed, including the rationing of food, fuel and material. This was not a life that Eve had envisioned for herself after the adventures of being in the Wrens. She decided to become an air hostess, a 'Star Girl' on British South American Airways, flying from London to Santiago in Chile, a twenty-day return trip requiring six stopovers.

After some basic training in how to ditch the plane in an emergency and in serving food, Eve was fitted out with a uniform that had been designed by Norman Hartnell to emphasise the girls' curves. They were issued with silk seamed stockings and told that they were allowed to wear flat black shoes while flying but should be elegantly shod at all other times.

Eve's first flight took off on 26 March 1947. She was not allocated a seat and during her breaks she would lie down on the mailbags in the hold. The planes only flew at ten thousand feet and at 250 knots per hour, their engines emitting an ear-splitting drone as they were buffeted by every gust in their path.

Their first stopover was in Lisbon. The next, after an eight-hour flight, was in Dakar in Senegal, West Africa. Mum graphically describes the effects of the gruelling flight: the nausea, the swollen ankles and intermingling smells of Jeyes Fluid and vomit. A glorious two-day stopover in a dilapidated hotel called the Majestic followed, with eccentric fellow guests, sandy beaches and warm, clear seas. After Dakar came a terrifying nine-hour flight over the Atlantic to Natal in north-east Brazil, and from there another seven hours to Rio and a two-day stopover. Finally they flew to Montevideo and on to Buenos Aires, a world away from grey post-war Britain before landing in Chile.

In August 1947, an Avro Lancastrian airliner named Star Dust disappeared while flying over the Andes. Eve had been scheduled to be on the next flight of that very plane. The tragedy was followed by another in January 1948, when the Star Tiger disappeared between Santa Maria in the Azores and Bermuda. Then the Star Ariel disappeared between Bermuda and Cuba, giving rise to the legend of the 'Bermuda Triangle.' The reason for the planes' sudden disappearances was a faulty pressurisation system that caused them to disintegrate in mid-air.

Even so, this Star Girl carried on flying – when weighing up the odds between personal safety and adventure, there was really no contest; adventure won out every time. Thankfully British South American Airways were to be taken over by the British Overseas Airways Corporation and they switched to the pressurised Avro Tudor airliner, but by this time Eve was embarking on another chapter altogether.

7

LOVE IS THE DEVIL

Love is both the devil and the angel; we crave it and we fear it. One thing is for sure: none of us can control it and very few of us escape its clutches entirely. Love can also refresh a family dynamic: just when everyone is settled in roles, along comes someone from outside and stirs up the pot. It's no coincidence that some of the greatest stories start with either a wedding or a funeral. Drama lurks where the relationship order is disrupted; watching how the sand settles is where the fun lies.

Let us look back at our story so far. We've witnessed the lives of Joyce/Mona, secluded in the wilderness of the Scottish Highlands, and then the Branson family, not of the landed aristocracy themselves but at ease in the world of shooting parties, stately homes and servants. We've followed Ted through six enriching and shattering years of war; having been undoubtedly respected as a soldier then finding himself, at twenty-nine, unqualified and unemployable.

We've also had an insight into the lives of the Jenkins family, with their emphasis on education rather than material possessions: Granny Dock with her athletic prowess and competitive, restless spirit, and well-to-do Rupert, his confidence crushed by the First World War. And then, of course, young Eve, a product of the two of them, neither shackled by her class nor defined by her education, and utterly unafraid of what lay ahead.

As children, we loved hearing the story of how our parents first met. It was nothing particularly extraordinary, just a day when the gods were smiling down, with both of them in the right place at the right time and open to making connections.

Eve was helping a friend at a drinks party while resting between trips to South America. She was standing behind the bar at the far end of the room when she saw Ted enter. She was immediately attracted to him, with his cheerful demeanour, thick blond hair and graceful posture. One of the many letters of condolence we received after Dad's death, sixty-five years later, stated rather touchingly that 'When you talked to Ted at a drinks party, you could be sure of three things: that he would make you laugh, that he'd tell you something that you didn't already know and that you would leave feeling better about yourself.' I'm sure that was as true back then as it would be for the rest of his life.

Eve grabbed a tray of nibbles, wove her way through the throng and, walking up to him, popped a cocktail sausage in his mouth, saying, 'The way to a man's heart is through his stomach.'

And she was right – Ted was instantly smitten. He invited her to the theatre, making the error of choosing the hit musical of the time, *Bless the Bride*. Sitting in the front row of the stalls, he couldn't work out why the cast kept glancing down at them, at one point even checking to see if his flies were undone. During the interval, Eve had to admit that she knew the show quite well, having been in its chorus during the war.

It's hard to imagine how ingrained the class system was in post-war Britain. Such thinking wasn't necessarily motivated by snobbery; it was simply regarded as the natural order of things. Unless you were living on the fringes of society, conventional thinking emphasised the importance of maintaining the status quo by ensuring everyone knew where they stood. A month or two after their first meeting, Ted invited Eve to Bradfield Hall for the weekend to meet his family. Blinded by love, he was oblivious to how his parents would perceive his new treasure, but the reality was that everything he was attracted to about Eve – her spontaneity, her classlessness – was designed to horrify them.

The weekend was a disaster. Eve had never been to such a grand house and looked to Ted for reassurance as they wound their way along the long drive and were welcomed by the butler. She didn't meet Sir George and Lady Branson until she entered the drawing room for drinks before dinner that evening, and their polite coldness was apparent from the beginning. It seemed that all their questions were traps, intended to expose her lack of education and humble origins. Poor Ted did his best to keep everyone's spirits buoyant, but his sister Joyce, forever under her mother's thumb, barely said a word all through dinner. The only saving grace was dear Uncle Bill, who gave Eve encouraging winks across the table when the going got particularly tough.

Wendy and Joe arrived the following morning along with their two young children, Michael and Jill, who offered plenty of distraction. Wendy and Eve instantly bonded, both feeling the weight of Sir George and Lady B's disapproval, Wendy helped Eve see the funny side of everything. She was thrilled to discover that Eve was even more hopeless at the English language than she was, and on Sunday took great pleasure in her in-laws' reaction when she told them what had happened in church that morning.

'After the service was over,' explained Wendy, 'Ted wanted to show Eve around the church so we all stayed behind for a little tour. Reverend Appleyard was full of information, telling us the history of the windows and various brasses. He invited Eve to follow him up the steep pulpit steps so he could show her his pride and joy, the medieval oak-carved lectern. When they got down from the pulpit, Eve shook the vicar by the hand and said, "Thank you for showing us around your church, Reverend – I particularly enjoyed seeing your beautiful rectum!"' The Branson seniors were not amused.

My parents' courtship was interrupted by Eve's long trips to South America, and before long both of them began to hate the weeks of separation. They'd found their match; Eve called Ted her Prince Charming, and was utterly in love. However, each time they went to stay at Bradfield, his parents reminded Ted of his dire financial position and told him they had no intention of helping him set up a family home. They bewailed the fact that he wasn't interested in marrying the wealthy heiress Wanda Whittington, who clearly had a soft spot for their blue-eyed but impoverished son.

As ever, Wendy came to Eve's rescue and boosted her flagging confidence. 'Oh Evie,' she would say. 'Don't worry – those old fuddy-duddies may want Ted to marry a solid Suffolk Punch, but you'll win out in the end. He's found his Palomino filly.'

Ted convinced Eve to give up her job as an air hostess. Planes were dropping out of the sky; it seemed suicidal to continue. With no income and a certain amount of trepidation about his future career, he proposed to Eve. Blind with love and full of youthful optimism, they were married on 14 October 1949.

Ted knew that his final law exam results would be issued while he and Eve were away on honeymoon in Majorca. Hoping to add an extra sprinkle of magic to their fairy-tale romance, he asked his father to ring him with his results. 'Are you sure you really want me to disturb your honeymoon?' his father asked anxiously.

'Yes please, Dad,' Ted confidently replied. His father did as he had been asked and called his son on opening the envelope. The young couple returned to London to face an uncertain future, for Ted had failed.

Eve recalled her happy summer in Shamley Green during the war and they managed to find and buy a workman's cottage in the village, overlooking the cricket pitch. It was in an atrocious state of disrepair, with ceilings so low that Ted couldn't stand up in any of the rooms, and the floors were so rotten that he had to tiptoe around with his head bent low, like Fagin out to pick a pocket or two. Nowadays it would be condemned but happily, health and safety laws didn't exist back then. Ted enjoyed the fact that he could lie in the bath while changing the electrical fuses.

Before the mid-1960s, conception was an ever-present danger. Eve discovered she was pregnant only a few weeks after returning from Majorca – a doctor had issued her with a Dutch cap and given her sticky instructions on how to use it, but something had failed. With no qualifications and Ted still unable to earn, it dawned on them that until his career was up and running Eve would have to be the family provider. Across the village green, an elderly man called Sir Philip Gibbs lent her a garage, where she began to give after-school ballet lessons, an ill-fated attempt to bring in a steady income.

The young couple plucked up the courage to tell Sir George and Lady Branson about the baby's imminent arrival. Aware that this news might not go down well, Ted suggested that they drive up to Suffolk to deliver it in person. It crossed my mind that Mum might have been exaggerating when she wrote of her in-laws' reaction – she described how she overheard them saying to Ted, 'We told you not to marry that flibbertigibbet,' and how she walked around the garden sobbing her heart out and being consoled by her desperate husband. However, her misery was confirmed to me when cousin Michael, who was a young boy at the time, recalled hearing his parents Joe and Wendy, who were also at Bradfield Hall that weekend, threatening to leave if George and Mona carried on being so beastly to Eve. Mum said that their reaction to her pregnancy made her only more determined to succeed.

Apart from the misery of his exam retakes, Ted and Eve spent a busy few months preparing for their first child. They couldn't afford a car and so drove around on a motorbike with Eve, her belly becoming more swollen by the week, bobbing along in the sidecar. A gang of friends came to help them lower the floors of the cottage and replace the ancient wiring, rendering their home habitable for their new arrival.

Rationing wasn't to end for another four years, so they had to supplement their paltry meat allowance by breeding rabbits in hutches in the back garden, and they would also swap the meat for eggs. Eve loved to grow vegetables – nothing exotic, but plenty of perpetual spinach and potatoes. Their dream almost came to a sudden end one day. Always preparing for a rainy day, they'd been hoarding petrol in old cider bottles in a drawer in the kitchen – why in the kitchen, goodness only knows! Early one summer morning, heavily pregnant and sleepy after a restless night, Eve padded downstairs to boil the kettle for a cup of tea. She lit a match and whoosh, the petrol vapour in the drawer ignited. Eve screamed for Ted, who rushed in and opened the drawer, managing to slam it closed again just as a bottle exploded. A microsecond later and both of them would have been covered in burning petrol and shards of glass.

As the baby's due date loomed, Ted was feeling under pressure. The stress of trying to pass his wretched Bar exams while simultaneously restoring the cottage caused an enormous boil to erupt on his cheek. Oh dear – the folly of a little knowledge. He decided to draw the poison from it by pouring boiling water into a cider bottle and holding the mouth of the bottle against the offending boil, understanding that as the water cooled it would reduce in volume, creating a vacuum that gently lanced the boil. His cheek was duly sucked further and further into the bottle, until it was stuck and dangling from his face. He then had to lie with his head on the kitchen table and cover himself with a towel, while Eve gleefully tried to shatter the bottle with a hammer. When the bottle was eventually smashed and the vacuum was released, Ted's boil had turned into a bulbous angry purple egg protruding inches from his face. Eve went into labour there and then.

In truth, Mona Branson was sensitive to the couple's plight. She was at pains not to indulge her son, but she couldn't stand by and see the little family struggle so. When she paid them a visit to see her new grandson Richard, she quietly slipped Ted some cash so he could build a garden shed for his wife's new venture – Eve was going into the fancy goods business.

The following years were exhausting, but idyllic. We can follow the family's progress by looking at the photographs. At first there are plenty of black and white snaps of baby Richard, forever beaming his toothy smile. Four years later, the now-colour images include his sister Lindy – always pretty, but even back then her smile was more tentative than her boisterous brother's. Eve, petite and with no signs of weight gain from her pregnancies, stands with a dancer's posture in 1950s frocks, staring straight into the lens with her chin down, ever the starlet. There aren't so many photos of Dad, who was always behind the camera, indulging his hobby. If Eve ever took a photo of Ted, he inevitably looked relaxed, a pipe hanging from the side of his mouth and his eyes twinkling. There are photos of their 'Bumpety-bump' car, an ageing Austin Traveller complete with running boards and an oak finish that would just about manage the trip to Devon and back for their summer holiday with Granny and Granddaddy.

While scavenging for scraps of the past that would give me an insight into their real lives, not the smiling-in-photographs lives of Rupert and Dock, I found a piece of typescript. Rupert had been an in-patient at St Thomas's when it was commemorating its four hundredth anniversary, having had the then-shattering operation of having his prostate removed. He was asked to write about one small facet of hospital life. Apart from his childhood poem, these are the only words I have from my gentle grandfather's pen:

Vespers

It is evening, two minutes to eight o'clock, and visitors to the ward, having seen their relatives and friends and left their gifts of flowers and fruit, are leaving silently and quickly.

A red screen is placed by a probationer nurse in its warning position covering the glass swing doors, a signal to all passing outside that the ward is now attending to its own affairs. One after the other the lights over the beds are put out by the patients themselves, and an unusual hush seems to spread along both sides of the long room. Apart from two lamps, heavily shaded with green baize, above sister's desk and the medicine cupboard, one bright light only remains above the table in the centre.

Outside, at the far end, beyond the long vista of darkened beds, can be seen through the windows and over the stone balcony, the swiftly running river, dark and forbidding, and beyond the faint tracery outline of the building of the Mother of Parliaments, with rows of bright lights reflected in the hurrying waters below, suggesting that another late sitting is in progress.

In the ward, the nurses, still looking as dainty and fresh as when they came on duty many hours before, hurriedly complete whatever they are engaged in, and then silently gather around the screen and the end beds of the ward.

Across the river, the Nation's clock commences to sound its warning of the approaching hour, and on the first echoing clang of eight, a slim figure, dressed in the darkest of blue under her snow-white apron, with lace cap and bow – sister, beloved by all – slips quietly through the doors and passed like a wraith through the semi-darkness to the centre table.

As if by a signal, all the nurses kneel down towards her – the beautiful colouring in their lovely faces, the white aprons and the irregular grouping against the background of the dimly lit scarlet screen and green shaded lights form a picture both exquisite and unforgettable.

Then in absolute silence can be heard sister's sweet voice leading the saying of the Lord's Prayer – a short pause and then, clear as a bell, come the words of that most comforting of evening prayers: 'Lighten our darkness, we beseech Thee, O Lord, and by Thy great mercy defend us from the perils and dangers of this night, for the Love of Thy only Son, our Saviour, Jesus Christ.'

A short valedictory prayer and then: 'Good night, everybody.' These restful words, such a fitting ending, seem to carry with them in their simple sincerity a special message of comfort and encouragement to all those who still have a long road to travel before rejoining the busy world outside. It is over. Some of the lights reappear. Duties are resumed, but in a rather quieter tempo, for in a surgical ward the nurse's work never ceases, day or night.

PART TWO

1959–1983

1

PEAR DROPS, ROBOTS AND BUDGERIGARS

With a certain trepidation, almost sixty years after my birth, I sit pencil in hand, poised to draw a map of my childhood village. I close my eyes and within seconds I'm there, back in Shamley Green, the village that was virtually my entire world for the first decade of my life.

Now I'm back there, skipping across the village green. An elderly man with his sleeves rolled up walks slowly behind an enormous noisy lawnmower, painting lines of alternating light and dark. The smell of freshly cut grass holds promises of a long hot summer stretching before my three-year-old self. As my map evolves, new memories appear with each stroke.

Protecting the cricket pitch is a low chain fence, the perfect height to stand and wobble on, supported by a grown-up's hand. The pitch is surrounded by benches, the resting place for those watching fiercely fought matches with the neighbouring villages, Shalford, Wonersh or Shere. Occasionally you hear a joyous 'Howzat?' but otherwise the players are silent and hardly seem to move.

I remember the two pubs, the Red Lion with its thick carpet, chintz curtains, dark stained furniture and wall lights, the bulbs covered with little lampshades trimmed with pompom braiding. The Red Lion was always empty, apart from someone propping up the bar on a stool, talking in low tones to the overly made-up barmaid as she polished the glasses. Up the hill, between the church and the garage, sits the Bricklayers, all scrubbed tables, dartboard, jukebox and the smell of beer and cigarette smoke. This was where the villagers went to drink.

I was born in June 1959, by caesarean section at Mount Alvernia Nursing Home in Guildford. It was an era when the grey years of rationing were receding, but still remained ever-present in people's minds. Money was tight. My father, his dyslexia playing on his confidence, remained uncomfortable talking in public and was struggling as a barrister. The poor man hated commuting: he first took the train from Guildford to London, then queued for the long wooden escalators to take 'the Drain', the short, crowded tube line that linked Waterloo Station to the City. He would then be faced with the clerk of his chambers, Crown Office in Inner Temple, who would inevitably hand him less lucrative briefs than those his confident colleagues would receive.

Mum's plans to supplement Dad's meagre earnings by starting a workshop to make fancy goods in the back garden were coming to fruition. Granny Mona's money had paid for the shed and bought the basic tools needed to get the business started. Dad used his practical skills to make the basic objects while Mum, having scoured local shops and markets for cheap remnants of materials, braiding and old prints, would decorate them.

My beleaguered father would get back from his crowded commute and go straight into the workshop to run multiple sheets of eight by four-foot hardboard through his noisy circular saw, transforming them into hundreds of rectangles. He would then glue them together, one on top of the other in a Heath Robinson-like contraption, to make the outer shells that Mum would then decorate and turn into tissue-box covers. Another winner at the Fancy Goods fairs were Mum's tea trays. Dad would make hundreds of frames that would then be glazed. Mum bought job-lots of 'antique' prints that would give them an air of grandeur, the felt backs a feel of luxury and the little brass handles precariously screwed onto each side a suggestion of practicality.

Easteds, our workers' cottage overlooking the village green, was wedged snugly between cottages belonging to two other young families, the Gows to one side and the Davises to the other. Despite our nagging money worries, there was always laughter and company, with the mums happy to care for each other's children when needed and the dads helping with gardens and household jobs. My earliest memory is of being popped into a wastepaper basket and thrown thrillingly from one daddy to the next, my giggles encouraging the men to throw me ever higher.

At the end of the terrace was Mrs Avenal's sweet shop, and her mere name makes the memories flood back. I must have been three when my big sister Lindy bet me two pennies' worth of pear drops to go into the shop on my own, promising to follow me a few minutes later to come and pay. I remember entering that dismal shop, the doorbell tinkling, the light barely passing through the neglected window and walking across the expanse of cracked linoleum floor. And the smell of Mrs Avenal, a memorable mix of dried urine and sherbet, filled my nose with fear and disgust. I could hear her shuffling along a dark passage towards me. I saw her hand pushing the plastic curtain to one side before her warty, whiskery face peered down at me.

'What can I get you, dear?' she croaked.

'Two pennies' worth of pear drops please,' I managed.

She turned and began to climb a wobbling A-frame ladder to retrieve the right jar. It seemed to take an age. My mind was racing. How was she going to get back down holding the heavy jar? And where was Lindy? I suddenly thought I was going to pee myself. What should I do? Lindy had sworn she would come.

Eventually, after much effort, Mrs Avenal poured the sweets into a tiny paper bag set on her scales and fiddled with the weights, scooping in more sweets and then taking one out. Still no sign of Lindy. I looked at the bag of sweets rattling in the old lady's shaky hand as she held it out to me, before panicking and running for the door. I raced home, yelling at Lindy and pleading with her to tell me why she hadn't turned up, but she just threw her hands up in the air and roared with laughter. 'Only joking!', she said. I never went into Mrs Avenal's shop again. It was my first lesson in shame – the shop closed soon afterwards. Mrs Avenal was no more.

Richard was already away at his boarding prep school, Scaitcliffe, when I was born. Life became electric when he came home. His best friend was a boy called Nik Powell, who lived in a cottage at the end of the green. They were forever going off on adventures, losing their bikes in rivers and getting stuck up trees. Nowadays, hyperactive children are diagnosed with Attention Deficit Hyperactivity Disorder and are considered somehow handicapped; but my parents, although stretched by their super-charged son, revelled in his enthusiasm and tried to channel his seemingly ceaseless energy.

Each hour of the school holidays revolved around setting Richard challenges.

'Rick, please could you bike to the post office in Guildford to catch the last post with this brief?'

'No worries, Dad.'

'Can you go down to the river to catch some trout for supper, Rick?'

'Will do, Mum.'

'The Vicar asked to see you about helping Judge Jellyneck with his garden.' And off he'd merrily go.

No one was safe if Richard wasn't kept busy, especially his little sisters. Lindy and I would sleepily pad upstairs to bed, shouting last goodnights to Mum and Dad. And as we fumbled our way to turn on the light, Richard's creepy hand would be waiting for us on the switch.

'Aaarrggghh!' he would shout, the terror skinning us alive. I remember him reading us tales by Alfred Hitchcock as our bedtime story, loving the effect he had on us as he described chilling scenes of fiendish murder.

Poor Lindy. Being closer to Richard in age meant she bore the brunt of his practical jokes. Although never unkind, he just couldn't resist pulling a leg if one was there to be pulled. Rather than get used to the teasing, Lindy became more and more sensitive to it. I don't blame her for occasionally taking it out on me – I must have been a nuisance to have around, and I'm sure I deserved to be kept in order.

The winter of 1963 was bitter. Snow lay on the ground throughout December and January, and well into February. Richard spent the Christmas holidays building an igloo, complete with a tunnel entrance, and I was his little four-year-old elf helper.

The role of little helper was one I played throughout my early childhood. Lindy spotted that I was eager to please and turned me into her robot. 'Robot, come here,' she'd command.

'Beep, beep,' I would reply as I walked, stiffly, towards her. She would turn me around, press a few imaginary buttons on my back and then say, 'Robot, go and make me a cup of tea.'

'Beep, beep,' I would happily say, and off I'd go to do her bidding.

I beeped around for months, doing her odd jobs – making her bed, fetching her homework and turning the oven off if she was cooking. Then, one day, reality dawned and I told her my batteries had run out. It was the end of an era – my innocence was slipping away. But I still had plenty of lessons to learn.

When I was nearly five years old, in the spring of 1964, our family moved across the green up Wood Lane, to Tanyard Farm. My father was reluctant, but Mum persuaded him that we should move, enticing him with the promise of outbuildings for his workshops and reassuring him that she would take on all responsibility for managing the house. He'd have been happy to remain at Easteds, but we children were growing – besides, Mum had vision. Dad's beloved Uncle Bill had died, leaving him his fishing rods and a legacy of £4,000, and they managed to get a mortgage for the other £10,000 they needed. The timber-framed house stood on a small hill, fifty yards back from the lane. Like many English farmhouses, each generation had had a hand in building the odd extension, or raising ceilings and adding windows. Tanyard Farm was a hotchpotch with an Elizabethan heart and Edwardian wings, surrounded by a muddle of timbers, brick, stone and tile.

As soon as we moved in, Mum set Dad to work knocking down the wall between the dark dining room and the study; light soon began to pour in. And once he'd got started with his sledgehammer, Dad couldn't stop.

'Let's take off all the modern rendering around the fireplace,' he enthused. 'The old stones behind it are so beautiful.'

Once he started, he couldn't stop. He happily spent the whole weekend bashing away. Late on Sunday night and in a cloud of dust, he yelled with excitement as he exposed an ancient bread oven beside the inglenook fireplace.

'Evie,' he called, as his hands felt around inside the oven. 'I've found treasure – some old manuscripts!'

'What is it, Teddy?' she whooped.

We all drew in our breath, as Dad carefully worked one of the books free and brushed off a thick layer of brick dust. 'Well, I'll be damned,' he laughed. 'I've broken through to the bookshelf in the study next door. It's one of my old *Halsbury's Laws of England*!'

Tanyard Farm was to be our home for twenty-five years. After an initial flurry of decorating, during which Dad developed tennis elbow from painting the walls, and the building of a conservatory, no more changes were ever made. Yards of velvet purchased from

Mum's business suppliers were enthusiastically pushed under the needle of her aged sewing machine and across the dining room table to make curtains. I watched in wonder as the headings were stitched on and the strings pulled tight, ruffling the fabric. She'd then ask me to help her thread the curtain hooks onto the heading and we'd hook the curtains on the metal hooks sliding along the rails. Mum then pinned up the hems, weighing them down with pennies. Once hung, the curtains were never hemmed and the pins slowly rusted into the fabric, while I'm sorry to say that the tempting pennies were removed by little hands and spent in the village shop.

The heavy oak front door, with sturdy bolts that my father would slide home with a reassuring thud each night, opened directly into the low-beamed dining room. One Edwardian extension was converted into a separate 'flat' and was soon occupied by tenants, in return for a number of hours of housekeeping per week. There were four other bedrooms, a family bathroom and my parents' en suite, which was never used due to its dodgy plumbing.

My parents' bedroom, which seemed like a world of its own, was dominated by a bed large enough for the entire family. Family snuggling-in-bed days were reserved for Christmas or the rare occasion when Dad had a blinding hangover and we'd all pile in asking him very loudly how he was. It was a sacred space, a private island of security. I rarely saw my parents in bed together; by the time Dad woke me with a 'Wakey wakey – it's another beautiful day,' and I'd padded my way along the corridor to climb into bed beside Mum, Dad would be getting dressed. I'd watch him standing beside his mahogany dressing table, first lighting his pipe and then putting it to one side as he attached a stiff collar to his white shirt with collar studs. After buttoning up his shirt, he'd relight his pipe, tuck his shirt tails between his legs and somehow slip on his pinstripe trousers and hook his braces over his shoulders, without the tails coming out from under him.

Childhood diseases felt like a real treat; mumps, measles, whooping cough and scarlet fever meant that we were allowed to spend entire days in that bed. Being ill meant being singled out for Mum's special attention, and she would bring me peeled and segmented oranges and bottles of warm Lucozade. It was the only time I remember her reading to me – and always the chapter on the Spartans from the children's *Encyclopaedia Britannica*.

Once, when I was being driven to distraction with measles and feeling particularly sorry for myself, Mum comforted me by saying, 'I'm going to let you in on a magic trick, Nessie. If ever you're feeling ill or scared, imagine you're in a boat, sailing towards the sunset.' My parents' bed became my galleon, a make-believe refuge.

Their musty walk-in wardrobe also provided hours of entertainment, and I loved rolling from Mum's side to Dad's. The chore of doing the laundry with our strange, primitive washing machine resulted in a practical approach to cleanliness: clothes were rarely washed, so smelt deliciously musty: a parent-y combination of tobacco, hairspray and wool.

Above the rails of clothes was a deep shelf sagging with dried foods, candles, tins of beans and jars of slowly solidifying Nescafe. The recent Cuban Missile Crisis had reminded my parents of the war, and this time they were certain they weren't going to be caught short.

At the back of the cupboard, behind the coats, was a cast-iron dark-green safe. When we were older, Mum used to give us 'a little something from the safe' for Christmas: a pair of family cufflinks, say, or some Maundy money collected by Granny Mona. She would then insist on taking the precious gifts back for safe-keeping, and much to our amusement, we would often be given the same present again the following year. Hidden in a box behind the shoe rack was Dad's collection of *Health and Efficiency* magazines, a strange little publication apparently aimed at naturists. As an inquisitive six-year-old I puzzled over the wholesome photographs of men and women playing badminton, and of women standing next to a caravan, one foot on the plastic doorstep, smiling directly at the camera. All, without exception, covered in nothing but goose pimples.

Jobs were the only activity I remember the whole family participating in. Tanyards boasted four acres of land and an abundance of ancient farm buildings. There was a vegetable garden and a herbaceous border to maintain, an orchard to mow and endless fences to restore. In what would have been the old barn's courtyard there was an enormous swimming pool that had been dug by soldiers returning from the First World War to the humiliation of unemployment during the recession of the 1920s.

My parents would have been overwhelmed by the maintenance of such a sprawling property if it hadn't been for Mum's knack of getting people to work. She could turn the most mundane chore into an adventure. From the minute we woke up, she'd be marshalling her work party, which included everyone staying in the house that day. Over breakfast (always something eggy on workdays), she would explain the challenge ahead, drawing us in by asking for suggestions of how we should go about the project. After tying up our hair in tea towels, like 'land girls' during the Second World War, we'd gather assorted brooms, scythes, wheelbarrows and trowels, and off we'd troop.

One of our jobs was scrubbing the pool each spring, a task that entailed lying on our tummies, our sleeves rolled up and brushes in hand, scrubbing for our lives as the water drained away. If you scrubbed before the algae dried, it would save hours of work. Once the pool had been emptied, scrubbed and dried, drums of powdered Snowcem cement paint appeared and we would be supplied with brooms. We would mix the Snowcem with water before tipping it out at the pool's shallow end and running along with our brooms, spreading the paint like players polishing the ice in a game of curling.

Other jobs included cutting down trees, chopping up logs and stacking them to dry for the following season. We'd also sweep the barns of cobwebs and restack the hay bales, and we'd squeal as mice – or, as once happened, a family of rats – ran around our feet. Mum worked harder than anyone, leading the charge with tales of finding treasure behind the ancient beams and with stories from her childhood.

At lunchtime, noticing that her army was flagging, Mum would melt away, returning via the vegetable garden to pull up a few lettuces, with a bag of sliced brown Sunblest bread, butter and a jar of Marmite. I see now that she realised we would lose our momentum if we went back to the house to eat, so she'd find a makeshift table and get to work wherever we happened to be, spreading lumps of butter onto the bread, followed by a dollop of Marmite and after casually flicking the slugs off the gritty leaves she would fold everything together and hey presto, heaven on earth. Dad would admire the morning's work while sucking on his pipe. 'Jolly good,' he'd purr. 'Jolly good.'

By this time, having failed his Common Entrance exam first time around, Richard had finally been accepted by Stowe School, and returned for the holidays full of frustration. No boarding school could cater for his challenging ideas and extraordinary energy, and he found traditional teaching methods agonising. He couldn't bear to waste time watching team sports, attending chapel or queuing for everything from food to showers. At fourteen, he was already trying to disrupt the system. My parents encouraged him to play by the rules, but Richard would have none of it. He had survived prep school because of his love of sport, but early on at Stowe he had damaged a cartilage in his knee and was left climbing the walls in frustration.

Mum encouraged him to write. He entered and won an essay competition judged by Gavin Maxwell, the writer best known for *Ring of Bright Water*, a memoir about befriending an otter on the west coast of Scotland while coming to terms with his homosexuality. Richard was euphoric when he received a letter from Maxwell inviting him to stay for a weekend, but Mum made her blond, blue-eyed young son decline the kind invitation.

* * *

Whether it was a result of his genes, the era he was born into, witnessing our parents' struggle to make ends meet or a love of beating us all at his favourite board game, *Monopoly*, Richard was determined to make his fortune, and my earliest memories of him revolve around his focus on business success.

One summer holiday, Dad was thrilled to see that Richard wanted to follow in his footsteps and open a museum of curiosities.

The two of them spent hours in Swallow Barn dusting off Dad's childhood collection, setting up trestle tables and arranging the display. Unlike Dad's museum, Richard had painted a big poster in red paint, which read, 'Entry fee 2/6p.' By the end of the holiday, the tobacco tin by the poster contained just three half-crowns: one from my father, one my mother and one from Auntie Joyce, who had come to stay one weekend. A lesson had been learned: no business sells itself, and promotion is essential.

When Richard came home for Christmas, he decided that his next venture was going to be breeding budgerigars. The sheets of hardboard used to make the tissue-box covers came in handy, as he and Dad spent days building stacks of interconnecting hutches, each with its own little nesting box. I watched in wonder as a budgie battery farm evolved in front of my eyes, and was excited when the first fluffy arrivals were introduced to their new homes. Richard had done his sums: each budgie cost two shillings and was expected to produce six chicks per year. Seed for each bird would cost two shillings, giving Richard a profit of ten shillings per budgie. My labour would be free, an economy he would soon live to regret.

Richard went back to school, expecting to witness his growing fortune at *exeat* three weeks later. I had loved the little birds and felt very grown-up when Richard told me that feeding and watering them was my responsibility. Though I was determined not to let my big brother down, my curious friends and I were drawn to the prohibited nesting boxes, playing mummies and daddies with them and counting their tiny eggs. It was sadly inevitable that one day, in our excitement, we would forget to close the cage door, and when we did, not one budgie failed to make a bid for freedom.

Richard's third childhood attempt at business was sadly no more successful. We'd grown up with tales of a distant relative who had planted trees in Burma and watched his fortune grow. This story appealed to Richard, who bought two hundred Christmas tree saplings, all under six inches tall but with a potential to grow by a foot per year, with each foot representing a pound in profit.

Our Easter holiday was spent digging holes and tucking these nuggets of potential gold into the soil. It was a whole-family task, and my role was to run up and down the rows with a small tin watering can. Again, Richard returned to Stowe at the start of the Easter term and returned to financial ruin: rabbits had entered the enclosure and nibbled the top of every single tree.

Down a single-track lane, next to the blacksmith's forge and beyond the wooden bus shelter and the ancient oak tree with a hollowed-out trunk that was big enough to conceal at least three smoking teenagers, was the post office, a treasure trove of felt tip pens, glues with squidgy rubber stoppers, packets of rubber bands, boxes of drawing pins, balls of string and parcel tags of all sizes. Mum was keen to teach us the lesson of her childhood: that we should save for a rainy day. I relished being taken to the post office every Saturday morning, my pocket money held tightly in one hand and my post office savings book in the other. I'd stand on tippy-toes and slide the book towards the lady behind the grille.

'Could you put one shilling into the book please, and give me one shilling change?' I would squeak self-consciously. My father would then stand patiently by as I agonised over the choice of sweets. Twelve pennies to spend and so much choice! I could buy eight Black Jacks for a penny to get my money's worth, though I wasn't so keen on them, or a Cadbury's Curly Wurly and a Mars Bar. A gobstopper could last weeks if I sucked it for an hour or two and saved it for the next day.

Ten years later, that rainy day did arrive – a torrentially stormy day, in fact. When I scrabbled around in my bedroom cupboard, desperate to find my long-forgotten savings book, page after page stamped with tiny deposits. With a heavy heart I took it back to the post office, now standing eye to eye with the postmistress, and made a withdrawal of £34, emptying the account.

'I hope you're going to treat yourself to something special, dear,' she said, while counting out the money.

'Sort of, thanks,' I managed, stuffing the notes into my pocket and walking out the door.

2

PEAFUCKS AND ROEBUCKS

All little sisters are painful at times, but for my gentle big sister Lindy, being sent away to boarding school and leaving me at home must have been torture. She says now that she didn't feel jealous of me, but Mum's letters to her, full of tales of the fun we were having, must have rubbed salt into her sensitive, homesick soul.

Boarding school is becoming an anachronism in the twenty-first century; even in its modern, less brutal form, with cosier accommodation and modern communications, it is still an old-fashioned idea to send your offspring off into the hands of strangers for their formative years. To send your children away from home at the age of thirteen – or, heaven forbid, at seven or eight years old – is counterintuitive, to say the least. However, back in the mid-1960s it was still the norm for people of a certain background and with the resources to drive for a couple of agonising hours and then lug trunks and tuck boxes up stairs and down corridors, before delivering their weeping children to a cavernous, barely heated dormitory, give them a last hug and flee to the car, not daring to look back for fear that they might be rushing after you. You then weren't allowed any contact until *exeat*, the school's permission for a weekend's absence, some three weeks later – it was thought three weeks was the time it would take your wretched child to break emotional ties with home and establish new ones with their school.

There is a theory that many boarding school veterans experience midlife crises in their early forties, when their own children reach the age when they were so cruelly separated from all they love and their long-buried trauma is dredged up. At this age, parents crave love and affirmation, so they can tear down the barriers erected thirty years before, when they lay on a bunk bed and silently wept into their pillow, swearing that they would never allow themselves to open their hearts and suffer this kind of pain again. Whatever form the trauma takes, many therapists are kept in business thanks to this brutal tradition.

Lindy was nine when she was sent off to Wispers, an old-fashioned girls' school in West Dean House in West Sussex. The palatial mansion was leased from the estate of Edward James, the poet known for his patronage of the Surrealists, and the dark stone building still housed much of his art collection. Lindy would get quieter and quieter as we drove over the South Downs, and by the time we passed through the magnificent wrought-iron gates and crunched up the drive, she would be inconsolable. She then faced the trauma of not only saying goodbye to Mum, Dad, me and our dog Suki, but of seeing me jump back into the car. I remember her waving to us, her puffy face trying desperately to smile. She would also cry on the way home for the holidays, because she hated leaving behind her art room, vegetable patch and friends. She loathed the constant upheaval of going back and forth.

Lindy returned for the Christmas holidays with a new vocabulary, budding breasts and an interest in dressmaking: she'd become a virtual stranger, but of course, I never wanted to leave her side.

'Lindy,' I whined. 'I want to use the ironing-board now. Look, my dolly's dress needs ironing. It's my turn!'

Lindy had erected the board and plugged in the iron, keen to press the seam of a dress she was making. 'Just let me get on, please, Nessie.'

'No, no, it's my turn now!' I wailed.

She stopped. 'Put your hand up here, flat on the board,' she said.

I did as I was told, keen to please her. First, having tested that the iron was only lukewarm, she placed it on my hand, hard enough that I couldn't wriggle out.

'If you scream for Mummy, I'll turn the knob up and then you'll *really* learn to stop annoying me,' she smiled, her hand hovering over the dial. I caught her eye, uncertain whether she was joking. I was beaten.

Our parents had strong ideas of good parenting and they had high expectations. They were tough on us, but we never felt a lack of love. They always made us aware that we were responsible for our own actions; this allowed them to give us untold freedoms, while knowing that we couldn't let them down. They refused to get involved in our little sibling squabbles and instead told us to sort them out among ourselves. In fact, they'd be livid if we involved them – they were convinced that we would reconcile over our joint irritation at their lack of attention.

I really loved Lindy, I really did, even when she once grabbed me from behind while we were doing the washing up and held a carving knife to my throat, grinning like Jack Nicholson in *The Shining* and whispered in my ear, 'You don't know if I've gone mad, do you Nessie?'

I could never be quite sure.

* * *

By 1966 the menagerie at Tanyards was growing. Both my parents had a real empathy for animals and Mum, having been deprived of pets as a child, was determined to make up for it now. Snowy, a jet-black New Forest pony arrived for Lindy, followed by Tommy, a Welsh mountain pony for me, and Suki, a pudgy Labrador puppy, soon to be mated by many a lusty village mongrel. Dad built a dovecote for some white fantail doves, though they rapidly succumbed to a similar fate, attracting every wood pigeon in the area, and their piebald chicks became targets for our air rifles, as we tried to keep the flock white. By the summer of 1967, although our barns were already full of peacocks, bantams and silkies, Dad was sent to Guildford's livestock market to buy four guinea fowl to complete the collection. Unfortunately, he left the auctioneer instructions to buy 'four' without realising that they came in batches of a dozen; his meek manner meant that, rather than cause embarrassment by admitting his mistake, he crammed all forty-eight birds into the back of his Vauxhall shooting brake and drove home with them squawking all around him.

One of our summer rituals was going to the Surrey County Show – I relished the moment of leaping out of the car and hearing the incomprehensible show commentary being carried over the breeze. Full of expectation, we'd follow other families walking towards the action, the smell of generators, horses, livestock and frying onions becoming stronger as we reached the crowds. There was so much to see, from sheepdog displays to show-jumping, from vintage tractors to day-old chicks, dyed all the colours of the rainbow.

One year, late in the afternoon, as the shadows grew long and the final rosettes were being awarded, Mum and I were walking back to the car, when she stopped still for a moment and then walked swiftly towards a brightly painted gypsy caravan. I was overcome with shyness, having spotted a number of scruffy children my own age, and was reluctant to follow her, but Mum pulled me along by the hand.

'Oh, Mummy, what now?' I whined.

'Stop thinking about yourself, Vanessa,' she said, her standard reply to any sign of self-consciousness. She, on the other hand, was in her element – she loved talking to people from different walks of life. A craggy-faced, long-skirted, elderly traveller was squatting on the bottom rung of the ladder that led up to the front of the caravan. She had very few teeth.

'What a beautiful caravan you have,' Mum said.

'Oh dear, oh dear,' the lady wailed. 'It's just so sad.'

'What's going on?' Mum replied, squeezing my hand and sensing a story.

'A policeman has just been here – they're going to kill our Humpty,' the old lady replied, rocking back and forth.

'Who's Humpty?' Mum asked, ever impatient.

'He's gone off to find someone from the RSPB and they're going to kill him. He said we're not allowed to keep wild birds in cages.' On cue, the surrounding children began to wail.

The woman beckoned us up the ladder and towards the back of the chaotic caravan. There, in the gloom, was a magpie in a cage. He cocked his head to one side, scanning us for possibilities.

We looked out of the caravan door, there was no sign of the authorities. 'Quick, give him to me,' Mum said. 'We'll save Humpty!'

'Let me cover him up,' the old lady muttered, throwing a blanket over his cage. Down the ladder we went and off we set, weaving our way through the departing crowds, expecting at any moment to get a tap on the shoulder, before collapsing into the car in a fit of giggles.

Mum grew to love that wretched bird, and it loved her in return. They became inseparable. From the day he arrived at Tanyards he was free to fly away, and we all wished he would, but he never did. He took enormous pleasure in tormenting us; even our long-suffering dog wasn't exempt. Suki would be lazily dozing in the sun, when Humpty would cock his head, hop forward and peck at the end of her tail. Suki would get up, turn around and settle down again, but Humpty would repeat the trick. The poor dog would once again calmly get up, turn around and go back to sleep, but Humpty would strike again and again until Suki eventually got up and walked away.

Humpty didn't like men, especially those holding newspapers in front of their faces – the crazy bird would dive towards the paper at breakneck speed, making it impossible to carry on reading. All summer long he drove us to breaking point. Meals on the outdoor patio were challenging as he'd hop between our plates, taking a peck here and pooping there as we flapped him away. We all laughed at his antics, but you could never relax knowing he was waiting in the shadows.

None of us trusted Humpty, except for Mum. He would sit on her shoulder, and woe betide any of us who tried to get close to Mum or went to kiss her. Mum's party piece was to feed him nuts from her mouth, until Dad told her about the dangers of psittacosis, a disease that humans can catch from parrots – it seemed far-fetched, but maybe Dad was displaying a rare moment of jealousy himself. Humpty's end was never verified, but we all suspected that our neighbour Gary had quietly wrung his neck. After all, everyone has their limits.

Dad had exchanged the eight-acre lake of his childhood for an ornamental well, which was hidden under the steps leading to our front door. To most people it was just a miniature pond, but to my father it was the essence of life itself. He took such pleasure in getting the balance of nature right, explaining the need to keep the water oxygenated with Canadian pondweed and a small pump. He introduced freshwater snails, goldfish, stone islands for frogs and a lily or two. He marvelled at never having to feed the fish, loved seeing dragonflies appear in the spring and whooped with joy whenever he spotted a great crested newt that he'd christened Kinka in honour of King Canute, the ancient king who did or didn't hold back the tide.

The pleasure my father took in nature was contagious. He taught me to look under nasturtium leaves, each one wriggling with caterpillars that would soon become peacock or red admiral butterflies. He showed me the greenfly on his roses and explained how encouraging ladybirds, which lived on the greenfly, reduced the need for pesticides. We plunged our arms deep into the compost heap, feeling how much heat is generated by decaying organic matter. Next to the roses was a wooden water butt where Dad would collect rainwater; every morning he'd rub it into his scalp, in the vain hope that it would restore his thinning hair.

Each spring Dad would notice the swallows arriving from their long migration north from South Africa. As they circled over the pool in the evening light, he would rush to open the doors of the barn and coo, 'Welcome home, my lovelies – you need a long rest now,' as they swooped into the eaves. He was also a horse whisperer. I was amazed to see him calm Snowy down after he was spooked one day, working his magic by gently stroking the distressed pony's muzzle and breathing deeply into his ear until they were breathing in unison.

Dad had no problem reconciling his love of animals with his love of shooting them and always eagerly looked forward to autumn, when the shooting season began. He and Mum would set off for Blandford Forum in Dorset, where they 'shared a gun' on a large country estate. Mum took pride in Suki, who was the star dog of the shoot, having been trained to retrieve the previous summer.

They would return in the evening and lay the day's bag on the dining room table: a brace of pheasant, a woodcock and maybe a hare or two. Dad would then pour himself a gin and tonic and light his pipe while happily contemplating their day, before setting to work dismantling his shotguns and cleaning their barrels. The smell of gun oil and gunpowder mingling with Dad's Three Nuns tobacco, wood-smoke from the fire and the drying blood of the freshly shot beasts, still encapsulates these moments of utter contentment from my childhood.

Setting aside the numerous litters of mongrel puppies that my poor father had to place reluctantly in weighted sacks and drown, Dad's rule was that you have to eat what you kill. Thanks to him, by the age of eight I could skin and gut rabbits, pluck pheasants and cut the breasts off pigeons with the alacrity of a farmer's wife.

As a family, we weren't cut out for the horsey world of gymkhanas, hunting or show-jumping; we were more the hacking-the-ponies-on-the-heath-behind-the-house-and-setting-obstacle-courses type of family. Goodness knows what we were doing with poor Snowy when Richard fell off him one year, but I fear he was showing off to Lindy's friend, Sally Franklin. As the pony bolted away, Richard was left lying on the ground, laughing. We all ran up to him as he pleaded he was injured.

'Get up, Rick,' we giggled.

'Honestly, I can't,' he spluttered through intakes of breath, but we didn't believe him.

'I really can't move,' he insisted, a grin still on his face.

Thinking the game was going on a bit, Lindy gave him a sisterly kick in the side. We were getting mixed messages from him, but decided to play along with the game. We found a plank that would stand in for a stretcher, laid it down and rolled our hooting brother onto it, before carrying him down to the house to find Mum and Dad. He went off to hospital in an ambulance, insisting that the crew left the back doors open so he could wave to people as they went past. Richard had broken his pelvis. He was on crutches for the rest of the summer.

Without being able to send Richard on long errands, the entire family was once again at the mercy of his practical jokes. Mum, Lindy and I being so trusting meant he had a field day.

One day, in a moment of remorse at never reading to me, Mum suggested that I join the travelling library – a van laden with books that came to the village every fortnight. Her plan was that we would go there and pick books to read together. We went once to take some books out but somehow didn't find the time to return them. Some months later, a brown envelope landed on the doormat with my name written on it and Richard came into the kitchen, brandishing the letter in the air.

'Nessie, a letter to you from the library,' he said. 'Shall I open it for you?'

How exciting – my first-ever letter!

'Yes please, Ricky,' I grinned.

'Dear Vanessa Branson,' he read in a serious voice, 'your library books are now two months overdue.' I felt the smile slip from my face. 'We are sorry to tell you that this is a very serious offence and you will have to go to prison for one whole year.' Rick was thrilled at the success of his joke but somewhat disconcerted when I fell to the ground, pretending to faint.

Mum and Dad's approach to health and well-being was pretty much aligned: they had faith in the human body's natural power of recovery and believed you should push it to its limit. They understood that when you were exhausted you had a reserve tank of energy to call on. Complaining of being tired was not on the agenda; a good night's sleep would replenish empty batteries. Whingeing about feeling hot or cold was considered bad form, too.

'It won't kill you' was Mum's response if we complained it was too cold to be sent outside to play, despite our chattering teeth and knocking knees. In my mother's world, bodies were self-healing and self-cleaning. We had a bath once a week, and she thought that soap was unnecessary because it dried out the skin. I didn't own my own toothbrush until I went to boarding school, aged ten, and until then, if I did brush my teeth, I used the family toothbrush that we all shared. No tubes of sweet Signal for the Branson family; rather a pot of Eucryl Smokers Toothpowder. Our parents were firm believers in the power of fresh air, green vegetables and mind over matter. We didn't have any need for bathroom scales; the subject of weight just didn't come up.

Aspirins or antibiotics were reserved for close encounters with mortality. I can't remember ever going to the doctor, though I do remember the agony of having my tonsils out. It was a fairly routine operation in the 1960s, but after the nodules were snipped out, your throat was eye-wateringly painful. The only palliative offered by the nurses was the promise of jelly and ice-cream for supper, a rare treat that was never on offer at home. Looking back at my last fifty years of work, childbirth and adventures, I am eternally grateful to my parents for imbuing us with an enduring confidence in our bodies from such a young age. To be free of fears of illness and food obsessions is a gift for which I will be always be grateful.

Mum and Dad's approach to parenting was aligned, too. They wanted their children to be 'radiators, not drains' and would often remind us that no one likes a sulky child. If our faces ever fell into a relaxed expression, one of them would catch our eye and give us a grin to remind us of our lapse. Richard had a hanging bottom lip, which gave him a perpetually gormless look. I think most other parents would have accepted that it was just how their child was, but not Mum and Dad. It didn't take many hisses of 'BL' to remind Rick to pull up his bottom lip at all times. It may have been irritating for him when he was young, but I'm sure he's grateful for it now.

Dad told us that when we were barely able to walk and were eager to sit on his lap, he wouldn't stoop down to lift us up but would instead encourage us to climb up ourselves. He also explained that crying is a primitive mechanism to attract attention; if we fell and hurt ourselves, he would expect us to stop as soon as he picked us up and inspected our grazed knees. If we didn't, he would put us down again until we'd stopped making a noise.

I remember the thrill of learning to ride a bike, shouting at my parents to come and watch as I whizzed down the hill from the orchard to the driveway, before misjudging the difficulty of riding on loose gravel and falling off. Blood was pouring from my forehead. Dad picked me up and inspected the wound while Mum ran into the house to get a plaster. Well, I presumed it was going to be a plaster but in fact she returned with the cine camera.

Lindy had also learned the importance of being stoical – even though she was far more sensitive to teasing than I was, she could be quite tough on me. One time we were in the bath together, cutting the squeaker out of a plastic toy so we could squirt water at each other from the hole, when I managed to stab myself in the hand. The pain made me take a sharp intake of breath. Lindy looked at the bathwater, which was turning red with blood, and laughed, 'Don't cry Nessie! Laughing is just the same as crying. Look, laugh like me!'

I started to giggle through my tears as we placed towels on the gushing wound, laughing uncontrollably at the mess we were making of the bathroom. The awful truth is that even now, if anyone tells me a story of woe, the more appalling it is, the more I laugh. This usually results in the poor person laughing along with me, too – but not always.

My parents abhorred laziness, and the only time there was the suggestion of a slap from my father was when, as a teenager, I dragged my feet over helping Mum with the hoovering. He shocked himself, and me, by sort of smacking me up the stairs, while emitting the chastising noise that he used to make when rubbing puppies' noses in a puddle they'd made on the carpet.

I must have been about eight when our home menagerie became really exciting. Mum had met someone who ran a children's zoo, and he'd asked if we would take in any animals that were struggling. 'Animals,' he said, 'who needed extra love.' How could Mum say no? Anyway, I came home from school one day to find a bundle of red blanket on Mum's lap with a tiny hand sticking out from one end of it, clinging on to her shirt.

'Shh,' she whispered, as I blundered into the room. The hand was clenching and unclenching and I stared in wonder at its minuscule fingernails.

'Guess what I've got here, Nessie?' Mum asked, raising the little bundle to her shoulder. My mind raced. Could it be a little brother or sister? If it was, it had pretty strange hands!

'Go on, guess!' said Mum, enjoying my confusion. I stood there, my mouth agape as she slid the red blanket from a miniature marmoset monkey.

'Say hello to Minette,' said Mum. 'She's not very well, but we'll make her better again.'

How we loved that little monkey! She had a few happy times wreaking havoc around the house, but her default position was to lie in a box on the kitchen floor, looking mournful. Our local vet in Cranleigh, having failed to think what might be wrong with her, suggested that Mum took her to see the chief vet at London Zoo. Later that night, Mum returned home with a resigned sadness in her eyes. Minette, she learned, had suffered from rickets caused by a lack of vitamin D and calcium in her diet, and her bones were soft and liable to fracture. Mum conceded that no amount of love was going to improve her condition and agreed with the vet's advice. Little Minette was put down there and then, and Mum returned empty-handed.

Never one to mourn for too long, Mum contacted her friend at the zoo a couple of days later, to see if any other animals needed some extra love.

'We do have an interesting dilemma,' was the response.

'Oh yes?' said Mum, gleeful at the possibility of a new challenge.

'We have a large white rabbit that has formed a strong attachment to an orphaned roe deer,' he continued. 'but the fawn is too nervous to be surrounded by excitable children. Would you please take them in, and try and accustom the deer to people?'

'Bring them around this minute,' replied Mum.

The two friends were housed in one of the stalls in the barn. Dad put up a makeshift barrier made of chicken-wire weighted down with logs, and we were made to swear that we wouldn't frighten the timid doe. I spent hours squatting by their stall, my arm stretched through the wire to stroke the animals. Every night they would sleep snuggled up together, the deer curled up around the rabbit.

I'll never forget the summer of 1967. Richard was sent off to France to improve his French, and his exchange student, Alexandre, came to stay with us for a month in return. I don't know what he thought of our family, but like many young people who crossed our path all those decades ago, he has remained a lifelong friend. Richard showed little interest in learning French at sixteen, but our parents had told him that, unless he managed to get at least three A-levels, he wouldn't be allowed to leave school, so he soldiered on with his studies.

Richard had already begun working on a school magazine and had ambitions to roll it out nationally. He and Alexandre were busy hatching plans, and the house began to reverberate with the sound of the Beatles and the Rolling Stones. Trudy, a sixteen-year-old from Holland, also came to learn English. She and Richard became inseparable, and at the end of the summer she decided not to go back to Holland to complete her studies. Instead, she pitched a tent in the Stowe grounds and spent the winter term camped there, 'helping Richard with his magazine'.

We made a strange party on our daily procession down the lane to the village. Our peacock, Charlie, had taken a shine to one of our large white ducks. My father knew that ducks can only copulate successfully on water, so decided that it would be worth the experiment of walking the unlikely lovers down to the village pond and see what happened – he loved the idea of producing a clutch of little 'peafucks'. Towards the end of the day, when the lane was quiet, Mum would take Bambi by the lead, with Handsome the rabbit hopping alongside. The duck would waddle ahead, followed by an eager Charlie.

Once we were near the water, the lustful peacock would pounce, nearly drowning the duck in the muddy shallows. Once he'd had his evil way with her, he would clamber off her back, his tail clogged with mud, and walk back to the house as gracefully as he could. The duck would then have a brief paddle around the pond and before following her mate home.

There was much excitement when the duck laid a clutch of eggs. She valiantly sat on them for weeks, but they never hatched. As the summer came to a close and the nights drew in, another sad story was unfolding. Handsome had started to hop out of his stall and one night, he didn't hop back. Bambi, inconsolable with grief, refused all food and, no matter how much time Mum spent stroking and cajoling him, the delicate creature slowly faded away before her eyes.

3

FOR BETTER, FOR WORSE

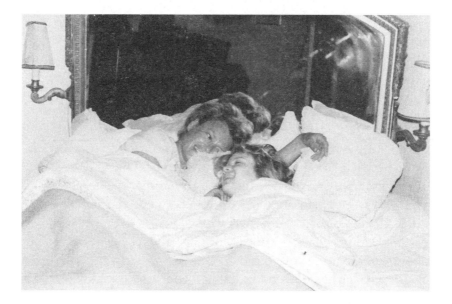

Sussex, 2009

Alarm bells rang when I received a call from Dad while I was organising my parents' sixtieth anniversary dinner. He was suffering: his spine and hips were crumbling in on themselves. He seldom gave in to self-pity, but the more he needed a caring partner by his side, the more Mum was absent. She'd long advocated that the formula for a successful marriage was spending plenty of time apart, and boy, she was embracing her own advice with enthusiasm. She hated to be reminded of her own diminishing future, hated seeing Dad in pain and was always busy. Nursing had never been

Mum's strong suit. When Dad had previously had operations and needed looking after, Mum had called in Granny Dock to help.

After hearing the tone of Dad's voice, I jumped in the car and drove ninety miles down the A3 to have supper with him. My heart bled when I saw this once-mighty man grappling with self-doubt and depression.

'I'm not sure what to do,' he said, when we'd sat down for supper. 'Our marriage is a sham.'

'Daddy, let's think this through,' I said, my mind racing with ghastly visions of my parents getting divorced as they approached their nineties.

'Your mother is always either away or making plans to be away,' he lamented, his usual humour absent. 'I don't think I can stand it any longer. And to compound it all, Mum rang up Elizabeth to tell her, in no uncertain terms, to leave me alone and stop taking me out to the pub for lunch.' Liz was a recently divorced friend of Richard's, a good forty years Dad's junior. They enjoyed each other's company, but it was hardly a romance.

'It was so embarrassing' he continued. 'What on earth does she think I'll get up to? I can hardly walk!'

'Oh, Daddy,' I said. 'I know Mum has always been hard to pin down, but she loves you so much – she just hates to see you suffer. Your marriage has been remarkable – you should look back over the past sixty years and feel a real sense of satisfaction.' I took him by the hand and looked into his sad eyes. 'Let's be honest, you two have had more than your fair share of adventures together, and look what you've achieved. Besides,' I continued, 'you can still take Liz out for lunch. I won't tell Mum, I promise.'

* * *

Back in 1966, with Lindy and Richard exiled to boarding school and Dad commuting to London, Mum made her first bid for freedom. She still had her 'studio' in the shed in the back garden, but her interest in fancy goods was waning and the business was now manned by Coley, a kindly lady who came in each day to make up the orders. Mum had read an article in *The Times* titled 'Unspoiled Menorca': in 1966, this small Balearic island was rarely visited by tourists, and there was only one flight from Barcelona to Menorca each week. She set off on her own to investigate and shocked Dad by returning with the deeds to the plan of a house in Binibeca, one of the first developments of its type. Each house was designed in the traditional Spanish style, with tiled roofs, whitewashed walls, and balconies overlooking the sandy cove.

Mum soon set up Binibella, a property company renting and selling houses in the village. I'm sure she hoped to supplement the family coffers, but her real motivation was the opportunities that this new venture would bring. Her children were all of school age and she was keen to make the most of her new freedom.

Until the age of seven, Shamley Green was my world, apart from the two weeks each year when I was sent to stay with Mum's parents. On reflection, it seems strange that neither Richard nor Lindy joined me, but they took advantage of getting rid of the baby of the family and went boating on the Norfolk Broads and spent time with Aunt Clare and her husband Gerard. As a consequence of these separate holidays, I always had a closer bond with my grandparents, while Lindy and Richard were closer to Aunt Clare.

I relished my seaside holidays with my organised, efficient granny and my gentle, hen-pecked grandfather. They now lived in the clifftop Hampshire village of Barton on Sea, in a modern bungalow called Cleve Cottage, the name being a combination of their daughters' names. At one end of First Marine Drive, in an even tinier bungalow, lived my stone-deaf great granny, who was by this point in her late nineties. At the other end of the road was a Christian holiday centre, a dour-looking building that echoed with the noise of chanting and singing. Rather than being uplifting, there was something ominous about it. At Cleve Cottage everything revolved around the pips on the radio that was always tuned to the clipped English tones of the Home Service.

Granny and I would visit her mother before walking along the bubbling-hot tarmac road towards the sea, past the booth that sold lilos and shrimping nets, and down the steep steps onto the pebbly beach. We would paddle together and then while I munched on digestive biscuit and Cheddar cheese sandwiches, batting away the odd beady-eyed seagull, I would watch my fearless, athletic Granny as she dived through the waves and swam into the distance. Once we were back home, she would teach me to knit and make wool pom-poms and I'd help her make salads and stick bags of Green Shield stamps into saving books.

One summer, our routine was disturbed by the death of Uncle Jack, Granny's brother. He had spent the vast majority of his life abroad as a music teacher, and finally as a headmaster in Trinidad. He had contacted Dock expressing concern about his health and said he was planning a trip back to England. Dock had booked him into Enton Hall, a health farm in Godalming that was the inspiration for 'Shrublands', the health farm visited by James Bond in *Thunderball*. It described itself as a 'dietetic and osteopathic health centre and organic farm' and she was convinced that this was what her brother needed, but it was sadly too late and he died on the way to England. There was no funeral. I remember trying to put myself in Granny's shoes, not being able to get my head around losing a brother, but she seemed quite unruffled.

'Granny,' I asked, 'are you sad that your big brother has died?'

'Oh well, Nessie,' she said, 'I'm afraid he was a heavy smoker.'

We went up to Great Granny's bungalow to tell her about the death of her son. She had the TV on and was watching a game of football. Everything had to be written down for her on her notepad. 'BROTHER JACK HAS DIED OF A HEART ATTACK,' wrote Granny, after which Great Granny read the news and dismissed us with the back of her hand. I saw her holding back a tear as we left the room, but later that afternoon she scuttled around to Cleve Cottage. 'Who was it who died at the football match this afternoon?' she sweetly enquired.

The only time I wasn't happy at Barton on Sea was when my grandparents were playing their interminable games of golf and I had to tag along. One day when I was four, after a few holes, they left me in a shelter saying they would be back 'shortly'. Shortly feels like an age when you're four, and I began to worry.

The next players came along and, thinking I'd been abandoned, took me back to the clubhouse. It wasn't long before my flustered grandparents found me there being entertained by the barman. I was never left to wait again, but it gave me some insight into the childhood my poor Aunt Clare endured.

My grandfather was a kind, quiet but distant figure. My last memory of him is of playing a game of catch on the pavement outside Cleve Cottage, with the sound of hymns pulsating towards us on the breeze.

'Can we do this for ever and ever please, Granddaddy?' I asked.

'Well maybe not for ever,' he smiled, 'but we can do it again when you come to stay next summer.'

'Do you promise, Granddaddy? Cross your heart and hope to die?'

'Yes, Nessie. I promise,' he replied.

'Cross your heart and hope to die,' I insisted.

'Cross my heart and hope to die,' he replied with a chuckle.

Sadly, die he did. Years of reconciling the horrors of war, followed by the effort of living in a difficult marriage, finally overwhelmed him and he had a massive heart attack, aged just sixty-six.

Predictably, Granny took his death in her stride. At the time she tried to comfort my inconsolable Aunt Clare, saying, 'It really was time he went; his teeth were beginning to need attention.' When she later told me that Rupert's funeral was one of the best days of her life, I don't think she meant that she celebrated Grandaddy's death, but rather that it opened the door to a completely new life. She dusted herself down and drove from the church to Enton Hall health farm. Life was short and she was determined to live every minute of it to the full.

* * *

There were two schools in Shamley Green, a state primary and a fee-paying pre-prep school, thus cleaving the village neatly down the middle. All three of us were sent to the posh school, Longacre, which took boys up to the age of seven and girls up to eleven.

At four years old, we were dropped off in a standard outsized uniform of greys and blues, with felt bowler hats for girls and caps for the boys.

A quirk of memory is such that, while I'm sure Mum drove me to and from school on most days, I can now only remember the days when I had to walk. I'd trudge down Woodhill Lane, across the village green and up the hill to school, a long walk for a small child. I remember thinking at the time that it wasn't fair to expect me to do this. I would cut across the playing fields and enter the main building through the back door, where we would all be welcomed by Longacre's indomitable headmistress, known to everyone as Chum.

Chum was squat and square but not squishy at all, her curvaceous torso restrained in some sort of corset. With her puffy features and tufts of facial hair, she could never be described as a beauty, but she had a kind face and we were all rather devoted to her. She loved 'her' children in return, which is more than could be said of Robert, the school's silent and put-upon groundsman. Chum was openly hostile to him, barking orders and muttering 'stupid man' under her breath. Mum told me that Robert was, in fact, Chum's husband – she'd married him when he was on leave during the war, and had regretted it ever since.

If Mum was in when I got home, you never knew what would happen. 'Quick, Ness,' she said once, 'I hear the flood water is rising and that the River Wey has burst its banks. Debenhams is under water – let's go and see what's happening.' And off we'd drive. Mum didn't want to shower pity at others' misfortunes – she just wanted to share in the drama. Any excitement, whether a fallen tree or a burned-out garden shed, and she was there.

I'd often hear her berating my poor father as he entered the house after a long day in London.

'How's your day been today, Teddy?' she would ask.

'Hello darlings,' he would say, as he headed to pour his first G & T. 'Oh, fine, just the usual – nothing out of the ordinary.'

'Don't be so boring, Teddy,' Mum would reply. 'Something must have happened. Tell us a story!'

Dad would scan through his day and come up with some small morsel to satisfy his wife's insatiable needs. 'I was the prosecuting counsel for a sexual assault today,' he began, before pausing for effect, knowing that he had our attention. 'Some chap sitting on the upper deck of a London bus had picked up his neighbour's hand and placed it firmly upon his lap. His defence was that she must have mistaken the sausages he was taking home for his tea for his member!'

Dad took a sip of gin and tonic, before continuing. 'My witness was a sterling girl,' he went on, taking his time. 'She clinched the man's fate when she looked the judge in the eye and said, "Your honour, I've been a butcher's daughter all my life and never have I come across a sausage with a throb in it!"'

Every evening brought some little snippet to make us laugh. 'My gum-chewing witness was given a stern telling-off by the judge today. He was told to stop masticating. I've never seen someone whip their hands out of their pockets so quickly.'

'Oh Teddy, I do love you,' Mum would chirp, wrapping her arms around him and snuggling under his shoulder.

One day, Richard had wanted to see Dad in action in court. They had driven to London together. They were driving home across the Surrey Hills in a howling gale at dusk, when Dad saw a branch from an enormous oak tree coming hurtling down towards them. He braked hard and yelled 'Duck!' and Richard instinctively did as he was told, as the branch crashed down on the bonnet and windscreen of the car. Both Dad and Richard had to be freed by the fire brigade but they were largely unscathed, apart from some cuts from the shattered windscreen. The fire brigade cranked the roof up enough for them to drive the car slowly back home, without the windscreen. They drove up the drive tooting the horn triumphantly, happy in the knowledge that they had a good story for Mum.

Weekends at Tanyards were never dull. Richard would come home often, to discuss *Student*, a magazine he was planning to launch. He'd been editor of his school magazine at Stowe and decided that there was a need for a national magazine dealing

117

with issues that would interest young people. He enlisted Granny Dock to help with the typing and sold advertising from the school telephone box. The first issue, published in the spring of 1968, dived right into some controversial topics. In his first editorial, Richard wrote, 'The views of any student, politician or journalist must be tolerated, not only because some of them may, for all we know, be on the right track, but because it is only through the conflict of opinion that such words as knowledge or wisdom can have any meaning.'

From the crypt of St John's Hyde Park, he and his business partner, our old Easteds neighbour Nik Powell, along with his editorial team of Jonathan Gems, Robert Morley and Paul Forbes-Winslow, interviewed the leading thinkers of their generation. Many of them came to sit animatedly around the kitchen table at Tanyards, eating Mum's wholesome grub and drinking Dad's distinctive homemade wine.

I don't remember any creative classes at Longacre School – no plays, dance or poetry, and no singing other than hymns in assembly. I do remember trying to learn French verbs without knowing what a verb was, and being singled out for extra reading classes.

My true education took place in the Tanyards kitchen, listening to this group debating the pressing matters of the time: abortion, contraception, the legalisation of cannabis, pornography, homosexuality, Vietnam, Franco's Spain, the women's liberation movement, South Africa, Biafra, race, art and culture. We discussed Richard's interviews with people such as James Baldwin, Vanessa Redgrave, Don McCullin, David Hockney and Henry Moore, plus archbishops, vice-chancellors, rear admirals, comedians and activists.

I only made two friends at Longacre: Belinda, whom I nicknamed Beatle, and a girl named Mags. At the end of school one day, Beatle said she didn't want to go back to her house because her mother was very ill and home had become a place of misery. 'Come back with me,' I offered. 'We can ask my mummy to call your mummy when we get home.'

We slipped out by the back entrance through the playing fields and walked hand-in-hand across the green and back down the lane to Tanyards. It was winter and getting dark. We must have realised that we were doing something naughty because as soon as we got home, Beatle curled up on an old armchair in the barn and I covered her up with a blanket and went to join Coley in the studio, before becoming so engrossed in making a picture out of material off-cuts that I forgot all about her. An hour or two later, her deeply stressed father came storming in, shouting and threatening to take off his belt and thrash me within an inch of my life, a fate that he said awaited poor Beatle.

Coley and I were speechless. She clutched my hand and we walked to the barn, where we found Beatle still curled up under the blanket, sound asleep. I will never forget her backwards glance at me as her father yanked her arm and frog-marched her to their car. Coley never said a word to my parents; we both understood that we had seen something that should never happen to a child. Beatle's mother was to die soon afterwards.

Beatle was very clever and destined to go to St Catherine's, the academic girls' school in Bramley. I took the eleven-plus in a forlorn attempt to beat the system, but my desperately poor reading skills meant there wasn't a hope in hell that I would pass.

My other friend was Mags. Her parents seemed very old to us – her mother was a teacher at Longacre and her father was dying of some dreadful lung disease. She was adopted, a concept I found hard to grasp, and though she loved her adoptive parents, we often fantasised about who her biological parents might be. When I went back to her house, we would skip through the sitting room past her dad, who was inevitably slumped in a wing-backed armchair watching television, his face covered by an oxygen mask. 'Hi Dad,' Mags would sing, hoping he wouldn't stop us. He would take in a difficult breath before managing to wheeze out a word in response. Her mum would be in the kitchen, making us tea and toast before sending us out to play. It was dawning on me that some families had no music, no teasing and no laughter.

We would flee the house and go off to play in the local sewage works, where we would happily ride around on the bars of the massive water purifying plant as it sprinkled pure piss through drums of stone and sand.

One day, Mum was invited to be guest speaker at one of the Longacre School sports days. I realise now that Chum had recognised something inspirational in her, and I was inordinately proud as she walked up to the podium and talked with contagious enthusiasm to a hundred captivated children about the importance of building solid foundations under everything you do.

Apart from schoolwork, my Longacre days were blighted by another horror – two girls in my class called Lottie and Laura. After Mum's talk, they attempted to make my life a misery by undermining my confidence at every opportunity. They both lived just off the village green, close to Tanyards, and acted as gatekeepers to my freedom in the village. I understand now that their home lives were wretched – one had an alcoholic mother and the other an anorexic one – so someone had to pay.

It's easy to bully someone and go undetected, with the odd hiss here and the odd sneer there. Continually asking 'What's so funny about that?' and rendering your cheerful banter leaden. You can move your victim's coat onto another person's hook, put a pool of water on her chair or hint to the others in the class that she smells, all things that while seemingly insignificant on their own are cumulatively enough to make a young girl turn inside out with misery. Once started, these girls were relentless.

I will never forget the bravery of one of the shyest girls in the class, Louise Elms, who once blurted out, in a fit of anguish, 'Will you two just stop picking on Vanessa!' There was a sudden silence as all the girls in the cloakroom stood still, in awe of her courage. I will be always be grateful to her.

It was early autumn, and Lindy challenged me to swim. I'd been trying to learn all summer but hadn't dared to swim out of my depth. In the previous months, I'd had one unsuccessful lesson with a creepy man called Mr Pilkington. He'd been booked to give us a few sessions, but when I told Mum that he didn't wear pants under his baggy shorts and that he seemed to relish the moments when he exposed his hairy thingy to us while looming above us at the edge of the pool, Mr Pilkington never returned to complete the job.

Lindy bet me a pancake that I wouldn't be able to swim a length of the freezing pool, and with that prize in mind, I managed one length and then, like Forrest Gump, just kept on swimming. I swam and swam, with Lindy counting: one length, two lengths, and so on, until I reached one hundred. She made a fresh batch of pancakes as a reward. What joy to have mastered swimming and to be wrapped in a warm towel, while munching through a pile of pancakes cooked by an admiring big sister. I've loved long-distance swimming ever since.

Looking at photographs of myself as a child, I'm sure that people would now say that I 'identified as a boy'. With my cropped hair, swimming trunks and ankle boots with elastic at the side, I never aspired to be a girl and I took pleasure in being physically strong. I chose to think of myself as being completely different to my sister, who exaggerated her feminine vulnerability and took great care of her appearance, experimenting with clothes and make-up. She would become coy in front of boys, but as far as I was concerned, I was one of them.

* * *

The winter term was over and the Christmas holidays lay ahead, and as the decade had got into full swing, life became more colourful. By 1966, Dad was gaining in confidence as a barrister and was being offered more lucrative cases by his chambers, while Mum was excited about her new business. The house was full of family Christmas rituals. Lindy was stirring cauldrons of fudge with a long wooden spoon – the smell of boiling condensed milk and sugar, mingling with woodsmoke, will always remind me of Christmas.

Mum dusted off the decorations from the previous year, including little cardboard snowmen with round tummies ready to

121

be filled with handfuls of Quality Street chocolates. Richard was sent to the woods to cut down a suitable sized Christmas tree, before we girls smothered the less-than-perfect tree with so much tinsel that no one would notice its missing branches. Dad spent hours twiddling the tiny glass bulbs on the coloured lights to try and 'get the damned things working again', while 'A Swingin' Safari' by Acker Bilk played on the record player. The pile of presents under the tree was growing satisfactorily, including one very large and heavy one to me from Lindy.

It even snowed that year, and once again, a sheet of hardboard came to good use. Placing it on the snow shiny-side down, we would sit three abreast on the board and shoot down the hill at breakneck speed. There was no way to slow down and no steering mechanism. It was breathtakingly good fun. Unfortunately Richard, going solo, shot straight into a barbed-wire fence, and had to spend the rest of the holidays with his face covered in plasters.

The Christmases of my childhood were heaven on earth. Dad had usually spent the year fermenting his frankly undrinkable but gratifyingly alcoholic homemade wine, and taking people up to the bathroom where it was concocted was his party piece. On top of a rickety chest of drawers were two twenty-gallon glass flagons, one full of a red liquid, the other a cloudy yellowy white. The flagons were stoppered with cork, into which a U-bend airlock was inserted. Dad stirred the brew by leaning against the chest of drawers and swilling the concoctions around the huge flagons. He was thrilled by the chemistry and marvelled at how cheap his wine was going to be. There was also an added bonus: knowing what was going to be on offer, most guests generously bought an extra bottle of wine as a gift.

On Christmas Eve, we'd all pile into the Vauxhall and drive to Corry Lodge for supper with Auntie Joyce. We'd be dressed in our Christmas best, which for me meant a clean pair of trousers and a jumper. Before we went up the drive, Mum would ask Dad to stop the car while she ferreted around in her handbag for a hanky that reeked of her metallic Rive Gauche perfume. She would spit on her hanky and rub it over our faces, ensuring that we were looking our best for Joyce. Joyce would make a fuss over us and prepare a feast of turkey followed by a flaming Christmas pudding studded with sixpences and served with dollops of cream and brandy butter and ladles of gooseberry fool. The food was served on beautiful hand-painted family plates, the drink from cut-glass decanters and champagne flutes. We would then race back to Shamley Green in time for Midnight Mass with a congregation of mildly tipsy villagers full of red wine and good cheer.

Waking on Christmas morning, the first thing I did was root around the bottom of my bed with my foot, hoping to feel a stocking weighed down with hard presents. There it was – Father Christmas had come! I'd run my hands up and down the knobbly stocking, in our case a shooting sock, the expectation almost unbearable as I waited for Dad to wake and get Mum her cup of tea, before we all piled into their bed to see what Santa had delivered. All families have their Christmas rituals, and Mum's genius at delaying gratification defined ours. After church we would be allowed just one present, with a smoked salmon sandwich and a glass of champagne. Then we'd give the house a quick hoover before sitting down by the fire in the dining room and slowly working our way through the pile, one present at a time. I saved the big box from Lindy until last.

'What do you think it is, Nessie?' my family asked.

I opened the outer layer and found another box within.

'There must have been some mistake,' they laughed, as I ripped open the second box. Then there was a third box and then a forth and so on, until in the very heart of the box I came to my prize, a tin mug. I laughed, trying to cover my disappointment. 'Very funny.'

We then went across the green to spend Christmas evening with the Talbot Wilcoxes – Peter, Jenny and their four children – in their elegant Georgian house to play parlour games. As the grown-ups steadily drank their fill, we would play charades, murder in the dark, sardines and Nelson, a marvellous game that you could only play once. Those of us in on the joke would gang up on some poor visiting guest, for some reason always known as 'a waif and stray'.

The game worked like this. Someone would dress up as the admiral and be placed on a chair in the centre of a darkened room. The waif would then be blindfolded, spun around a few times and led into Nelson's lair. The guide would speak respectfully to Nelson, asking if he would mind being introduced to the waif. Nelson remained silent.

'This is Nelson's knee,' the guide would say, drawing the blindfolded victim's hand onto the knee. 'And this is his good arm,' whispered the guide, as he took the hand up Nelson's body. 'This is his bad arm,' he would continue, as Nelson proffered the stump of an elbow. 'And these are his lips.' This would start to feel distinctly weird to a blindfolded person. 'This is his good eye,' continued the guide, as he allowed the waif to gently feel Nelson's closed eyelid. Then, gently prying the index finger of his victim forward, he'd say, 'and this is Nelson's bad eye,' while plunging his finger into a pot of Vaseline. Oh, the shrieks of joy at the poor waif's horror as his finger slid into the slimy goo.

'Time to go home,' said Mum. 'Always leave a party when you want to stay for more.'

She'd repeat her conviction that Dad would still be at the party she'd met him at, had she not come into his life. 'Come on, Teddy, time to go!'

Another family Christmas ritual was the bitter accusation from Mum and denial from Dad about him flirting with Jenny T. W. Dad would light his pipe while steering with his knees, and the car would fug up with the acrid smell of gas from his flip-top lighter, smouldering tobacco smoke, boozy breath and Rive Gauche.

'I saw you sitting on the floor, stroking her knee,' Mum would snipe.

'Oh come on, Evie, it's Christmas,' Dad would reply. 'I just had my hand on her knee for balance.'

'Enough, the two of you,' we would chorus laughing, as the car wove its way down the country lane and back to the house, which was lit only by the Christmas tree lights and the dying embers of the fire.

Forty years later, I met Lucy T. W. at a party, and we laughed about our family Christmases and our parents' behaviour back then. Peter, her father, had died a year or two previously.

'You know, Nessie, we always suspected your mother of having an affair with my father,' she said.

'Ha!' I replied. 'In our family, we always suspected *your* mother was having an affair with *my* father.' What a laugh!

A week or two later, while flying to Necker Island with Mum and Dad for our annual family holiday, I bobbed up from the back of the plane to see them in Upper Class.

'I must tell you something funny,' I said. 'I bumped into Lucy T. W. the other day, and their family myth is that you, Mum, had an affair with Peter!'

They both stared at me, startled rabbits in headlights, not knowing what to say. Oh Lord, I thought to myself, it's true. Mum had accused Dad of flirting with Jenny to cover her own bad behaviour. Later in the holiday, she explained that the 'affair' had amounted to a walk on the heath one afternoon, but that she had always relished her emotional connection with Peter. To conduct a clandestine relationship in the 1960s would have had its own complications and would have been virtually impossible in a tight-knit village community. No wonder Mum organised to spent part of her life away from my father.

With Lindy and Richard away at school, and Mum focusing on Binibella and training to become a lay magistrate, I was becoming increasingly isolated. My only friend within walking distance was Mishi Blower, who lived a mile up a steep track, deep in the woods above Tanyards. I loved going to stay with her in her tiny woodsman's cottage, but it had no television. Mishi and I had an arrangement with the family in the big house down the track: on Thursday nights we would brave the dark and knock on their front door. Someone would silently let us in and we'd traipse down a long corridor to join the family and watch *The Man from U.N.C.L.E.* No one ever laughed out loud or said a word to us and, after the show, we would leave the TV room and make our way back to the cottage. It gave another insight into how other families lived.

I began to dread going to school. At first Mum told me to get a grip, reminding me how lucky I was. But I was bored, being bullied and utterly miserable, so didn't feel lucky at all. Mum then told me to pull myself together and stop sulking, but by the age of ten no amount of self-pulling was going to cheer me up.

I developed a 'breathing disorder', a wheezing, panicky inhalation that would disappear as soon as I was snuggled up in the studio with Coley. It was also at around this time that I first became aware of a growing resentment from Mum when I looked to Dad for support. It was nothing dramatic, just a subtle sensation that I was getting in the way when Dad came home at the end of the day and she wanted to have a drink with him and discuss their day. Three of us for dinner each night just wasn't working – it was time I too went to boarding school.

4

Trunks, Kicks and Shoplifting

Mum drove me to Box Hill School one spring afternoon, the air full of promise as we hurtled down densely wooded lanes. The previous week, I'd been issued with the regulation, plenty-of-room-for-growth summer uniform. I was the only new pupil that term, having left Longacre in the middle of the school year, thanks to the relentless misery inflicted on me there. I have no idea why I was sent to Box Hill, but I know that Mum had taken advice from a schools' advisory agency called Gabbitas and Thring who, knowing of my academic shortcomings and happy demeanour, suggested a co-educational establishment, believing

I would thrive in a less stuffy environment than the one Lindy was being forced to endure.

The school was a founder member of the Round Square group of international schools that included Gordonstoun in Scotland and Aiglon College in Switzerland, all of which placed an emphasis on a robust physical approach to education. Come rain or shine, we boarders, the boys shirtless, had to run a daily circuit around the main building within five minutes of waking up, before standing under a cold shower on our return. Apart from that, Box Hill was like any other second-tier boarding school, a place people sent their offspring between the ages from eleven to eighteen, to be educated but more importantly to get them out from under their parents' feet during their troublesome teenage years. Not all parents would have thought 'out of sight, out of mind' regarding their children, but I had the distinct feeling that mine did.

Mum was convinced that you should 'shuffle your children out of the nest' before they wanted to leave, thus ensuring that they would always want to return home. She would often repeat the mantra 'you've got to be cruel to be kind', firmly believing that, by wrenching us from the comfort and security of home, she was helping to build our characters.

Mum was full of positive chatter as we drove through the Surrey Hills towards Mickleham, a village at the foot of Box Hill. However, through her breezy indifference, I could sense her anguish at sending her youngest away. I had our miniature whippet, Sadie, on my lap, and stroked her silky ears the entire way. We drove up the drive and parked under the flagpole opposite the imposing Victorian red-brick building, then lugged my trunk up a flight of stairs into a long dormitory filled with metal-framed bunk beds topped with thin horsehair mattresses, one of which had my name stuck to it.

'You lucky thing, Nessie,' Mum chirped. 'You're by the window.'

'Super,' I said, wanting to sound cheerful and not let her down.

For some reason we had arrived early and the dark, empty corridors echoed with expectation. Then a slow-witted girl came up to us and said hello, giving Mum an excuse to make a hasty exit – she gave me a brief hug, a cheery tap on my nose, a wink and was gone. The girl, keen to befriend the new arrival, asked if I wanted to go for a walk around the grounds before the others arrived. I agreed, and managed to regain some composure as she explained the complex school hierarchy. We should call Mr McComish, the headmaster, 'Mac', day pupils were called 'bugs' and school food was to be avoided at all costs.

On our return, the drive was full of cars and the chatter of children catching up after the holidays. Seeing this melee was both daunting and exciting. 'I can cope with this,' I thought, 'and I'm not going to feel homesick.' Then, entering the front door, I came face-to-face with Sadie the whippet. I picked her up and buried my face in her neck, inhaled the warm doggy smell of Tanyards and became inconsolable. Groups of pupils surrounded me, patting my back and saying kind words, taken aback at this strange new girl with cropped white hair, wearing chunky boys' shoes and weeping while clutching a trembling dog. This was not the first impression I had been hoping to give.

Mum had realised what had happened half an hour into her drive home and had no option but to turn the car around. I was waiting in the school hall when she entered, her face streaked with tears, and without saying anything took the dog from my arms and turned for the door.

Everyone remembers their first night at boarding school as if it was yesterday. The pain of knowing that you will not be in your own bed, surrounded by your own knick-knacks and smells, or seeing your parents, for a whole month, is challenging enough; but then the realisation hits that there is no one there to defend you and that you have to fend for yourself.

Aware that I was becoming stifled by Dad's blind adoration, I'd asked to go to boarding school because I yearned for the space to develop as an individual. I distinctly remember relishing the thought that I now had the freedom to make my own mistakes as I lay in bed, listening to the other nine girls in my dormitory whispering to each other after lights out. They all knew each other well and were merrily chatting about their holiday antics. They also talked about boys, periods and Tampax. I had a rough idea about the birds and the bees from the mating antics of the menagerie at home, and Lindy had mentioned 'the Curse', but I'd never dared ask her what it was. Now these girls were hooting with laughter, trying not to attract the attention of the matron prowling the corridors. Maybe boarding school was going to be fun after all.

I soon learned my way around the school, with its quad of prefabricated classrooms and the art and carpentry workshop, which were all dominated by the mock-Gothic main building. The sixty boarding girls slept in the main house, while the boys slept in a modern block opposite. Within the walls were the library, with its desultory collection of books, their spines broken and covers ripped; the staffroom, thick with cigarette smoke and the sweet smell of dunked Rich Tea biscuits; and a dusty ballroom. The refectory was a hideous 1960s extension, designed with no sympathy for its Victorian neighbour.

In the shadow of the woods was the gym, with its ladder-clad walls, wooden horse and the lingering smell of unwashed socks, raw rubber and urine. A sunken expanse of lawn stretched along the sunny south side of the main house, the scene of many exhilarating games of all-school, bone-crunching British bulldog. Beyond the lawn and crumbling ha-ha lay the playing fields, large enough for a football pitch, the athletics track and a slightly decaying obstacle course, and beyond the fields was the Mickleham Bypass.

I remember very little about my four years of lessons there – not one inspiring teacher or one subject captured my imagination. Not only was the school an academic wasteland, but we lost all the team games we played against other schools. However, rather than smart with humiliation, we chose to play up to our reputation, celebrating the ever-greater losses: 'We lost 13–1 to Farlington at netball this afternoon. 'Well done, guys – it's a record!'

I realise now that Box Hill's strength lay in its diverse intake. After the protected world of Shamley Green, I became friends with people from Malaysia, Venezuela, Saudi Arabia, Yugoslavia and

America. There were children of dethroned royals, of film stars and gangsters, as well as direct-grant pupils who had been failing in the state system and came to a small private school to be put back on the right track. My friends included girls from children's homes, bright East End Afro-Caribbean kids who had fallen in with the wrong crowd and political exiles from the Middle East. Having such a wide range of friends from all socio-political and economic backgrounds was life-enhancing and defining.

The one payphone in the hall inevitably had a queue of three or four kids waiting to ring home during breaks or free time, which made it impossible for parents to contact their children. Between the twice-termly *exeats*, when we went home after lessons on Saturday afternoon and were back by 8 p.m. on Sunday night, and the three-day half terms, I had very little contact with my parents. Dad would take his annual leave during the first two weeks of June, when my parents always went to Menorca. My birthday was 3 June. My birthdays at Box Hill were marked by a call from Mum, frustrated by the effort of getting through. There would be a cheery rendering of 'Happy Birthday' followed by a gabbled 'I can't talk for long – this call is costing an arm and a leg!' I would replace the receiver shrugging off the disappointment, each sting of rejection reminding me to toughen up and not expect too much support.

Birthdays were never a big deal, even when I was living at home. We would mark them with a token gift on our place setting at breakfast, but I don't recall Mum ever organising a party in our honour. A few years later, I organised my own twenty-first in the barns at Tanyards. Never one to miss a trick, Mum suggested that the celebration double up as a fundraiser for a charity she was involved with. As a result, the invitation read, 'Ted and Eve Branson invite you to celebrate Vanessa's twenty-first, in aid of the Guildford Talking Newspaper for the Blind.'

One Saturday evening during my first term, in 1969, the girls' house was glued to the television, watching a magazine programme about the young people to watch in the coming decade. The TV studio was full of inventors, scientists, writers and budding politicians all eagerly answering questions about their plans for the future with considered, articulate responses. Then, to my embarrassment, I noticed Richard sitting at the front, slightly slumped and clad in a chunky roll-neck sweater. His face was obscured by a mane of matted locks, the beginnings of a beard and a pair of black spectacles, one arm of which was fixed at the hinge with Elastoplast. The anchorman turned to him.

'So, Richard... Branson,' the TV host said, checking his clipboard, 'do you have a vision for the 1970s?'

'Yeah, well young people are really going to, umm...' he answered, in his familiarly hesitant manner.

'What do you mean exactly?' the man with the microphone pushed.

'Well, I mean . . .' Richard floundered, and the man moved on to the next person. None of my schoolfriends realised he was my brother, and I didn't say a word.

Nowadays stories of paedophilia are regularly in the news, but back then I think most of us lived in naivety. We trusted and talked to everyone, and if we experienced a 'Mr Pilkington' enjoying the thrill of exposing himself to little girls, or witnessed a man in dirty mackintosh playing with his flaccid penis behind the railway bridge during our cross country runs, we would dismiss it as sad and fundamentally harmless.

I did take a stand, however, when confronted by a very ill and damaged science teacher. His name was Vincent Derbyshire, and our nudging grins at his unfortunate initials and dishevelled appearance turned to opened-mouthed disbelief when he introduced himself during our first lesson with him.

'My name is Vincent Derbyshire,' he snuffled with a strange lisp, 'and I come from outer space.' He had our attention now. 'I know that a number of you will find this fact hard to grasp but, trust me, it's true.'

'But sir,' we said, 'what do you mean?'

'I can't tell you all at the same time,' he continued. 'If you want to know more, you'll have to come for a walk with me, one at a time, after school.'

I went to my housemistress to inform her about this lunatic, but she laughed it off and told me to stop being ridiculous. I then called Mum, who said much the same. The man was so weird and his story so outlandish, that no adult believed me.

For our next science class, I smuggled in my cassette recorder, which back in 1969 was a bulky machine that only just fitted into my desk, leaving a two-inch gap because the lid couldn't close properly. I was terrified that the man from Mars was going to catch me. The rest of the class knew what was going on.

'Sir, sir, tell us what planet you're from!' we chorused.

'Well,' he said, 'I arrived here by spaceship from a far-away planet.'

'Why aren't you green, sir?'

'We have special powers, and can take on any form,' he lisped. He had lost all authority at this point. 'Look,' he shouted, 'I told you, if you really want to know the truth, you have to come for a walk with me after school.'

Bingo – we had him. I played the tape to my incredulous housemistress, and we never saw Vincent Derbyshire again. No one so much as mentioned the recording to me – whistle-blowing is a thankless task.

* * *

Back home for the long summer holidays, I realised that everything had changed. Even though I was only eleven, I'd experienced a wider outside world. The few kids of my age at Shamley Green seemed less interesting in comparison to my international friends. To make my sense of alienation worse, two bedrooms at Tanyards were now being let out to students from the Guildford Law School. Lindy and Richard had been 'shuffled from the nest' and Mum was utterly focused on Binibella.

That summer was the first time that I felt the shattering effects of loneliness. For two weeks Mags was away on holiday and Beatle had moved away following the death of her mother. I saw Mishi a couple of times, but we had little in common.

I had no one to call on, and my new schoolfriends were too young to travel to me on their own. I moaned a bit to Mum, who reminded me that I was incredibly lucky, with a pony, dogs and acres of land to play on. She told me I should write, but this was not an easy way to pass the time as a solitary eleven-year-old who had done so little reading. I made myself a den in one of the barns and tried writing a diary. I played snooker with myself and took myself for walks in the woods, but my head prickled with loneliness. Mum's PA, Evelyn, took pity on me – she'd noticed my budding breasts (she was not alone – I'd been nicknamed 'Sprout' at school) and drove me into Guildford to buy my first bra. I remember holding back tears as a virtual stranger passed me training bras through the flapping changing room curtain.

One day, I made a half-hearted attempt to train my old pony, Snowy, on a lunge rein, but he was over twenty years old by this stage and didn't have a clue what I was trying to do. Before long he had backed in my direction and given me a well-aimed kick in the chest. Thoroughly winded and gasping for breath, I lay on the ground feeling sorry for myself as Snowy stood by my side, nibbling on some grass.

Mags and I began our brief shoplifting career in the Guildford branch of WH Smith. We would catch the number 9 bus into town and then lurk suspiciously in the aisles before indicating to each other that the coast was clear and stuffing a rubber or pencil sharpener into our pockets. It was thrilling. Later that holiday we took the train to London. I had driven with my parents to see Richard a few times but had never arrived at Waterloo station with the whole city to explore. In our naivety we spent the day on the Underground, asking everyone that would engage with us where we should go shopping. We had return tickets back to Guildford but no money, and for some reason ended up in Fenwick's on New Bond Street, one of the most exclusive department stores in London.

I can't remember talking to Mags about any plans to shoplift, but I was well aware of what was going on in the changing cubicle next to mine and was thrilled by her audacity. We then sheepishly walked towards the exit when, with a few paces to go, the heavy hand of the store detective was on our shoulders. As he marched us to his office, I felt like my world had come to an end. My head pounded and sweat was pumping from every pore of my trembling body. My father often worked at Wells Street Magistrates Court barely a mile away, prosecuting petty shoplifters like us every day. The shame this would bring on my family was beyond my imagination.

The detective went through the bag Mags was carrying and found a top stuffed under a carefully placed raincoat. He pulled it out between thumb and forefinger, holding it up as if it were a dirty nappy.

'Now what have we here?' he asked.

Mags gave the performance of her life. 'Please forgive me,' she sniffed, beginning to cry. 'My father died last week and, and...' At this, she began to wail. I looked at the man's face to see which way this was going to go.

'My dear,' said the store detective. 'I'm so sorry.'

'I loved him so much,' Mags bawled, blowing her snotty nose into the hanky offered by the man. I sat there, completely speechless, until the detective stood up and walked us, this time with a protective arm around our shoulders, to the shop exit.

He waved us goodbye and Mags and I spun on our heels and ran for our lives. That had certainly been an adventure, but not one to be repeated. Mags should have become an actress – her father was indeed dead, but he had gone to meet his Maker several years before.

My loneliness came to an end when we Bransons boarded a plane bound for Menorca, which was quite a journey in 1969. We took a jet plane to Majorca and then a twin-engined propeller plane to Mahon Airport. The second flight was memorable – the aged plane flew through a storm and was buffeted about alarmingly. Lindy and I gripped each other's hands as we were tossed this way and that, my sister comforting me with the words, 'We're going to die, Nessie. We're going to die.' We clutched each other, giggling hysterically, and didn't let go until we were safely on the runway.

Casa Candy was a tiny sugar cube of a house, and I revelled in the idea of spending an entire month with the family in such close proximity. Lindy and I shared a room that was only just big enough for a pair of narrow bunk beds. The galley kitchen led directly onto the sitting room, with a built-in bench and dining table at one end, and a balcony overlooking the fishermen's slipway at the other. My parents had a bedroom that looked out to sea, and Richard slept in the boathouse below.

Mum loved fishermen as much as she loved gypsies, and soon after arriving she bought *Margareta*, a Menorcan fishing boat. Dad used to joke that the boat was the same age as him and deteriorating at about the same pace!

The challenge was on. Mum spent hours practising her appalling Spanish by talking to an endlessly patient fisherman and learned that the best time to fish was under a full moon. 'It's easy,' he'd assured her. 'You feed a slither of electric light flex down the shaft of a number of hooks, attach the hooks to each line and drop them overboard. When you jiggle them up and down, the flex catches the light of the moon and the fish will leap onto the hooks.' Then, as an afterthought, he added, 'Oh yes – but you have to be at least two kilometres offshore.'

The boat was washed down and Dad tinkered with the inboard engine and prepared the lines. He made sure he stowed a lead cosh on board to whack any fish we caught over the head, along with a bucket to store them in. Dad ensured that we had enough provisions to survive if the engine cut out and we drifted towards North Africa, which meant that, along with water and biscuits, a flagon of gin and a bottle of whisky were added. We were ready to go.

Dad pointed to the sky where two seagulls were circulating overhead. 'Do you know why you never see a gull flying on its own?' he asked. We racked our brains, trying to remember something we'd been taught at school. 'Shall I tell you?' he chortled. 'It's because one good tern deserves another!'

'Oh Daddy,' we groaned, as we cast *Margareta* off from her moorings.

I've always loved being outdoors at night and found setting off to sea in the dark absolutely thrilling. Being in a fishing boat with my entire family as we travelled across the late-summer waters of the Mediterranean under a starlit sky was like something from a dream. The trusty inboard throbbed reassuringly until the lights of the village were mere specks in the distance. Just when we thought the night couldn't become more magical, Dad pointed out a trail of phosphorescence behind us, as the heavy propeller cut through the sea.

When the village lights were almost invisible, Dad cut the engine, took a swig of gin and handed each of us a fishing line. We dropped them into the water and jiggled them about as instructed; within a minute, Lindy shrieked, 'I think I've caught something!'

'Pull up your line!' we yelled, and up it came with six squirming fish attached. We all whooped and then realised that our own lines were also being tugged. There followed a scene of carnage, as a multitude of silver fish flapped about on deck, resisting being coshed over the head by Dad. It took a while for us girls to dare to unhook the wretched things, their slimy bodies wriggled unhelpfully, their gristly mouths stubbornly attached to the hooks. Within half an hour the white deck was red and flecked with bits of fish. We had drifted alarmingly. There was now no sign of land. Our bucket was full and it was time to go home.

Dad wound the rope around the starter motor and gave it a yank; the engine spluttered but failed to fire.

'Ha, no worries,' he mumbled, as he re-wound the rope.

Another pull, another splutter.

'Ha, no worries,' said Dad again, as he relit his pipe, took another swig of gin and re-wound the rope.

'Third time lucky,' he said, pulling the starter with one last almighty heave, fearful that another false start would flood the engine. We all fell about laughing as the rope snapped and he flew backwards.

'Oh Lord,' he chuckled. 'Don't worry, we have biscuits, water and gin on board. Come on, Richard, we're going to have to row for our lives!'

Any other parents would have regarded our situation – being stranded several miles out at sea, at 1 a.m., on a leaky, wooden, blood-soaked boat – as a potential catastrophe, but not ours, who saw it as a team-building experience, a source of a good story and an awfully big adventure. Richard and Dad took it in turns to row the boat back to shore, while we passed an hour happily serenading them with 'What Shall We Do With the Drunken Sailor?' and 'We're All Going on a Summer Holiday'. Then, lulled by the rhythm of the rowing, I lay my head on Mum's lap and slept while we made our way home to the village, one stroke at a time.

Menorca in the sixties and seventies was bliss. I could run free, playing with the local children in the village, buying Spanish sweets from the local shop and swimming in the clear waters, or we would all jump in *Margareta* and chug along to the beach at Binibeca and eat paella under the shade of the beach bar. We messed about on the sea, towing each other behind the boat or using the 'aquanaut', a compressor that floated in a rubber ring on the surface and pumped air down thirty-foot tubes to us, as we explored the seabed wearing weight belts. While Lindy attracted every hot-blooded male into her curvaceous, sensual orbit, I joined families with children my age on the beach. It was here that I met Fiona Whitney.

Fiona's mother Roma, a former ballet-dancer, was doing handstands on the sand, and I couldn't resist showing off that I could do them too – rather bizarrely, nor could Jeffrey Archer, who happened also to be on the beach.

Fiona came up to me. 'Are you a boy or a girl?' she asked.

'I'm a girl,' I replied. 'What are you?' By the end of the day, we had become firm friends and I'd invited her to Casa Candy for a sleepover.

Fiona lived in London, and her parents dazzled me with their sense of humour. Her father John had a dandyish manner and was the first truly creative man who talked to me person-to-person, encouraging me to share inventions I'd come up with.

'They could work,' he said, 'but you must never forget one thing, Vanessa. Ideas are two a penny – it's putting them into action that matters.'

John had a strange little-boy manner that was evident in his relationship with Roma. She played the strict mother figure to his naughty boy and they called each other 'Tiny'. To me it was a strange game, but theirs was to be an enduring marriage and as I write this, over fifty years later, they're still acting out these roles in Dorset. John was then developing the TV series *Upstairs Downstairs* and would go on to be the founding director of Capital Radio, the radio station whose goal was 'to turn the capital into a village', and which provided the soundtrack to our early adult days in London. Fiona, six months my senior and an academic year ahead of me, dazzled me with tales of London and her Quaker boarding school, the Friends' School in Saffron Walden. On that very first sleepover we pledged to write to each other from our respective boarding schools, and five years of hilarious correspondence were to follow.

Meeting Fiona marked another turning point for me – I'd never come upon such an extreme personality before and was excited to walk on the wild side with someone who seemed to be, by turns, fearless and cautious. Life with Fiona was never going to be dull, but even my wildest ten-year-old imagination couldn't possibly guess just how interesting it would be.

* * *

My memories of home life from that time are blurred. I still suffered from moments of loneliness but, on the whole, the house was filled with energy and people. Mum had transformed an old grain shed under one of the barns into a cottage, which was rented to yet more law students. Richard was working and sleeping in the crypt of a London church, kindly offered to him by a vicar who was impressed with his youthful enthusiasm. He would come home at weekends, along with his band of young journalists, to have a hot bath and get fed. Lindy also came home for weekends; she was by now at Lucie Clayton, a secretarial college and finishing school, and would astonish me with tales of her lessons there, of how a lady twiddles her pearls in an alluring manner and how she steps out of a car without showing her panties.

Richard had tried to knock out a few of the crypt's arches, before discovering that they were made up of stacks of occupied coffins. As it became too claustrophobic, he managed to secure, under Mum and Dad's name, a lease from the Church Commissioners on a town house on Albion Street, just off Connaught Square. It was a residential-only lease, and on more than one occasion Mum and Dad received a panicked call from Richard, saying that the commissioners were coming for an inspection and we had to make a mad dash to London. We would sit in the drawing room, Mum sewing, Dad reading a paper and me playing on the floor – the perfect family tableau to distract the inspector from the chaos in the basement, where the office staff were hiding silently until he'd left.

It was on one of these occasions that Richard asked me if I would model for him. I must have been twelve and Virgin Records was about to be launched. The artist Roger Dean had been commissioned to design its logo, and I was to go to his studio. I entered with some trepidation, but Roger was perfectly nice and offered me a cup of tea, before casually asking if I'd go behind the screen to take my clothes off.

'I'm sorry, I don't understand,' I stuttered.

'Over there – the screen in the corner. It won't take a minute or two – I just need to take a few shots before working on them.'

I hesitated and seeing my utter bewilderment, Roger said, 'I think there must be some sort of misunderstanding. Richard said you wouldn't mind taking your clothes off.'

I apologised, barely looking him in the eye, and made hastily for the door. Nowadays, the image of a naked set of Siamese twins, the old Virgin Records logo, could be regarded as rather creepy, but back in 1971 it had a Garden of Eden innocence. I rather regret my prudishness now – it would have been wonderful to have my youth immortalised. For that sweet youth was about to pass.

5

DUSK OVER FIELDS

My four years at boarding school were generally happy, as Tanyards became a backdrop to my life rather than playing centre stage. Home was filled with law student lodgers, partying and laughter and I was always welcome, but I felt no obligation to appear and was free to come and go as I chose. In many ways, this benign neglect was the ideal way to grow up: I neither had to share teenage anguish with my parents nor hide issues from them, and I knew I was utterly loved and trusted. I remember admonishing my father on a couple of occasions for not celebrating some small triumphs of mine; he simply replied that he had complete faith in me and expected nothing else. Mum displayed no alarm if I told her I was staying with friends for the weekend or going to London for the day; on the contrary, she encouraged me to explore the world and to take pleasure in meeting new people.

I realise, as I write this book, just how much the Virgin story is interwoven through mine. It is impossible to tell my story without acknowledging how much it has enriched my life. Richard loved to share all his highs and lows and he surrounded himself with talented, energetic young people, who were excited about challenging the old world order. Sitting on the sidelines, I watched his often crazy antics evolve into the multinational business that is Virgin today.

The years 1970 to 1973 were especially busy for my brother, whose career was moving at a fearsome rate. Simon Draper, having arrived from South Africa in 1970, had knocked unannounced on Richard's door, introduced himself as the nephew of Aunt Wendy, the aunt that my father had picked up on the cruise ship over forty years earlier, and asked for a job. Simon's passion for, and encyclopaedic knowledge of, contemporary music gave Richard a new direction. Music was the cultural life force of the age and Virgin was going to be at its vanguard.

Student and its mail-order record business evolved into a chain of record shops, the first of which opened on Oxford Street and the next on Notting Hill Gate in west London. Richard bought a house nearby in Denbigh Terrace, just off the Portobello Road, from the comedian Peter Cook, who would later make a number of outrageous albums with Dudley Moore on the Virgin label.

Notting Hill Gate was a rather scuzzy area back then, the elegant, late-Georgian terraces having been broken up into flats that were run by slum landlords and filled with migrants, gangsters and struggling artists, including David Hockney and Jimi Hendrix. On Fridays and Saturdays, Portobello Road came to life as the market stalls fired up and the area pulsated with youth, creativity and music.

144

Virgin record shops were designed to be laid-back places, where music lovers could listen to records on headphones while slumping on bean bags. Virgin became the epitome of cool. Richard borrowed £35,000 from Auntie Joyce, who had cared for her parents her whole life and inherited the bulk of the family wealth after their death, and used it as a deposit on a mortgage for The Manor at Shipton-on-Cherwell, a sixteenth-century manor house, complete with walled gardens, a church and lawns that swept down to a lake.

One of the outbuildings at The Manor was converted into a state-of-the-art recording studio. Unlike the usual London recording studios, bands could stay in the cavernous bedrooms, hang out in the house and grounds in the daytime and record all night. One of the session musicians working with Kevin Ayers, the former frontman of Soft Machine, was Mike Oldfield. During the studio's downtime, Mike had been patiently laying down a record, overdubbing instrument after instrument; the result, from its thin opening riffs to its fulsome orchestral finish, was fresh and enigmatic. He had sent a demo tape to record companies but his music, so out of tune with the rock and roll fashion of the time, was turned down by every label in the country. Simon Draper was convinced by *Tubular Bells'* brilliance, and he and Richard decided to launch a record company to release it themselves. This was an audacious plan, as apart from the shops, neither of them had any experience of the music industry.

I remember Dad walking me across the village green to visit Judge Jellyneck, a retired high court judge who also played the violin. Dad wanted to ask his opinion of his son's first release. We sat together on upright chairs while the old man slotted the record onto his turntable and listened first to side one – twenty-five minutes – and then to side two – twenty-four minutes – in silence. When the album came to Vivian Stanshall's introductions of 'grand piano' and 'glockenspiel', and climaxed with the titular bells, the judge stood up to retrieve the record and replaced it in its sleeve, shaking his head.

Thankfully, the good judge wasn't the arbiter of cool back then – the DJ John Peel was. Peel championed *Tubular Bells* by playing it in its entirety on his radio show, *Top Gear*; after a slow start, sales began to rocket.

* * *

Growing up at Box Hill School, I wasn't aware of much supervision. Having witnessed my children going through boarding school at Marlborough College thirty years later, with electronic fobs monitoring their every movement and CCTV cameras watching their every encounter, I doubt that this level of scrutiny kept them out of mischief. In fact, being so closely monitored simply drove them crazy with frustration and made them want to fight the system.

In our day, by following a few rules (the most important being 'don't get caught') we could evolve into responsible grown-ups in our own time, by experimenting with aspects of our identities without the interference of adults. At the age of twelve, hanging out in corridors in huddles was our chosen method. We spent hours just knocking around, taking the mickey out of each other. We scaled the school's roof using our dressing-gown cords as safety ropes and explored the Victorian central-heating ducts, a network of pitch-black tunnels running under the main house. It was thrilling.

Occasionally a couple would start 'going out', which meant walking around the school hand in hand, and finding hidden corners for intimate conversation and some stroking and kissing. To my shame, I recall succumbing to the attentions of two boys in my year, one after the other. One took me into the woods and asked me, with youthful awkwardness, to stroke his enthusiastically erect but diminutive penis, and the other placed my hand on his bulging lap during Cinema Club. Neither encounter shocked me; I just presumed it was something boys did. I didn't tell any of my girlfriends all the same, for these early fumblings felt shameful. From then on, I understood that, however much you resist, you can't help but absorb a portion of the essence of every person with whom you share intimacy, and this remains with you for the rest of your life. So be discerning!

When I was almost fourteen, I began talking to a boy in the year above. I look now at the photograph of the striking young Iraqi boy and can clearly see why I fell so in love with him. And this was *real* love, by the way, no mere teenage crush. Nabeel was unlike any other boy in the school. He was born in Iraq to a British mother and an Iraqi father. The family had fled Saddam Hussein's Ba'ath Party, and their factories and homes had been confiscated. He told me that his uncle had been tortured, a fate beyond my understanding after my cosseted childhood at Shamley Green.

Nabeel had four brothers, all of them mature beyond years. I don't know what bookish, quiet Nabeel, with his shy smile and slightly diffident manner, saw in me, the carefree joker laughing around with gangs of friends, but I firmly believe that love unearths qualities that sense doesn't. Nabeel and I became inseparable. I went to stay with his family in Southampton and was struck by his gracious mother's acceptance of her middle son's young girlfriend; his father, I have to admit, was slightly speechless. Back at school, I took to sharing Nabeel's study cubicle, a privilege reserved for those taking their O-levels.

With his encouragement, I began to read, making my way through tomes that I would previously have considered incomprehensible. We prided ourselves in only reading Penguin Classics: books by Henry James, George Orwell, E. M. Forster, Vladimir Nabokov, Thomas Hardy, Jean-Paul Sartre and Émile Zola. We would lie on our backs under the dappled shade of the mighty beech at the far end of the playing field. With my head on his bare stomach, I was aware of his beating heart and rhythmic breathing. I revelled in his smell, his smooth brown skin and the downy hair that ran from his belly button down to the band of his boxer shorts, as his flat stomach sank beneath his hips. I would run my fingers over his chest, tracing a network of scars, the result of a childhood accident when making fireworks with his brothers in the basement of his house in Baghdad.

Is it any wonder that we wanted to explore every inch of the beautiful young bodies that we held so close? I trusted Nabeel entirely and am happy to carry his essence with me to this day. One day, during the dark winter term, we wordlessly went to the hidden, musty foot tunnel beyond the playing fields, the entrance of which was camouflaged by trails of vines and ivy. We laid our school blazers down on the compacted earth before wrapping our arms around each other, not losing eye contact for a moment. Nabeel lay on top of me and gently worked his beautiful being into mine. My God, it hurt. I held onto his back and cried out and laughed with joy, relieved that I would never have to go through that searing pain again.

Sex came instinctively to me, being the youngest of a liberal family, and I was excited about exploring this new part of life. Having never watched pornography, our generation slowly investigated and tasted the joys of skin on skin. All happened in its own good time, with each new coupling revealing fresh pleasures.

Nabeel transformed my school experience, stimulating an intellectual curiosity that otherwise may well have lain dormant. He also set me on the right track regarding drugs, denouncing anyone who was dabbling in them as idiots – he had seen the fallout from kids taking drugs in Baghdad. Over the years, his words of distain have echoed in my ears and, whenever possible, I've avoided those who are indulging, particularly those tiresome cocaine users who are forever on 'transmit' and never on 'receive'.

How different the world was back then, without mobile phones and social media. I'm trying to remember what Nabeel and I did during the holidays. We certainly didn't meet up – I think we simply clocked off for the holidays and clocked back on when term started again.

In a bid for more freedom, I made a home in one of the gypsy caravans at the far end of the garden at Tanyards, beyond the orchard. The brightly painted old caravan had a working wood-burning stove, double bunk beds, a table and a couple of chairs. I whitewashed the interior, put up some curtains, filched a saucepan and a few tins of beans from the house and spent many happy hours collecting firewood, reading and entertaining the occasional guest with beans on toast, which I'd cook on the open fire. Fiona Whitney would come down from London to stay, and we'd spend our days hacking through the woods on Snowy and Tommy and writing business plans for our future riding school.

From the caravan, I moved to the cellar of the main house. I didn't fancy having to lift up the trapdoor in the kitchen floor every time I wanted to go to my room, so I sawed a hole through the coat cupboard and descended down an old stepladder. My parents were reluctant to risk the cupboard route, which meant I had the cellar to myself, though the only natural light in my underground cavern came from two glass bricks covering the old coal chute. I painted the walls a deep purple and divided the space into two: one side was my bedroom, with a mattress on the floor, and the other was a study area. While dividing the room with plasterboard, I also disguised the greasy oil-fired boiler, hacking through panels of asbestos without pausing to consider the risk. The ancient boiler fired up twice a day, which filled the room with toxic fumes that helpfully camouflaged the smoke from the numerous cigarettes I was chugging through. The days of self-destruction had begun . . .

I'd bobbed up the ladder to have breakfast one morning just as Mum was leaving for work as a magistrate in Guildford. As she went out through the front door, she shouted back to me, 'Oh, by the way, Snowy's dead. Can you call the knacker's yard?'

The truth is, I had rather neglected Snowy, who had been living in contented retirement in his field. But the news was still somewhat shocking. I walked up the hill through the orchard. It was a crisp winter's morning, the ground rock hard. There was Snowy, lying on his side with his legs straight out, as if he had simply toppled over. His black fur was dusted white with frost. I lay beside him, wrapping my arms around his neck and wailing into his stiff body.

What I was crying for? I didn't know back then, but I now realise that my tears expressed a deep grief for the passing of my childhood. I wept for the days I'd spent making jumps out of

149

painted poles and Snowcem drums. The long summer days spent hacking across the heath and up the one-mile gallop. The days of taking picnics to the woods and stopping under the shade of trees to eat our squashed sandwiches before finding our way home.

I was crying for my present, too, and for having no one to share my grief with. I returned to the house, and scoured the Yellow Pages for the phone number of the knacker's yard, mistakenly looking under 'N'. My eyes swimming, I eventually rang Directory Enquiries, gasping between words as I tried to tell the operator what I was looking for.

After I'd eventually found the number, a rough old traveller turned up and asked me to slip a rubber collar around Snowy's rear legs. Then I watched as my shaggy old friend was winched into the back of the horsebox, his head bobbing up and down as it was dragged up the slatted wooden ramp.

What was in Mum's mind when she so callously told me about Snowy's death? Even now, I can't quite get my head around her lack of compassion, though I realise she was in a rush to get to work, and I guess I might otherwise have sauntered up to the field and found the dead pony myself. The truth is that death doesn't fit into a mind that's as focused on the positive as my mother's – she just wasn't able to deal with the conversation.

Whatever her motives, I think her harshness ultimately did me a favour; I've faced a number of challenges since then when I've had to pull myself together and call the metaphorical knacker's yard; every time, my mind returns to that winter morning and the knowledge that I can cope, because there is no other option.

In the summer of 1972, after audaciously courting the stunningly beautiful designer Kristen Tomassi, Richard convinced her to marry him. To my thirteen-year-old self, she seemed like a willowy, ethereal princess. Considering their youth and progressive beliefs in changing the status quo, the couple had a remarkably traditional wedding, in the church attached to The Manor – Simon Draper recently told me that Richard put on a good show in order to impress his bank manager from Coutts, who was guest of honour.

Lindy and I were bridesmaids, along with Kristen's sisters, and we all gathered by the church porch, feeling a little self-conscious in our long, peach chiffon dresses, as we waited for the bride to arrive. Then Mum, who had reserved a seat for Granny Dock, came out of the church, wondering where on earth her mother was. Richard and Dad then came out, too. Everyone's concern was palpable – Granny was driving up from the south coast to Oxfordshire and would surely have left in good time. She must have had an accident.

We all turned to see Kristen and her father appear in a garlanded Rolls-Royce at exactly the same time as a giant articulated lorry. Rolls and lorry pulled up outside the church gates simultaneously. Granny climbed down from the lorry's cab with as much dignity as possible, as the lorry gave a giant air-brake fart. The driver blew her a kiss and gave her a cheery wave. Her wide-brimmed hat slightly askew, she was hustled into the church just as the organ fired up. It turned out that she had crashed into the lorry thirty miles away and the kind driver had driven her to the church at breakneck speed, leaving her mangled car by the roadside.

In my teens, the pleasure of visiting The Manor was tempered by my shyness. I would wander around rooms filled with Chesterfield sofas, log fires, faded rugs and sleeping Irish wolfhounds, quietly observing but never quite fitting in. There would always be musicians, technicians, girlfriends and boyfriends mooching around. When entering a room, I'd wonder: should I say hello or try and be as cool as them? On one visit, I joined in a five-a-side football match with the band Queen, who were recording there; on another, I was there for Van Morrison's birthday dinner, a grumpy affair as he didn't approve of the flavour of the cake that had been made for him by the cook's ten-year-old daughter. An early insight into the complicated workings of the creative mind.

Happily back at Box Hill, I volunteered to direct the Eisteddfod (a talent show, for want of a better word) on behalf of my house. Box Hill was divided into four houses, and competition between us was intense, with points scored for all aspects of school life, from sport and academic work to social service and music. I was a Corinthian, and we were neck-and-neck with the Spartans – the house prize rested on the outcome of the show, and I was desperate to win.

During rehearsals I realised that I loved directing, and hit upon a cunning device to tie all the skits together. We placed a couch in the corner of the stage and had a psychiatrist talk to the empty couch, which raised the suggestion that he was also insane, as he plucked scenes from the contorted mind of his imaginary patient. By contrast, the Spartans' production was good but didn't entirely hang together. The judge gave us a glowing critique, and as I went to collect the cup at the end of the evening, with the whoops and cheers of the school ringing in my ears, I felt truly fulfilled for the first time in my life.

* * *

I've been rooting through my letters, diligently kept in box files over the years. There they are, my teenage years all laid out on the ping pong table. Letters from Mags, my ever-loyal friend who kept in touch from Bramley, along with short, morale-boosting notes from Mum with snippets of home news. There's not one letter from Dad but there are three from Lindy, including one that rather ominously apologises for teasing me so badly during the drive to school that 'she and Daddy cried all the way home'.

There are letters from friends, full of references to the LPs they were listening to – David Bowie, Marc Bolan, Bob Dylan and Cat Stevens – as well what they were getting up to during the holidays, including the odd foreign trip but otherwise a lot of listening to music and smoking in bedrooms. With the Vietnam War coming to its ghastly climax and the Irish Troubles rumbling, you'd have thought that the odd letter might have given them a passing mention but no, we focused on the close-at-hand.

A while ago, Fiona photocopied and bound our five years of school correspondence. It's a thick volume that captures the language of co-educational boarding school life in the seventies and our excited observations of status systems, rules and friends, as well as the first bras, periods, boys and young flirtations that obsessed our twelve-year-old minds. By fourteen, our enthusiasm was tinged with cynicism, first cigarettes and quarter-bottles of vodka. Finally there are long, hysterical letters from Fiona filled with drunken Saturday nights, fallings-out with best friends, topless frolicking under the stars, incompetent teachers making passes and the drama of being caught meeting her boyfriend at 2 a.m., which led to her being expelled.

Here's a taster – one of my last letters to Fiona, in which I was experimenting with a new-found intellectual pretention and highlighting the agony and ecstasy of those teenage years, as I switched from near-suicidal misery to romantic bliss on the spin of a bottle of Smirnoff...

Dear Fi

I was so happy to hear from you this morning. I thought you'd forgotten about me. It really has been getting depressing lately, both mentally and work-wise. There are just no working rooms here and no working atmosphere.

Last weekend was Nabs' birthday and I got really drunk, and I mean really drunk, on about three quarters of a bottle of vodka, and for my head that was quite a bit. All I did all evening was cry and cry and make a real fool of myself. It's funny, but I have a big hang-up. I've sort of grown a skin around myself against the whole system. All the people around me seem so involved in themselves – I just don't know who to mix with.

Nabs is in the same situation as me, so we really depend on each other which is bad really.

All my morals and ideas of life have changed. I want to go to university now, to study philosophy. I thought about it last Saturday. I need some aim in life and me and Nabs talked for hours on the subject and came to that conclusion.

You know, Nabs is the most amazing person. I just don't know how to explain it, but he has this real love for the countryside and beauty. Every afternoon we go for a walk

and sit on this bench on the top of the hill looking across
this valley and at the end there is the most exhilarating
sunset. It's all I really enjoy now. But deep down inside
I have some content feeling, which makes me feel inwardly
happy – silly, really.

Send me more news, Fi Fi.

Have you read *The Fall* by a man called Camus? It's
great, by the way.

Love ya

Nessa xx

Among the hoard of correspondence, I came upon a file entitled
'Very Old Love Letters' – now this was going to be interesting.
I lit the fire, put the kettle on and settled down to savour the
moment. There were a number of letters from boys I could hardly
remember, one or two from boys I'd met in Menorca who went to
different schools, and a couple from a neighbour of Fiona's that
we'd watch television with when I visited her in London.

At the bottom of the file, slightly damaged from a flood we
suffered in the cellar, I came across four long letters from Nabeel.
Three were written during the school summer holidays, which he'd
spent in Tunisia, and the last was written after he'd left Box Hill.
Reading his letters reminds me of the glory of coming of age: when
you realise that the world doesn't actually revolve around you;
when hormones flood your body and empathy and yearning
overwhelm you; when you see yourself reflected in the eyes of
your lover and like what you see; when you first experience the
wonder of looking at a sunset and its beauty moves you to tears.

I never had any confidence in my ability to write, though Nabeel's
letters are littered with pleas that I write back to him. I think we
understood, when he left Box Hill to go to a sixth-form college in
Southampton, that it was unlikely that we'd be able to sustain a
relationship. As the summer term drew to a close, we clung onto
each other, barely talking to anyone else. On the last day of term,
the entire school climbed onto buses for a day-trip to Littlehampton.
While the other kids spent their time at the fun fair, we walked up

and down the windy beach. I nestled under his arm while we listened to Bob Dylan sing 'Sad-Eyed Lady of the Lowlands' over and over again on a tinny portable cassette player and when the batteries ran first slow, then out, and we just lay on the pebbles in silence.

Nabeel wrote to me the following term.

Dear Vanessa,

God, I don't know how to start this. Basically I'm wrecking myself, I don't know what the fuck is up, 'but something is not right, it's wrong'. You know today at college I lit a cigarette and with it I almost screamed, I turned around, I wanted you there, do you understand? You weren't of course. But I suppose I'll fade from you soon, but you know for the second time since I've known you, I've missed you like hell. The first time was in Tunisia and now. These are things I think about and never say, yeah I suppose I've said 'I love you' etc. And I did, I haven't lied. But you are on my mind nearly all the time, do you know what I mean? I can't love you in a letter because it's impossible, but I miss you...

Please write back soon and say what you think, look here, don't feel sorry, don't be polite, be brutal if it's like that. I just have to know. I want you. It is as simple as that. I just want to know. I could get a girl around here when I felt like it, but I don't want them. I want you to sit next to me when I smoke a cigarette, to hold my hand and to kiss me and to talk to me...

One thing I want of you: be truthful for God's sake, it doesn't matter, you don't have to be nice, when you don't want something, say 'no'. I mean this, I'm hoping for the best but that is immaterial as far as you're concerned. I'd hate it if you felt sorry for me on this issue, say it like it is with no dilutions. I've loved you and I have to have your person as well as your body, one on its own won't do, not without the other.

ANSWER VERY SOON, RIGHT? PLEASE WITHIN A FEW DAYS. You have the time and don't fuck about.

I miss you with every cigarette.

155

Nabeel
Love is in this letter as far as it can go.

I never replied. Now, over forty years later, I wonder how I justified my youthful carelessness. I have no excuse other than the fickleness of youth – my childish emotional intelligence was ill-equipped to deal with such force of feeling. I fear that I simply thought there was a whole new world out there, waiting to be explored.

Nabeel sent me one more postcard, a reproduction of a Georges Braque from the Museum of Modern Art in Paris, a year or two later:

I just felt like saying hello to you. I hope you're ok.
Love Nabeel.
I'm alright here in Southampton. I'm being made into a doctor.

I didn't hear from him again until I tracked him down while writing this book, but that's another story altogether.

* * *

Sussex, April 2017

An afternoon spent reading love letters, forty-four years after receiving them, had an extraordinary effect on my mood and I felt awash with love again. The birds sang, my lips tingled and my eyes smiled, as I walked across the fields to meet Mum for supper in the Ship at Itchenor. As I reached the pub, I noticed a man sitting outside, speaking softly in French on his mobile. I joined Mum at a corner table beyond the bar, bought her a whisky and myself a glass of dry white wine and started to tell her about my afternoon. She shuffled closer as I quoted from the letters. I'm not sure how much she takes in, but love still touches her soul.

'Oh, Nessie, you are a little devil,' said Mum, her eyes sparkling. The French man, although 'boy' would be a more apt description, came in and sat at the table next to us. The letters were playing magic tricks and I soon brought him into our conversation. He was quietly spoken and in his mid-twenties, with tightly curled red hair, thick-rimmed glasses and a cable-knit sweater. His name was Arthur. We asked him what he was doing in Itchenor and learned that he'd just abandoned his PhD and was embarking on a fresh challenge. He'd borrowed money from his sister to buy a creaking one-hundred-year-old wooden sailing boat, and he was about to sail along the south coast to Falmouth, with plans to learn about boat restoration while living aboard.

Arthur was a poet and a dreamer, and his ethereal presence caught me off-guard. I saw him looking at me, and after waving Mum off with her carer who had come to collect her, he and I walked along the towpath. We walked in silence, listening to the sound of the curlews as they drilled their long beaks into the mud. We could have been teenagers about to have our first kiss – the connection I felt with this young man, younger than my son, was confusing, powerful and deeply moving.

We stopped at his boat's mooring and at a loss about what to do, we stood looking at each other. Where was this about to go? Without saying a word, we held each other in a long embrace, his cheek on my head and mine to his chest. I pulled away and looked him in the eye. 'Have a wonderful adventure, Arthur. Bon voyage.' And then, without looking back, I walked on down the towpath.

6

Aunt Clare's Story

October 2017

Robert Hoare, a distant cousin, sent me a text in the early hours
of this morning:

Hi Ness, Aunt Clare just died, have a drink for her. I'm
waiting for a nurse, hence no call.

I lay in bed for a while, absorbing the news. Against all the
odds – ten slim panatella cigars each day and zero exercise –
the stubborn Jenkins genes had kept Clare alive well past her
expected departure date. Even so, her death took time to sink
in. How could someone with such eccentric opinions and such a
forceful character simply cease to exist?

I thought about who to contact and texted Robert for a little
more detail, knowing that news like this is easier to receive when
sweetened with the knowledge that someone died without a
struggle. Robert had been Clare's nephew by marriage, and his
dedication and love for her went well beyond the call of duty.
He'd driven to her house most days after work, to sit and chat
and share a smoke, a gin and a glass of Robinsons orange squash,
and he'd also overseen the rota of carers who came and went at an
alarming rate – most of them not sharing Clare's particular brand
of humour.

He replied:

Me and Robert were there, it was very peaceful. We think
she smiled. x

Now I had some good news to relate. Clare revelled in the
company of men and adored her two Roberts, her neighbour and
her nephew. To have had them both there as she floated off would
have been blissful.

The boys had entered into the spirit of the occasion: knowing
what Clare enjoyed in life, they had dipped her toothbrush into
some gin and, while she gently sucked on the sodden bristles, had
waved a lit cigar around her head. She smiled as she took a final
breath and was no more.

I immediately texted Richard, Lindy and Milo, one of Lindy's
sons, who had lived with Clare and Uncle Gerard for a year while
studying to be a helicopter pilot. Although he had told endless

stories of the ageing couple sniping at each other and had finally chosen to sleep in the back of his van rather than go home to The Mill House and witness the eternal battle scenes, he'd retained a strong bond with his aunt.

When amiable Uncle Gerard died four years ago, it fell to me to help with his funeral and all that disposing of a human body entails. During the drive from Sussex to Norfolk, I thought about how someone who had just lost her partner of sixty years must be feeling. I imagined us spending the next few days gently reminiscing, while searching in books for the perfect songs, readings and poems for Gerard's funeral service.

But not a bit of it. All sympathy was brushed aside and any words of praise for her dear departed were batted away, as if to say, 'He's gone now, so no use looking back.' Before my arrival, she had asked her neighbour Mahari to call a nearby farmer. Clare wanted him to bring his JCB to their meadow, dig a deep hole and pop Gerard's body in before covering him up.

Mahari was somewhat agitated as she waited for me to arrive. 'Brace yourself, Vanessa,' she warned. 'Clare has taken Gerard's death quite – how should I put this? – oddly.'

She was sitting down in the conservatory overlooking the mill pond, surrounded by well-thumbed copies of the *Daily Telegraph* and the *Daily Mail*, her sleek whippets' unclipped nails clicking on the tiled floor.

'My darling Clare,' I said, bending down to kiss her through the clouds of cigar smoke and brushing a dog away, 'I'm so sorry to hear about Gerard.'

'Don't be,' she replied.

I thought perhaps I should bring up the subject later. 'How about a cuppa?' I suggested.

'Lovely, darling – I never say no to a cuppa.'

As a family, we had always revered Clare, with her forthright, no-nonsense approach to life. Her fine features were defined by a strong jawline and high cheekbones, that would in the latter part of her life become entrenched with deep crevasses, emphasised by years of nicotine deposits lining their depths. She was quick to condemn but equally quick to laugh, an infectious intake of breath that conveyed sheer joy.

After Gerard died, I took to visiting Clare three or four times a year. I would take the train from London and be met by cousin Robert, then endure an hour or two sitting with her in a fug of cigar smoke, batting off her dogs Poppy and Blue, who crawled on my lap, licking my face and taking opportunistic nibbles at my lunch. Clare's life had shrunk over the years and she now did little more than walk from her bedroom to her conservatory. Her interests had been reduced to watching her bird table and scanning her right-wing newspapers. No longer did she wander around her once-well-tended garden, and nor did she watch TV, listen to the radio or call anyone. She steered clear of anything that might touch her emotions.

How did this highly educated, well-read, funny lady become so brittle? And how could her outlook differ so from Mum's, her sister who was ten years her senior? She never forgot her early years of loneliness. She never forgot being sent away to boarding school, and she never forgot the years she spent hanging around at Thurlestone Golf Club, waiting for her parents to finish their round. And the sad truth is that adult life never allowed this clever, beautiful spirit to fly.

After leaving school, Clare joined the Foreign Office, where she met handsome, laconic, resourceful and kind – but also weak-willed and indulged – Gerard. They were just twenty-one when they married. Gerard had contracted tuberculosis during the war and, to everyone's horror, Clare contracted the disease on their honeymoon.

His family, wealthy distant cousins of the Hoare banking dynasty, gave them the Mill House as a wedding present. An exquisite Georgian village house, it looked over a millpond, with views across the water and over the meadows beyond that which resembled a painting by John Constable. The house had been immaculately furnished with block-print wallpapers and silk curtains, but once Clare and Gerard had moved in, they could barely afford food let alone for refurbishment, and their once-dazzling interior gradually faded before their eyes. The kitchen utensils became buckled with use, the curtains threadbare and shredded, the carpets worn and the walls crusted with the continuous onslaught that the two committed smokers inflicted on the house.

Their lives together had started well enough. Gerard and Clare were celebrated on the Norfolk social circuit, but after years of partying, drink played an increasingly central role. Gerard found it difficult to hold down a decent job, and their pain was exacerbated by the realisation that, after contracting TB, it was unlikely that Clare would ever be able to get pregnant.

The final shred of respect that Clare had for Gerard vanished when an adoption agency declared them unsuitable as parents, on the grounds of Gerard's excessive drinking. Clare realised that she could no longer rely on Gerard and started Black Sheep Knitwear. She'd been building a flock of Black Welsh Mountain sheep for years and now began employing ladies from the village of Ingworth to knit their beautiful brown wool into jumpers.

The family entrepreneurial spirit kicked in and Black Sheep grew into a successful business. Her biggest export market was the Japanese, who couldn't buy enough of her cable-knit chunky sweaters. She talked to me about the thrill of flying to Japan to meet suppliers and retail outlets. However, on her second or third trip to Tokyo, Gerard, back at home, drank with such suicidal fervour that he was taken by ambulance to the Norfolk and Norwich Hospital. Clare took to locking the drinks cupboard whenever she left the house, but no lock could prevent Gerard from drinking himself into oblivion if Clare left him alone overnight.

It's no wonder that Clare's bitterness grew into a hardened ball that, while well disguised during our family visits, was perfectly apparent to local friends and acquaintances. Their relationship spiralled downwards, and sweet Gerard lost his confidence to such an extent that he soon refused to travel further from the house than to the off-licence in their local market town of Aylsham, just three miles away. Clare's barely suppressed anger was a constant reminder of his weakness, and she expressed it in increasingly eccentric behaviour that would have been humorous to witness if it wasn't so tragic.

'We couldn't get divorced in our time,' Clare muttered on my arrival following Gerard's death. 'It just wasn't the done thing.'

'You had some happy times though, didn't you?' I asked hopefully. 'Some times of laughter in the early days?'

'I suppose so,' she admitted reluctantly, 'but he was never really my friend – not like Douglas.'

Time plays such tricks with our memories of past loves. Douglas Bader had been brash and rude, and he'd been a notorious bully to his juniors. I doubt Clare would have been any happier if she had ended up marrying him, but she could dream.

'Well, I remember some very happy times with you two,' I said firmly. 'Do you remember his collection of wind-up toys? The pleasure he took at setting them off!' Clare rolled her eyes.

'What shall we do for his funeral, Clare? It's probably time we started giving it some thought.'

She looked me straight in the eye. 'Oh, we're not having a funeral,' she said.

I waited until Gerard's youngest sister Rosie arrived before broaching the subject again. Rosie was eighteen years younger than Gerard and had adored her big brother. She was also fond of, and very patient with, her sister-in-law.

'It would be lovely to do a little something for Gerard, Clare,' Rosie said gently. 'Nothing fancy – just a little ritual as the family gather to say goodbye.'

But Clare sat bolt upright, not budging on her refusal to hold a send-off for Gerard. We tried humour, we exerted moral pressure and we let her sleep on it, but she refused to budge. The following morning, Rosie and I put some concrete proposals to Clare.

'We could ask someone to write and say some words about Gerard,' we suggested optimistically.

'No, I don't think that's a good idea.'

'Maybe a simple poem then?' She shook her head.

'How about just a little music?'

At this, Clare threw her hands in the air, covered her ears and shouted. 'How many times do I have to tell you? I *don't like music!*'

Years of suppressing her emotions were at risk of being released, but she had managed to keep the lid firmly screwed down and had no intention of exposing a hint of vulnerability. In the end, the family reached a compromise of sorts, reading one poem and singing one hymn. Clare was driven to the crematorium by Robert Hoare and sat upright throughout the service. She refused to stay for a drink in the pub afterwards.

When I last visited Clare a few months ago, I asked her what the happiest time of her life had been. She leant towards her packet of cigars, slotted one between her painfully contorted fingers, lit it and took a deep draw of the acrid smoke. As she slowly exhaled, she said, 'Now, I think – I don't think I've ever been happier.'

Mum rings me every hour, asking why her sister, nine years her junior, has died. She's not sad exactly, but rather incredulous that a death could have happened. There's always been a shortage of sentimentality in our family, and grief and disappointment are put into the same basket. I'm taken back to an eventful family holiday in Menorca, in August 1997 when the call came through that Granny Dock had died while we were partying on the terrace. Mum relayed the news to us all. Granny had reached ninety-nine, and the quality of her active life had been much reduced, due to a stroke that had overwhelmed her as she was about to board a cruise ship in Cairo two years previously. Her death was a blessing, but the news still momentarily took my breath away. My father caught my expression and rushed to my side, not with a consoling arm but with a stern admonishment.

'Don't even think about crying, Vanessa,' he said. 'Your grandmother lived well. To cry is just thinking about yourself.'

'Please, Daddy, just give me ten minutes to let the news sink in, then I'll be fine,' I replied.

Half an hour later, my son Noah, then aged ten, rowed us back across the harbour to Vanessa's Folly, our old houseboat where we were staying. When we were safely away from the house, he dropped the oars and we wept in each other's arms.

How best to send Clare off? Who would come to wish her well on her onward travels? I knew what she wanted: no fuss, no religion, no music and no poetry. But we couldn't resist.

I officiated at her funeral, which was attended by a surprising number of well-wishers. Gerard's sister Clemency read a fitting poem celebrating man's love of dogs. We sang 'Jerusalem', of course, and I gave the address, praising the eccentricity and stoicism of that remarkable generation. Mum had come up to Norfolk by train flanked by three of my children, Louis, Florence and Ivo. As always, she was the star, dressed in a cashmere suit topped with a fur stole, her hair coiffed, nails polished and skin glowing. I looked down at her from while I was reading the address, suddenly all too aware of the different lives that she and Clare had led. After pushing the button to send her sister towards the furnace, I caught Mum's eye and we gave each other a simultaneous wink.

7

TWO SLIGHTLY DISTORTED GUITARS

My enthusiasm for university withered on the vine. Neither Mum, Dad, nor any teacher had even hinted that it might be a possibility. My parents had been serious when trying to convince Richard of the importance of a good education and of gaining some sort of professional qualification, but they had become more relaxed when the time came to encourage their daughters to continue their studies. Dad's fear of academia and Mum's conviction that life was for living meant that higher education just wasn't on our agenda.

Once Nabeel had left Box Hill, I decided that my boarding school days were over too. I spent a glorious year at St Mary's Tutorial College in Guildford, better known as 'Hobbs Crammer'. It was a tumbledown establishment run by a headmistress whose interest was clearly directed at encouraging a steady stream of students through her doors rather than concerning herself with the quality of their education. There were plenty of students there who, like me, had outgrown conventional school life. We were a motley lot and would bond over a ciggie on the pavement before entering the draughty Victorian building each morning. I turned up for classes covering my chosen subjects, and felt grown-up and free. My time at the college was unremarkable except for the fact that that I met two lifelong friends there, Sarah Batwell and Hamish Dewar, and that I was taught biology by Hugh Cornwell, who played in the local pubs at night with his band, The Stranglers.

Sarah would zip around the Surrey countryside and pick me up from Shamley Green in her white Triumph Herald convertible. She would later teach me how to drive, and with only one proper lesson, I passed my test two weeks after my seventeenth birthday. Then, thanks to Mum loaning me her Mini, I too had the freedom of the open road.

Hamish and I met for lunch every Friday and would sit in the gardens of the Jolly Farmer pub beside the River Wey. Hamish was quietly spoken, a youngest son with two older sisters. I was immediately struck by his kindness and gentle curiosity, an unusual quality after the boisterous atmosphere of Tanyards, where everyone talked over each other while hammering their points home. Hamish had been expelled from Sherborne School, having been caught flogging weed to his fellow sixth formers. He was quietly ambitious and stretched Hobbs's academic capabilities by being the first ever student to attempt an Oxbridge exam there.

Hamish's mother had recently received a breast cancer diagnosis, and he had been coming to terms with this when his father suffered a devastating stroke, rendering him virtually speechless – all he could say was 'yes', 'no', 'damn', 'bloody' and 'blast'. Over enormous plates of jacket potatoes and baked beans, Hamish and I would try to make sense of what his family were going through.

Aside from the challenge of his home life, Hamish had another conundrum: once he had passed his Oxbridge exams, he would need a reference from the Sherborne headmaster. Knowing this wouldn't be forthcoming, he asked his old drama master if he would write him a reference on Sherborne headed paper, hoping the university wouldn't notice the difference. This kindly teacher agreed, on the condition that Hamish never took any drugs again.

The freedom I experienced at this time is hard to describe. My home life was filled with student lodgers during the week and Richard and Lindy, plus their partners and friends, at the weekends – our kitchen table seemed able to expand to accommodate any number of people.

I would observe my sister closely with the blind love of a younger sibling. With her full Branson smile, perfect teeth, wide eyes, high cheekbones, glossy auburn hair and flawless skin, she was undeniably beautiful, but I learned that being so attractive can be a mixed blessing. The combination of having gone to girls' schools and the effect she had on men meant that it was difficult for her to have platonic friendships with them. The power she exerted over men was exhilarating, but could also be a handicap.

Lindy was living in a one-bedroomed first-floor flat on Ifield Road, on the Chelsea–Fulham border, which Mum and Dad had recently purchased as a London bolthole. Although she was a talented artist, her friends tended to be focused less on culture and more on business. She also had a penchant for racing drivers and spent a good deal of her weekends at Brands Hatch, but her heart eventually settled on Robert Abel Smith, a smooth-talking old Etonian who ran a furniture removals company. We all adored Bertie: his relaxed charm and easy nature more than compensated for his presumption that dirty dishes miraculously washed themselves and flew back onto the dresser.

Even at the time, I was aware of the advantages of being the youngest member of the family. Richard and Lindy were so much older than me that they were almost like a second set of parents, but unlike the more cautious role that parents feel they have to take, they broadened my vision. My wonderful siblings took risks on my behalf and pushed boundaries, and I worshipped them both. They were exemplary role models, even if, having witnessed the paths they took, I chose to walk down different roads.

Lindy and Bertie were soon engaged to be married. Feeling somewhat uneasy after attending their wedding rehearsal on the eve of their big day, I went to see her that night.

'Lindy, do you mind if I say something?'

'No, of course not,' she hummed, carried away on a cloud of joy as tomorrow's nuptials drew near.

'It's just, well, I'm not sure...' I tentatively started.

'Not sure about what?' she asked.

'Do you really want to say "love and obey" in your vows?'

'Oh yes,' she swooned. 'I think men should be the ones to wear the trousers in a relationship.'

I thought about the generations who had worn our family wedding dress, including our strong-minded granny and great granny. I also thought about our mighty mother and about how I wanted my future relationships to play out – and decided to say no more.

Until this point, the world at large rarely encroached on my adolescent life. The Three-Day Week and the power cuts of the early 1970s had provided cosy candlelit nights by the fire. In our house, the only suggestion that we might be personally affected by the threat of conflict was that the shelves in Mum and Dad's wardrobe would sag a little lower under more tins of baked beans and sacks of muesli. The news affected other people's lives, but not mine. But then, one Saturday night in October 1974, everything changed.

Ten or twenty of us were having a party at our friend Pete's house. It was the usual stuff of Saturday nights – the odd swig of illicit vodka with JJ Cale on the stereo, furtive smoking and enthusiastic snogging. I think Pete and I were under a blanket when his parents walked in and turned the lights on and the music off.

We scrambled upright.

'Something really quite terrible has happened,' his mother told us quietly.

We stood blinking in the light, more concerned about being busted than whatever they were about to tell us.

'No one should be alarmed, but we want you to line up behind the telephone in the hall and ring home to let your parents know that you're alright. The Horse and Groom pub in Guildford has been bombed, and many people have been killed and injured. The Seven Stars was bombed too, but the people inside had been tipped off and no one was hurt.'

'Bramley, three one double three,' came my father's slow, clear voice as he picked up the phone.

'Hi Dad, it's Ness – we've just been told about the bombs in Guildford.'

'Oh Lordy,' he replied. 'Not very nice, but I wouldn't let them worry you.'

The IRA bombings became a fact of life from then on, but it became a point of honour not to adjust our behaviour in any manner; I have the same attitude to terrorism to this day. Sadly, the Guildford pub bombings resulted in the passing of the Prevention of Terrorism Act, which was used by the Metropolitan Police to force false confessions from a group of innocent men. The Guildford Four, as they became known, were convicted and jailed for over fifteen years before their convictions were quashed.

After leaving Hobbs, I spent a happy but fruitless year doing a bilingual secretarial course at Guildford Technical College. I couldn't spell in English, let alone in Spanish, so the idea of getting a job as a secretary was ridiculous, but I did learn a few important lessons. There were thirty girls in Miss McKenzie's class, and we would sit in rows behind enormous electric typewriters, transcribing our shorthand dictation. We were taught how to use carbon paper in triplicate, and I was forever

Tippexing out mistakes and accidentally sticking all three sheets of paper together in the process.

During one breaktime, I was telling one of my friends that I had no intention of becoming a secretary, but rather saw the course as a stepping-stone to doing something more interesting, when I suddenly received a hard wallop to the back of my head. I turned around and was shocked to see the heavy typing manual in the hands of an angry-looking student.

'How dare you presume that the rest of us are in the lucky position of having the option of doing something other than becoming secretaries?' she hissed, before running from the room in tears. That encounter taught me a very humbling lesson.

During the holiday, on Christmas morning, I bent down under the kitchen sink to get the washing-up liquid and felt unexpectedly nauseous. While my family was joking around at the breakfast table, I managed to quietly throw up in the compost bucket. Did this mean what I feared it meant? 'Don't panic,' I thought to myself, 'you can deal with this'. Later that day, while singing 'Away in a Manger' in church, the full implication of the situation I was faced with began to sink in.

The house was full and the phone in the hall made privacy impossible – talking to Mags would have to wait. After the interminable festive period was over, she and I pored over a Predictor pregnancy test and watched as a blue line appeared. We called our friend Zoe, whom we knew had had a termination, but she couldn't talk – again, the phone-in-the-hall problem. As soon as we returned to college, Zoe slipped me a piece of paper, on which she had written, 'Wistons Clinic, Brighton.'

Over the coming days, I began to feel increasingly panicked. There was a distinct possibility that I was going to become overwhelmed by what I was facing. The main emotion I felt was humiliation: after all my posturing to my family about how grown-up and capable I was, to allow myself to get pregnant was idiotic. I wanted as few people as possible to know, and I didn't want any fuss. I didn't need counselling and I certainly didn't want sympathy; I just wanted to get on with my life, and I knew what I had to do. I called Directory Enquiries from the college payphone, and then the clinic – I made an appointment and was told I would need to bring £68 in cash and an overnight bag.

I'd had a brief liaison with a racing driver acquaintance of Lindy's. When I rang him to ask if he would pay for half the termination, he freaked out and told me he couldn't raise the necessary £35. His conscience eventually got the better of him, but I realised that I was on my own with this one. I had no idea how on earth I was going to find the money, but then I remembered my childhood post office savings book, with its hundreds of tiny deposits.

Rather than going to stay with Mags for a weekend of revision – the excuse I'd given Mum and Dad – I went to the post office, slipped the book over the counter and withdrew my entire childhood savings.

'I hope you're going to treat yourself to something special with this, dear' the postmistress said as she slipped the notes under the grill. And then, with all the effort I could muster and desperate to avoid a panic attack, I took the train to Brighton. It was then that I had to access the toughness that I'd learned when I'd called the knacker's yard. Have courage and push on – there is no option.

Walking into the clinic was terrifying, and I felt agonised as I approached the reception and said, 'I'm here for a termination.' However, I was met with efficient kindness at every stage. No one judged me for my stupidity, no one showed sympathy and no one suggested I was doing the wrong thing. My ears rang with white noise and I could feel my heart racing, I was soaking in sweat and my temples throbbed. British law dictates that you have to talk to two doctors before a termination, who then sign a consent form, and each interview was blessedly perfunctory; the doctors understood that as a sixteen-year-old, I was incapable of being a good parent, and to carry an unwanted pregnancy to full term would be both mentally and physically devastating. I then dressed in a hospital robe; there were forty of us, all silent and stressed as we lay on hospital beds in a massive ward. We were then given a pre-med before being wheeled down to the theatre, one at a time, for a general anaesthetic and the ten-minute procedure.

The relief I felt when I came to was immense. The surgeon did a ward round before signing each of us out. The gratitude we all felt towards him was quiet and genuine. We shared our stories over a cup of tea and a biscuit before leaving: at least a third of the women had travelled to Brighton from Ireland. The extra expense they'd incurred, in addition to the guilt and secrecy that they'd experienced, made my story pale into insignificance. The majority of the rest of our group were perimenopausal women who had presumed they were past child-bearing age.

I vowed at that point that I would take no shame from the experience. Not one of us had taken the decision lightly – no one would have chosen to go through such a wretched operation, however respectful and professional the staff had been, had they had another option. Hundreds of thousands of women all over the world risk their lives by undergoing illegal backstreet abortions, and witnessing some people attempting to turn back the tide of progress and make terminations illegal once again fills me with both horror and sadness. The truth is that abortion is an unpleasant reality, but criminalising it will not make unwanted pregnancies go away.

While writing this book I've been reading excerpts to Mum, hoping to fill the expanding voids in her brain with vivid memories. She loves hearing stories of her youth, and giggles away when I read her the stories of how she met Dad, and of life at Tanyards. This morning, when I came to read the Brighton episode, I hesitated and considered skimming over it, but didn't. I like the idea of having no secrets between us now.

'Oh my darling Nessie,' she said as I finished reading. 'You poor darling – it must have been terrible for you.'

We stood up and she shuffled towards me, wrapping her tiny arms around my waist. She buried her head in my breast, and as we hugged I found myself silently weeping.

* * *

After leaving Guildford Tech, Sarah and I enrolled at Tante Marie Culinary Academy, a Cordon Bleu cooking school in Woking.

We learned a great deal there, including how to make an array of different pastries, what herbs went with fish and what went with meat, and how to blend sauces, whisk mayonnaise and fold meringues. We dressed crabs, jugged hares, stuffed chickens, potted shrimps, cured salmon, devilled kidneys and learned how to bake the perfect Victoria sponge. I was now the proud holder of a Cordon Bleu Certificate – the key to financial independence.

We soon arranged to cook for the Whitbread family and their friends in their hunting lodge near the banks of Loch Ness. They were a generous and warm group of people and it provided a wonderful introduction to the world of work for two young, inexperienced chefs. Not all the cooking jobs I had subsequently were quite so happy, but living in a number of different houses was quite an eye opener, for kitchens are the beating hearts of every household. No one can keep a secret from a kitchen. I witnessed disintegrating marriages in Yorkshire, ambitious politicking in Kent and abusive employers in Dorset. It was fascinating stuff for a teenager, but not a job I could see myself doing for long.

Like many children, I had always loved building dens and would transform any space into a snug with the odd plank of wood or length of fabric, whether I was hanging a sheet over a table as a toddler or decorating the caravan and the cellar as a teenager. Could I possibly turn this interest into a career? To investigate the possibility, I enrolled on a three-month foundation course in interior design at the Inchbald School of Design in Chelsea, and went to live with Richard and Kristen in their house on Denbigh Terrace, just off the Portobello Road.

Where a sixteen-year-old fits into the home of her twenty-five-year-old brother and his new wife is an interesting question, and one I didn't think about at the time. Kristen had designed the narrow four-storey house with classic American elegance and I lived on the top floor, with my own en suite bathroom, though the luxury never quite compensated for the lack of belonging I felt. I can remember their cleaner Mary harrumphing at my presence, and her precocious four-year-old daughter would come and sit at the end of my bath, staring at me while I lay in the water, feeling distinctly exposed.

'Mummy says it's a real pest having you living here,' she would say, looking for a reaction.

It was 1975, and the energy surrounding Richard and Virgin Records was incredible. I never knew who or what I would find on entering the house after a day at college – if only I'd kept a record or taken a snap of everyone who passed through the house. Richard was often away, signing up bands in the States or spending time in The Manor, and I barely saw Kristen. To earn some pocket money, I'd occasionally cook lunch or breakfast for Richard and Simon Draper, but I soon realised that living in London required serious money.

I began waitressing in the evenings at Monsieur Thompson, a small bistro on the corner of Kensington Park Road and Blenheim Crescent, fifty metres from the Portobello Road. That fifty metres would become the centre of my universe a few years later and still now, three decades later, joyous memories come to me whenever I walk those pavements. Everyone should wait tables at some point in their lives – you'll forever be an appreciative diner afterwards. Serving in restaurants is hell; you're either appeasing grumpy chefs or grumpy guests. I'd only eaten in a restaurant a couple of times and had little idea of what was expected of me. The *Evening Standard* got it just about right when they reviewed Monsieur Thompson. 'The waitress makes up in willingness what she lacks in efficiency,' wrote Fay Maschler. My first review.

One Saturday night around then, Richard and Kristen threw a fancy-dress party. I can't remember what I dressed up as – to be honest, I might as well have been a wallflower, I was so deeply out of my depth. I wandered through the thronging mass, afraid to be seen standing on my own and thinking that no one would notice me if I moved around. Dominique, who would one day play a key role in my life but was Richard's PA at the time, was there, the epitome of French chic in a tight striped T-shirt, with plaits, a miniskirt, and a string of onions round her neck, topped off with a beret cocked to one side. She was on the arm of Andrew Graham-Stewart, who managed the band Tangerine Dream. Also there was Ken Berry, Virgin's new finance director, and his girlfriend Binna, Rod Vickery, the company 'fixer' and, of course, Simon Draper. All the acts who were signed to Virgin at the time turned up too, along with all the bands who had recorded at The Manor. Roger Taylor from Queen was there, as well as Kevin Ayers from Soft Machine.

The party was mayhem, as parties could be in the days before mobile phone cameras: a seething mass of rock-and-roll eccentricity. Some people were shouting over the thumping music, while others were standing around and smoking. A cascade of people spilled out down the stone steps from the open front door. Inside, the narrow staircase of the tall townhouse was chocked with embracing couples – no room was out of bounds. The basement kitchen was crammed with partygoers helping themselves to a generous buffet.

As I pushed my way downstairs, I noticed Richard looking at Kevin Ayers across the kitchen table and could tell that something wasn't quite right. Richard flicked some rice at Kevin, who picked up a dollop of mashed potato and threw it at Richard. Before I knew what had happened, they were picking up handfuls of food and hurling them at each other, laughing but definitely aiming with intent. The kitchen went silent as they pounded each other with chicken, rounds of brie and soggy lettuce. There was laughter, but it felt strange and uncomfortable. Richard brushed past me on the stairs, wiping salad from his face.

'I'm off to New York tomorrow, Ness, so I'm going to stay in a hotel near Heathrow. Can you lock up after everyone's gone?'

As I was stood there, wondering how on earth I was going to deal with all these people, a bear walked up to me.

'Can I help you, Goldilocks?' he said, his kind voice muffled through the furry head of his costume.

'Yes please,' I replied. 'But who are you?'

The bear took off his head. It was Mike Oldfield. We sat and talked until the party had thinned out and then were able to sweep the stragglers out into the street. Mike and I were both social misfits: he was overwhelmed by his new-found success and I was too young and unworldly to be in this environment. He invited me to stay with him at his newly purchased manor house in Slad in Gloucestershire the following weekend.

On his return from New York, much to his misery and bewilderment, Richard learned that Kristen, his bride of less than three years, had left him and gone to live in Majorca with Kevin Ayers.

My relationship with Mike was a short-lived affair. He loved driving and would pick me up from Denbigh Terrace in his embarrassingly loud red Ferrari, which once ran low on petrol when we were on the M4. We roared into a petrol station and pumped the car full of fuel. Since Mike was newly wealthy, his accountants hadn't yet organised a way for him to carry cash, so I had to hand over my entire weekly pay from Monsieur Thompson, tips and all. We would spend weekends hanging out at his house and occasionally messing around in his recording studio.

Sally, his sister, keen to protect her brother from people whom she thought might take advantage, would sigh every time I walked into a room; as a result, I crept around the house, hoping not to bump into her. The one time I felt at ease was in the evenings, when we would walk to the friendly village pub and sit in the cavernous inglenook fireplace that was immortalised by Laurie Lee in *Cider with Rosie*.

Later, when we got back to his vast, under-furnished bedroom, our shy couplings were overseen by Mike's curious Irish wolfhound, who would sit at the end of our bed like a giant stone statue guarding the entrance to a tomb.

It was only when my children were almost adults themselves that I owned up to having once made a record. It was the B-side to the single of 'Tubular Bells'. I sang with Mike on a reggae version of 'Froggy Went a-Courtin'. I was Little Miss Mouse to Mike's Froggy. My goodness, I sound young.

8

FINDING BEAUTY

It was one of those spontaneous ideas you have while sitting in a pub on a freezing cold Friday night in the middle of winter. Hamish and I arranged to meet up in Florence, halfway into his month-long Italian 'grand tour', at midday on 1 April 1976, by the Fountain of Neptune in the Piazza della Signoria. A few weeks later, I'd saved enough money deep-frying chips and burgers at a tenpin-bowling alley for the airfare and booked myself an Alitalia flight to Pisa.

It took less than a minute to clear customs; my holdall contained nothing but a change of underwear, a toothbrush and a book – shamefully, given that I was about to discover the glories of the Italian Renaissance, *The Pirate* by Harold Robbins. I was wearing an ankle-length Indian cotton dress I'd bought from Kensington Market, black and red with an elaborately embroidered top panel inlaid with a twinkling mass of tiny mirrors, and a pair of vintage cowboy boots.

Once I'd left the airport, I flagged down a cheerful baker who was sputtering along in a three-wheeler van. On the way to Florence he offered me mounds of warm pastries and fired questions at me in rapid Italian. He dropped me off in the city centre, laughing and wishing me luck with my liaison. As I approached the magnificent stone fountain, I began to lose the confidence I'd possessed earlier in the day. After all, Hamish and I hadn't confirmed our meeting – I'd simply taken him at his word. Had he been sober enough to remember? And if he had, would he have thought I was serious about joining him? And would his travel plans have worked out so that he was even in Florence at this time? Of course he wouldn't be there – what an April fool I'd been! I sat for a while by the fountain, fantasising about picking up a dashing Italian one minute or of walking destitute around the city streets as if I was starring in a Fellini film.

Then I spotted my beautiful blond friend, tanned and leaner after a fortnight of lugging his art-book-filled backpack halfway around Italy. He stood smiling while brushing his unkempt fringe from his eyes. Of course he was going to turn up. After a minute of hellos he pulled out a map, laid it on the edge of the fountain and we planned our trip: five towns, including Perugia and Assisi, each with a multitude of churches and galleries housing the masterpieces on Hamish's 'must-see list'.

Hamish was studying fourteenth-century Italian Art and, unlike most of his peer group, he knew what he was going to do once he'd finished: he'd agreed to be apprenticed to a painting restorer called Dick Maelzer, who worked for the respected Old Master dealer, Edward Speelman. An in-depth knowledge of the history of art is essential for any restorer, and Hamish was focused on becoming the best in his field.

Once again, love was my great educator: Hamish's passion for both the history and the magic of creativity was contagious. Early on in our relationship we realised that keeping our love platonic was the best way forward, and we've remained firm friends to this day. On that trip he taught me that the fundamental lesson of art history is that artists are informed by the ideas of previous artists and movements. I also learned how much easier history itself is to remember when you can reference works of art: history comes alive in the clothes, traditions and battles laid out through oil on canvas. During that two-week expedition, I grasped the extent of the hold that religion had on Europe during the last thousand years and understood how the great dynasties exhibited their power in their patronage of the arts.

Hamish and I had virtually no money, and each evening we'd traipse around the less salubrious parts of the town we were visiting, knocking on the doors of guest houses and haggling with landladies until they reluctantly offered us rock-bottom prices. We'd then find the cheapest restaurant we could and sheepishly order plain spaghetti before smothering it with olive oil and the entire pot of grated Parmesan cheese left on the table. Hamish brought a book to the restaurant each night and would test me on what we'd seen during the day.

'What's this?' he'd ask, showing me an illustration of some masterpiece while covering the description. Once I managed to see the caption before he obscured it.

'Ah, I know this one,' I said, as he held his hand over the name of a delicately rendered crucifixion.

'You'll never get it,' he said.

'Ok, let me think,' I said, looking to the restaurant ceiling as if summoning the information from the recesses of my mind.

'It's an oil by Panell!' I whooped.

'Don't be ridiculous, Vanessa,' smiled Hamish. 'It's oil on panel, by Bronzino. You're busted.'

Hamish caught me out a second time. We'd spent several hours wandering around the Uffizi Gallery, marvelling at Rembrandt's tragic self-portrait and staring in awe at paintings by Piero della Francesca and Leonardo, when Hamish became transfixed by *The Annunciation* by Simone Martini. This gave me the opportunity to sneak off and find a corner in which I could furtively read the final chapter of *The Pirate*.

'Caught you!' laughed Hamish. He hasn't let me forget my act of philistinism to this day.

While flying home from Italy, I realised that I too wanted to study the history of art. I went for an interview with Lucy Knox and Roger Bevan, who were starting a school called The New Academy of Art Studies. Still glowing from my Italian trip, I surprised myself and my potential tutors when I explained that I wanted to become more knowledgeable about the arts so I could communicate their transformative qualities to the masses.

That academic year was tremendous; Roger and Lucy, who were barely out of university themselves, invited the lecturers they knew would fire our enthusiasm. The course romped through the history of fine, decorative, architectural and sculptural art, from cave paintings to conceptual works. We had four lectures a day from Monday to Thursday, with Fridays reserved for museum and exhibition visits.

Our lectures were held at the London Sketch Club on Dilke Street in Chelsea. It was here, towards the end of the year, that Antony Gormley delivered a lecture about Stanley Spencer. The sheer physicality of his description of *The Resurrection, Cookham* was utterly captivating. The sensual manner in which his expressive body rose upwards, his large hands re-enacting the sleepy villagers climbing from their graves, was seared into my impressionable mind – from that moment onwards, I knew that I wanted to work in the arts, and more specifically to work with contemporary artists who would make me look at the world through their eyes and challenge my preconceptions.

Antony took me to see his Higher Diploma show at the Slade School of Fine Art. One of his works, *Breadline*, consisted of a ten-metre line of bite-sized mouthfuls of Mother's Pride bread, their bitten edges facing forward.

'I'm hoping to open out our relationship to the material world by making an object into a journey,' Antony said as he paced up and down, his hands cupped in concentration. 'A line along which the viewer can walk.' I nodded, hoping to convey that I understood what he was saying. 'Buddhist meditation encourages an awareness of time as a sequence where one mind moment follows another, and this work makes a frame-by-frame movie out of bread, acknowledging mortality and our nature as consumers.'

A penny dropped somewhere in the recesses of my mind but I remained silent as he walked me around some of his fellow postgraduates' installations, explaining the ideas behind their work with a clarity that I could just about grasp. I didn't understand all the work by any means, but something about it drew me in. These students were some of the smartest of their generation, and it was clear that the conceptual language they were developing was going to be worth learning.

A few weeks earlier, on a crisp April weekend, I'd been to visit Hamish at his Downing College in Cambridge. We spent time in the book-filled rooms of Hamish's fellow students, listening to records and discussing events of the week over cups of tea. We also went to the Cambridge Union to see a debate about Northern Ireland. I had never witnessed young people displaying such erudition and confidence as those standing up to challenge the politicians. Later, after we'd been to the ADC Theatre to see a comedy revue, Hamish pointed out the silhouette of a man hunched in a wheelchair, beetling across the Downing quad.

'That's Stephen Hawking,' he told me. 'I take him to the loo sometimes when we're working near each other in the University Library. He's amazing.'

That one weekend opened my eyes to a life of limitless possibility. Being surrounded by these clever, engaged, funny, curious people while wandering around Cambridge's majestic streets filled me with an indescribable optimism and a real sense of possibility.

On the Monday morning, Hamish asked his friend in the next-door room to entertain me while he went to a lecture. Robert was six foot two and stick-thin, with unruly blond hair well below his shoulders. I immediately noticed his elegant fingers and neat fingernails, as well as his dreadful teeth – a saving grace, in my opinion, because I've always had a mistrust of men who cruise through left on the strength of their good looks. I'm sure Robert's heart must have sunk when he was asked to babysit Hamish's weekend squeeze; but he good-naturedly offered to take me for a walk to see the famous Cambridge Backs.

By now I was smitten with Cambridge and high on the energy pulsating from the students chatting on street corners, languishing on lawns or gathering in coffee shops. From Downing's courtyard, we wandered through Pembroke College, down Trumpington Street, over the river, past Queens' College and the Mathematical Bridge. Over the gently flowing water loomed King's and then Trinity College. It was easy to imagine my undergraduate father, late for swimming practice, furiously pedalling along these paths, his loyal Great Dane Appin gambolling along beside him.

As we strolled along the riverbank, Robert told me that this was where he and his parents had come for a picnic to introduce him to the idea of going to the university. I became aware of a busker with a guitar slung around his neck, strumming ballads while walking behind us. We walked in silence and, as we neared the Bridge of Sighs, the realisation slowly dawned that we were being serenaded. We caught each other's eye, laughed in embarrassment and carried on walking. The troubadour played on. Cupid had fired a direct hit.

I visited Cambridge every other weekend for the next two years, living the university life vicariously through Robert and my newfound friends, before melting away during the final few months of the academic year, as the hurdle of finals approached.

Robert finished with a good degree, but one not quite good enough to pursue the academic career he'd had in his sights.

The following few years were lived at a furious pace, as I made new friendships and consolidated old ones. I shared a tiny, one-bedroomed flat in Fulham with Ian Harrison, whom I'd met at Cambridge, with me on the sofa-bed and him in the bedroom. I subsequently moved into a grander flat in Kensington, paying rock-bottom rent to my landlady, in return for lying to her father. Whenever he telephoned to speak to her, I was to say that she'd popped out for a bottle of milk and would call him back on her return. On no account was the poor man to know that his trust-fund daughter was actually living in Knightsbridge with her boyfriend.

On graduating from Cambridge, Robert shared an unmodernised cavern of a flat in Sloane Street with a fluctuating number of friends. There was his old Marlborough schoolfriend Tim Evans, whose uncle owned the flat, who was studying medicine and had a revolving cast of blond beauties back to his room. Hamish lived there too, along with his dress designer girlfriend Anna, who specialised in making wedding gowns. A frequent visitor was another old school friend, Bodley Ryle. Bod was working in Hatchards, the bookshop on Piccadilly, and was also no slouch in picking up girls.

So many life-long friendships were made during those years. That gloomy basement might not have offered the best sleeping accommodation but boy, you could have a good party there. Everyone was broke, but money never seemed to be an issue. We were blind to our privilege and took the safety nets that our caring parents provided for granted. Every one of us had welcoming families offering the free use of washing machines, hot baths and Sunday lunches, as well as stocks of baked beans to take away for the following week. Apart from these home comforts, we were blissfully unaware of the advice that our parents were subtly offering, in the hope that they would nudge us to make the right life decisions. Most importantly, we were oblivious to the freedom that our childhood beds gave us, waiting to offer silent solace following job or relationship failure as we licked our wounds before heading back into the fray.

The year after graduating, the fledgling year, is a tricky one for many. It's a time when you're desperate to show that you can fly after gaining your degree but more often than not you crash-land a number of times before soaring into the future.

History had been Robert's passion, but working in publishing was his dream. While he was looking for a job, he spent a dispiriting six months on the dole and volunteering for Amnesty International. My parents were uncomfortable with my boyfriend's left-leaning politics and were taken aback by his brash over-confidence, though I understood that much of this bravado was maintaining his flagging sense of self-worth while he tried to find a job.

The Devereux family lived in the north of England, a few miles north of Morpeth in Northumberland and just fifty yards off the A1. His mother Barbara was a much-loved English teacher in the local comprehensive school, while his father Humphrey had a painting and decorating shop on an estate just outside Newcastle. Humphrey was what you might politely call an eccentric, and took pride in taking contrary views and winning arguments with hapless opponents such as council officials or waiters. I'd never witnessed a relationship like theirs: Barbara was skilled at ensuring that Humphrey's temper didn't get the better of him and would stand behind him, stroking his back while winking at us over his head. She was clever, sympathetic, quick to laugh and we became instant friends. She would talk to me about her complicated marriage; she seemed to carry the responsibility of the family finances and its emotional stability on her tired shoulders, a heavy burden that she clearly found exhausting.

On my first visit to Robert's family, Humphrey picked us up from Newcastle Station in his van. The seats were covered with wallpaper samples and paint charts, which he swept onto the floor before inviting us to sit. When he ran through the first red light, I couldn't help but let out a little yelp from the back seat;

but after the second and third, I realised that this was simply Humphrey's driving style. The family home was a five-bedroomed mock-Georgian house, set in an acre of garden. It was cosy, but certainly not opulent. I was given Robert's old dayglow-daubed bedroom.

Humphrey, Robert and I gathered in the sitting room for tea and Barbara entered with a tray of hot buttered crumpets, whispering that Clare, Robert's sixteen-year-old sister, would pop in to introduce herself, before going out to meet her friends in town.

'Clare's desperately self-conscious,' Barbara continued, 'so please don't make any comments on how she looks.' We all agreed and Clare coyly entered the room. She gave Robert a hug and then turned to her Dad, who immediately said, 'Golly, aren't you looking smashing! Are you wearing make-up?'

Clare's composure melted as she fled from the room, mascara running down her cheeks. Humphrey simply shrugged his shoulders and looked theatrically nonplussed, and from that moment I realised that my relationship with Robert's father was never going to be straightforward. However, little did I know just how complicated it would prove to be.

* * *

At around that time, Mum had an accident that sent shockwaves through our lives. Dad was suffering from kidney stones, and while he was on leave from work and waiting for his operation, my parents offered to take Richard's steel-hulled houseboat, *Arthur*, down the Grand Union Canal from Reading to Little Venice, in the heart of London. On entering a lock, Dad asked Mum to tie the boat to a metal bollard on the towpath. He thought the boat was in neutral, but it was actually still in forward gear. Mum placed a coil of rope over the bollard. In an instant, the rope snapped tight around her right hand, squeezing off her index and little finger and badly mangling the rest of her hand. She was taken by ambulance to King Edward VII's Hospital, where she and Dad were admitted to adjoining rooms, him for his kidney operation and her to have her hand saved and patched up as best as possible.

The pain Mum suffered was indescribable, as was the guilt Dad felt at causing it. I would visit one of them and then the other, and realised that they were struggling to connect with each other. Mum was also confused about the role she was to play at home, her last child having been shuffled from the nest. She celebrated her freedom while harbouring feelings of grief for the past. She took up a few hobbies perversely challenging to someone with two missing fingers: calligraphy, tapestry and the piano.

By this time, Lindy and Bertie were living in Brook Green with their new baby, Ned, and Richard was enthralled by a new love, Joan Templeman, whose bewitching beauty and Glasgow common sense was destined to play a vital role in the Virgin story. We should trust in love's instinct to see in another what others don't see and to recognise that another person can complement our own strengths. With this fundamental premise, love can withstand many a storm – I witnessed it with my parents and again with Richard and Joan, as they became an anchor for our generation.

Mum became increasingly demanding. The accident occurring alongside her menopausal years made for an uncomfortable combination. She'd ask me to run errands that entailed driving through London rush-hour traffic unnecessarily, becoming agitated if I suggested alternative options, and there was also her ever-present irritation at my easy relationship with Dad. I can only think that my solipsism as a seventeen-year-old wrapped up in boyfriend problems, on top of the anguish she was experiencing herself, justified Mum's behaviour. When Richard invited my parents and Lindy and Bertie to join him and Joan on the holiday of a lifetime, flying first on Concorde to Singapore and then onwards to Bali, I was not invited, I suspect because of some failure of communication on Mum's part.

To compensate, Richard suggested that I go to New York to help Ken Berry, who was setting up Virgin America. Ken had recently bought a rambling house on Perry Street in Greenwich Village for Virgin's head office.

'The house needs a women's touch,' Richard told me, kindly giving me some responsibility but not realising that I felt more like a girl than a woman. There was no further discussion, and a week or two later I found myself sitting in a back seat of a Laker Airways plane, chain-smoking for the entire flight across the Atlantic. I was to stay there for a month.

When we're young, we're unaware of just how life-changing experiences can be, and travel can further reinforce their impact. I'd been to New York once before, visiting for a day during a Christmas holiday with Kristen's family in Southport, Connecticut, an hour to the north. I was in awe of everything about New York, from the height of the buildings and the background thrum of subway trains to the pavement vents that belched steam while checker taxi cabs, their horns honking, bounced over potholes in the roads. Southport was much more civilised, with piles of boxed gifts under the Christmas tree and frozen mist hanging over the silent ocean. Kristen's neighbours were the Richardson family who owned Vicks, the vapor rub brand, on one side, and the composer Leonard Bernstein and his wife Felicia on the other – carols sung around the piano were certainly memorable that Christmas.

Deep into setting up Virgin America, poor Ken was somewhat perplexed at suddenly having to accommodate his business partner's little sister into his schedule. Neither of us knew quite what was expected of us; instead of tackling the monumental job of giving the house the 'woman's touch', I filled my days by attending free lectures at the Museum of Modern Art, the Metropolitan Museum of Art and the Frick Collection. With barely a cent to my name and not comfortable asking to borrow a dollar or two from Ken, these lectures were my only daytime activity. The talks were wonderful, but I was becoming aware that spending so many days walking around on my own, barely eating, and going to gigs each night, was unsettling my equilibrium.

While queuing at the café at MOMA one day, I found myself chatting to a friendly man who then joined me while I sipped my coffee. He introduced himself as Hartley. I told him of my new-found passion for art and how I was spending my days in New York. He explained that his mother was an artist and wondered if I would like to meet her; before I knew it I was getting into a cab with this total stranger and heading for the heart of Harlem. That district was notorious in the seventies as a police no-go area, and the streets were alive with men standing around drinking, dealing drugs and arguing animatedly. Old ladies were sitting on stoops as plastic bags caught in the wind swirled above their heads. I remember realising that I'd broken the first rule of self-preservation in getting in a stranger's car, but my concern was trumped by the excitement of stepping into the unknown.

We walked up the litter-strewn staircase of a five-storey apartment block, and as we neared the fourth floor, the air became thick with the smell of linseed oil and turpentine. Hartley called to his mother as he opened the door and my jaw dropped; I had never seen such a space. There were paintings propped against the walls all the way down the corridor, and in every room. Yet more paintings, mainly portraits and many of them nudes, were nailed haphazardly to the walls.

An elderly woman walked towards us, holding out a welcoming hand and offering us tea.

'This is my mother, Alice Neel,' said Hartley. 'I hope you like what she does – I'm sure she'll be happy to show you around.'

I spent the entire afternoon with this confident woman, who was well into her seventies. Alice explained how she had come to painting and how her work had been affected by the death of her daughter and subsequent years of depression, including prolonged spells in lunatic asylums. She wanted to challenge the social norms of what was depicted in art, and at that time she was focusing on painting nudes of pregnant women, many of whom were local friends who she invited to sit for her. She explained that she found these paintings exciting because pregnancy is such an important part of the human experience.

'It is something that primitives have often done but modern painters have shied away from because women are always depicted as sexual objects,' she asserted. 'A pregnant woman has a claim staked out: she is not for sale.'

Being in this powerful woman's presence, surrounded by her paintings, grounded my thoughts. Her insights into allowing yourself periods of reflection were at odds with the messages I'd been given while growing up of thinking about others and exuding positive energy. It was perfectly OK to be walking the Manhattan streets, allowing ideas to ferment gradually.

In 2014, I was invited to a dinner to celebrate an Alice Neel retrospective at the Victoria Miro Gallery in London and was coincidentally seated next to Hartley. 'Do you remember meeting a girl in the coffee queue at MOMA a lifetime ago, and taking her up to meet your mother?' I asked him.

He looked at me somewhat perplexed, then smiled and smacked his forehead with his fingers. 'Yes, of course,' he laughed. 'What on earth was I thinking of!'

'It was a life-changing encounter,' I reassured him. 'I'm so glad that I have the chance to thank you for it now.'

My month in New York passed all too quickly, with weekend trips to San Francisco, Washington and Miami to listen to music; Ken was actively looking for artists to sign to the Virgin label. We walked to the Mudd Club to see The Police play an early version of 'Roxanne', and when Sting paused slightly longer than expected before rasping, 'Roxanne, you don't have to put on the red light', the hairs on the back of my neck stood on end. Ken was concerned that The Police were going to be one-hit wonders, and Virgin subsequently only signed Sting for his music publishing rights.

We would go to CBGB, at 315 Bowery at Bleecker Street, to see an astonishing array of raw talent including the Patti Smith Group, Blondie, Talking Heads and the B-52's. We'd inevitably have a drink with the bands after their set; these ambitious, hard-working kids were all relentlessly cool, but they couldn't hide their eagerness to get to know the people behind this new record company with the strange name, a company that was looking to sign new acts. I was attempting to look as cool as them and praying that I was passing myself off as a hip record company exec. I needn't have been so self-conscious because everyone was playing with their identities at the time, but I still felt like an imposter. My month in Greenwich Village had been unforgettable, but I was happy to get on the plane home.

Robert had called to tell me that after months of rejections, two publishing houses, Macmillan and Penguin, had offered him a job on the same day. I realised how much I was missing my clever, opinionated, supportive boyfriend – he was waiting for me, and so was working life. A new chapter was about to begin.

9

WORKING GIRL

London, May 2017

Every six months or so, museum groups visit my house to hear a talk about my voyages around the art world while we tour my collection as we drink glasses of wine. Tonight, it's the turn of the Contemporary Art Society. Some of the works are more saleable than others, but to me they're all equally precious, souvenirs that represent four decades of life immersed in creativity. It is questionable whether our lives are dictated by the planets, but one thing is certain: I was born under some lucky star to be working in the fertile world of 1980s London.

At that time, a confluence of forces came together to whip the calm waters of the British art scene into a wave that was to build over the next three decades, a convergence of innovative teaching and politically motivated, educated and ambitious working-class artists, fuelled by the patronage of voracious collectors. And I was there from the very first ripple.

* * *

I started an apprenticeship with Wells and Fitzgerald, a traditional picture-framing workshop in the eaves of a three-storey Edwardian industrial block on Kingley Street, between Carnaby and Regent Street. My education in art, far from finished, was polished by hours of discussion with dealers. We'd lay the paintings or drawings out on an expansive plan chest and discuss each work, deciding how to show it at its best by selecting the most appropriate frame mouldings and mounts. What was the work's provenance, and who was the artist referencing? We'd discuss the condition of the work, the medium and the labels pasted on the backs of the old frames. We worked with Old Master dealers like Colnaghi and the Fine Art Society, for the auction houses Sotheby's and Christie's, and for a few Cork Street galleries – Waddington Galleries, Bernard Jacobson and Edward Totah.

The process of sawing mitre joints for the frames, cutting the glass and slicing through boards to cut bevelled windows, before decorating the mounts with gold lines and watercolour washes, hinging the works behind the mounts and finally knocking the drawings into the frames and sealing them up, was immensely satisfying.

When Rocky, my fellow apprentice, told me that he had just taken out a twenty-one-year mortgage, I was incredulous. How could you agree to spend twenty-one years of your life paying a sizable chunk of your salary towards paying off a loan? I decided that, however much I enjoyed working at Wells and Fitzgerald, the life of a picture framer was not for me. I wanted to start my own business.

I had no capital and was still far too wet behind the ears to open my own a gallery, so I rented a tiny room in the Wendy

Wisbey Acting Agency for child actors in Chiswick, and set up Poster Brokers, buying, framing and selling vintage posters. I just about managed to cover the meagre rent. As old Wendy Wisbey and her equally ancient sister were barely able to teeter down the stairs from their first-floor office, I'd offer to open the front door for them. It was always a drama. Streams of eager mothers would thrust their children towards me, and I'd explain that I wasn't in fact Miss Wisbey and give them time to brush their clothes down, square their shoulders back and launch into their routine again once they'd entered the old ladies' office. What wasn't quite as entertaining was having to sit on the edge of the sisters' urine-sodden chairs as I helped them with some office glitch or other – it was time to move on.

It takes a particular set of characteristics to work on your own, and I don't possess any of them. The energy generated by working with the right people is contagious. I often think the same holds true for friendship, and so often the line between colleague and friend is blurred. Rewarding social encounters can feel like miraculous exchanges of energy, and looking back I realise that my life has been blessed with many of these miracles.

At home in Surrey, after the years of Christmas evenings with the T. W.s had become tinged with tension, we began to join the Hutley family for games and merriment in their Victorian pile. Anne Hutley, the mother, was eccentric, warm and generous. She would take my hands in hers as she questioned me about my relationship with spirituality. The family saw humour everywhere, and Charlotte, their oldest child, has always been an extraordinary friend. We bonded over a joint party we gave to celebrate the marriage of Prince Charles and Princess Diana in July 1981, a 'Wed, White and Blue' party. It was a beautiful day, an excuse to celebrate love and friendship and to snigger at that ridiculous dress!

My early twenties were golden years for making friends. David Teiger, a retired management consultant who was now an art collector, had heard of my interest in art and told me to contact him every time I was visiting New York. He became not only a great friend but also a mentor and guardian angel. I'd tell him when my plane was due to land at JFK and he'd send his driver to pick me up. He'd get tickets for a Broadway musical and would take me out for dinner, where he'd grill me about my business plans and attempt to give my ideas focus.

David had wonderful tales from the world of New York galleries. He told the story of his six-year-old son Douglas, who had once joined the dots, with indelible felt tip marker, on a painting by Andy Warhol called *Join the Dots*. When David called Andy to see if he would consider repainting the work, Warhol took great pleasure in replying, 'Dear me, David. It seems you no longer own an Andy Warhol painting – you now own a major work by Douglas Teiger.' Warhol never replaced the canvas.

Louise Hallett entered my world like a whirlwind. I've never known anyone with an energy like hers. While we worked on our first joint exhibition, I was in awe of her ability to survive on virtually no sleep and to manage the perfect balance of nicotine, caffeine and alcohol. With terrifying speed and a barely disguised impatience, Lou tried to teach me the skills necessary to run a gallery and how to hang and light an exhibition in order to show the works off to their best advantage. She also knew how to catalogue works and, above all, she knew how to clinch a sale.

Looking back over the decades, some of my working relationships have evolved into the most enriching friendships. I'd moved my framing workshop from Chiswick to Fulham and was joined there by Kate Flannery, who introduced some much-needed administrative rigour to my tiny organisation. Kate's love life was a running soap opera and our days were filled with raucous tales of her misadventures while we puffed our way through packets of Marlboro cigarettes and – strictly after 5 p.m., of course – quaffed cans of Pils lager.

With the help of a loan from his grandmother, Robert, along with two friends, bought a terrace of condemned cottages next to the railway viaduct in Walworth. The tiny houses shuddered with every passing train and were in serious need of modernisation, but with a price tag of just £4,000, no one was complaining and these dilapidated shells provided his first step onto London's golden housing ladder. I donned some workman's overalls and seized the chance to try out my design skills, grouting tiles, hanging wallpaper, helping with the rewiring and generally transforming the ruin into a comfortable home. Us Bransons have limitless energy when faced with a project we want to get our teeth into. Some might call it passion, others obsession, but we like to think of it as 'focused enthusiasm'.

The house was featured as a double-page spread in *Brides* magazine, which led to it being sold, sight unseen, to a major returning from the Falklands War: the work had paid off handsomely.

Robert had moved from Macmillan to Virgin to take over the publishing company there and was working insanely hard. He'd spend long hours at the office, but we played hard too. We'd often attempt to recharge our batteries at Tanyards, but weekends there would more often than not turn into a party, as the house filled up with unexpected guests.

Saturday night dinner parties would descend into wine-fuelled debates about the state of the world; Robert often provoked apoplectic responses from my usually balanced father, which would delight the rest of the table. One evening Mum argued that listening to people talking about how to sort out the issues of the day was boring, boring, boring. 'It's no good just talking about it – do something about it,' she said, giving us each a sheet of paper and a pen and instructing us, for reasons known only to herself, to write a letter to the Shamley Green parish magazine. I can't remember what the rest of us wrote, but Rob's letter simply said, 'Is there more to Shamley Green than bricks and mortar?'

When people in the village found out about his letter, there was uproar. How dare this upstart Londoner come down and insult them in this way? To make amends for offending village sensibilities, Mum set up the 'Bricks and Mortar Colts Cricket Club', a much-needed initiative that provided a feeder team of younger players for the ageing village team. Once again, Mum's genius for conjuring calming rabbits from the hats of discontent came to the fore. Our friends Donald Mason and Paul Chesney, who were renting Tanyard Cottage, were volunteered to be head coaches.

Fiona Whitney, her school career having come to an abrupt end, was now a secretary for Rank Xerox and living in north London with her boyfriend Eamonn. They came to stay one weekend, and Donald and Paul invited us all over for a Saturday night drink. Fiona and Eamonn stayed and partied into the night while Robert and I returned to the main house and went to bed. The next morning, we were woken by a phone call. It was Eamonn, calling from London.

'Tell Fiona that all her belongings are in plastic bags out on the street,' he said, before hanging up. An hour later Fiona came running into the house, wrapped in a small towel. 'Oh God, what on earth have I done?' she giggled, before bursting into tears. It transpired that she had ended up in bed with Donald during the party. On hearing that Eamonn had thrown her out of their flat she threw caution to the wind, and on Sunday night she slept with Paul. The following week she met one of the producers of the 'Star Wars' films in a London nightclub and by the weekend she had flown to Los Angeles with him, where she lives to this day.

Robert and I were a good team, and our life together was based on trust. Infidelity didn't cross either of our minds and we supported the other's dreams, not complaining if one of us had to work late or go abroad. He also had an interest in art, and listened patiently to me talking about my work. His brilliant critical mind complemented my practical skills, and his extraordinary focus was crucial in helping me see projects through.

Robert developed a deep and mutually respectful relationship with Richard, and having them working together kept me in touch with how Virgin was evolving. We made some lifelong friends during the early years of the business, and our friendships were consolidated by fiercely competitive weekends in the Alps in which we skied ourselves to jelly during the day and played bridge late into the night.

Photographs from the time show Robert and me tanned and with shaggy hair, an easy happiness shining from our eyes. Here we are in September 1980 travelling around Turkey, walking into the abandoned ancient city of Ephesus just ten days after the military coup, the only visitors. And here we are driving through France in my white Mini, camping on the way to join the rest of the family in Menorca. We were laying down memory upon memory of shared experiences, and it all felt too good to be true.

Rob and I travelled to Morocco in 1981 and stayed at La Mamounia hotel in Marrakech. We selected a guide from a group sitting on the wall outside the hotel; Mohamed introduced us to the magic of the city, with tales of meeting Churchill as a street urchin and of the ladies pulling at the testicles of the sheep carcases on sale in the souk, to check that they were properly attached and thus that the meat was from a ram and not a ewe. He told us tales of henna being applied on the night before weddings, from where the term 'hen night' arose, and how the visiting caravans of Tuaregs arrived on camels and stayed in fonduks, courtyard inns deep in the heart of the medina. He also told us of the Moroccan belief in djinns and omens, mystics and holy men, and about their tradition of taking care of those less fortunate than themselves. Little did I know, back in 1981, that Morocco, and Marrakech in particular, would be responsible for some of the greatest chapters in my life and that Mohamed would remain a friend until this day.

Marrakech, the labyrinthine Rose City, is hidden within thick medina walls. A thousand crumbling, mud-built houses, separated by narrow alleyways, where everything is for sale and everyone is trying to sell you something. The holy medieval city, where customs of old are upheld; where children look you straight in the eye and readily proffer you a cheek and a kiss when saying hello; where people smile if you accidentally bump into them and diesel-pumping mopeds hurtle by, brushing your clothes as they pass. In this mysterious city, where a front door, its paint flaking, conceals opulent interiors while next door a family sleeps ten to a room. Where elegant storks build nests on rooftops, looking down on cool tiled courtyards of such lush vegetation that it's hard to believe you're in the heart of the desert.

I was captivated, alive and in love. Robert and I drove over the mountains in a rattling hire car, stopping to eat an exquisite picnic the hotel had prepared on the roadside, and sharing it with a gang of dusty children. On to Ouarzazate and then to the Gazelle d'Or hotel in Taroudant, full of wealthy couples reviving their flagging marriages. With fireplaces in each room and pathways lit by candles, it was unfeasibly romantic. I had never felt so sexually charged, and revelled in spending time with my smooth-limbed, sensual boyfriend. How lucky we were not to be able to see into the future.

Concerned that I was throwing myself into a project in which I had nothing to gain, Dad asked whether Robert had offered me a percentage of the profit he'd made from the Walworth house sale. When I tentatively raised the issue, Robert replied that I should count myself lucky that he hadn't been asking me for rent. It began to dawn on me that I was at risk of being a complete sap – happily taking the role of home-maker and carrying much of the domestic burden, while also doing most of the design and some of the building work myself. With a partnership as strong as ours, with our complementary skills, I resolved that we should formalise our relationship. Although there were times when he threatened to overpower me with the force of his personality, I weighed these nagging doubts up against the positives: Robert was never dull and I couldn't imagine loving another man more.

My parents' marriage had been fundamentally happy and inspiring, and I presumed that Robert and I would enjoy a similar course. We were travelling along a rewarding road together and though we were perhaps going too fast at times, I saw no reason why our journey shouldn't be a committed one. Robert was more cautious and expressed concerns that I wasn't his intellectual equal. His memories of family life were of placating his angry father and consoling his distraught mother, which also prevented him from rushing down the aisle.

However, on 2 July 1983, a blazing hot day, Robert's twinkly eyed Uncle Tim officiated at our wedding service in Shamley Green's Christ Church. Tim had suggested that we learn our vows rather than repeat them after him, and I became overwhelmed by the moment and had to use one of Robert's hired gloves to wipe my tears and streaming nose. The Bricks and Mortar cricket team gave us an unexpected 'bat of honour' as we left the church, and the ancient churchyard was soon filled with our wedding guests. As the family had been a big part of the community for thirty-five years, half the village was there too, throwing confetti and wishing us well.

The reception was a huge success. Janie Davis, our wicked old neighbour from Easteds, gave a speech on my behalf, while Hamish, as Robert's best man, told suitably debaucherous tales from their Cambridge days. Then Richard congratulated Robert by throwing him in the pool, rendering our marriage certificate a soggy, illegible mess. Anna who was now married to Hamish, made adorable sailor suits for our page boys and bridesmaids. My gown, which was gloriously disintegrated with age, had been worn by brides in my mother's family for the previous 150 years. After the traditional reception, the marquee was given a circus theme for the evening party. We were married!

But then something terrible happened. We left the party in a hail of whoops for the Crown Inn in Chiddingfold, where we'd booked the honeymoon suite. When we arrived in the oak-beamed room, I swept my gown from the floor, expecting to kiss my groom, but he just stared at me and sat down on a chair in the corner of the room.

'Did I notice you having a cigarette during the reception?' he asked.

'Well, I may have had a puff,' I laughed. He didn't find it funny.

'You promised me that you would give up smoking when we got married,' he said. 'You know how much I hate it. Honestly, Vanessa, I'm disgusted by you.'

'Come on, Rob,' I replied. 'It's a not big deal. I've just pushed it back by a day.'

I stopped smiling, realising that he was deadly serious. He really was going to make a big scene about this, on tonight of all nights.

'How can I trust you if you behave like this?' he yelled. I was becoming frightened and could feel my throat catching as I started to make excuses about the pressures of the day, how I'd drunk champagne to give me courage and then lost my self-control…

'You're a weak-willed idiot,' he said. 'If you smoke again,' he continued, 'if you smoke one more time, I'll divorce you.' I lay curled up on the bed as he towered over me, snorting with derision. 'Oh God, now you're resorting to tears.'

I wrapped myself up in my dress, silent tears hidden behind my hands, winded by his aggression. The culture of our marriage had been set.

The Hutley family had loaned us their holiday house on the Maltese island of Gozo as a wedding gift. Our honeymoon address was Number One, Prison Street. An ominous beginning.

PART THREE

1983–1999

1

PORTOBELLO

And yet the man I married was dazzling. The characteristics that made Robert challenging to live with also made him compelling company. His powerful, competitive spirit extended far beyond the tennis court, and he was as happy engaging in debates about the ethics of blood sports as he was playing a game of chess. He would argue for the sheer jousting joy of it, his facility with language and confidence of manner more than occasionally compensating for the slightly dodgy facts he built his cases on. I revelled in his energetic company and wallowed in his sweet smell, the texture of his skin, his elegant hands and his open smile. He was generous with his time and his money, supporting the local community and lending his expertise to good causes further afield. He was culturally inquisitive, a great reader – insomnia supported his prodigious thirst for books – and let's be straight here, he was pretty damned sexy. This man completed me: his strength complemented my femininity and his intellect my practicality. I loved him deeply.

We baby boomers were the in-betweener generation. Germaine Greer had published *The Female Eunuch* in 1970 and Margaret Thatcher was now prime minister. Women were told that everything was possible, but the odds were still stacked against us. The times were a-changin' – but oh so slowly.

Having questioned Lindy about her willingness to 'love and obey' in her wedding vows, I thought nothing of changing my surname from Branson to Devereux, unaware of the impact that it might have on my sense of identity. Robert and I then fell into the trap of playing out the roles that husbands and wives subconsciously play, without ever discussing the effects that getting married would have on our relationship.

This uncomfortable role-playing, combined with the possibility of waking the honeymoon monster, squeezed much of the fun from our relationship. From the first day of our married life, I failed to acknowledge that I was hurting. Distant memories of being bullied as a ten-year-old bubbled up. I hadn't known how to confront my tormentors then, and I didn't know how to confront my husband now. I'm sure Robert was unaware of the effect his dictatorial style was having on me and I kept on smiling as if it was water off a duck's back, which must have infuriated him even more.

Robert didn't mean to stop being my friend, but he did so at a stroke on our wedding night. We were falling into the same pattern of behaviour as his mother and father, and I found myself occasionally catching someone's eye and winking if Robert's manner became particularly arrogant. Given the opportunity, his mother and I would sneak off for a smoke and do the *Guardian* crossword together. Smoking was my self-destructive self-preservation, my pathetic 'fuck you – I'm not going to be controlled by you' self-defence.

When you're newly married, you can't admit that you're unhappy to anyone – not even yourself. I was convinced that these were just teething troubles and that once we got into a rhythm we would find a way of communicating as equals, the oppression would lift and we would fly once more. However, the reality was that our patterns of behaviour became entrenched as we dug ourselves deeper into the mud.

Everything I did became an unconscious attempt to please Robert. He hated illness, dismissing it as a sign of weakness, so I became defiantly stoic. And he introduced the term 'MUT' or 'maximum usage of time', which to this day occasionally pops into my mind. Reader, you must be shrieking, 'Why did you allow this man to dominate you so?' The answer is that, back then, Robert was 90 per cent wonderful. My parents had always taught us to look on the positive side; holding one's own was never in their parenting manual. On the contrary, girls of my generation were taught that we were there to boost men's confidence, to make them feel and look good. Robert had commented that he thought the Branson family were dysfunctional because we never yelled at each other. Whatever your point of view, it seemed that we were programmed for different styles of married life and were ill-equipped to reconcile them.

Details, details, details. Despite all this, our lives were about to enter a fantastical period. Although the time was defined by work, the line between work and play was so faint that it sometimes felt impossible to tell them apart.

The draw of west London was strong, and soon after getting married we moved into a garden flat at 98 Oxford Gardens in Ladbroke Grove. The forty-foot-long sitting room was bookended with floor-to-ceiling windows and the ceiling was decorated with elaborate cornicing, beautifully set off by a marble fireplace. Off to the back was a narrow galley kitchen and downstairs, testament to the fact that the idea of children had not yet crossed our minds, there was one spacious bedroom and a bathroom.

It was the summer of 1984. Live Aid, Bob Geldof's visionary endeavour to raise funds for relief of the Ethiopian famine, harnessed all that was good in the music industry, ending with the thrilling performance of Freddie Mercury. 'We are the champions,' he sang, and indeed, everyone under thirty felt at that moment as if they *were* the champions of the world.

Word of a mysterious fatal disease that had affected mostly gay men from the East and West Coasts was filtering through from New York. My neighbour Tony Moore, a gentle artist, rang the doorbell to ask if I wanted to buy some of his prints.

'My God, you look ill – are you OK?' I asked without thinking, horrified at the sight of my statuesque friend, now reduced to skeletal proportions.

'It's nothing,' he sighed, giving me a resigned smile. I found out a few days later that when he became gravely ill, the ambulance crew had refused to pick him up.

The extent of the prejudice surrounding AIDS became apparent over the following years. Thankfully, most of this ignorance has now been eradicated. In the London I inhabited in the 1980s, we brushed up against the disease rather than being overwhelmed by it. However, I remember answering the door to a man canvassing for support to prevent an AIDS hospice called The Lighthouse from opening in our area. He tried to convince me that having such a building nearby would affect house prices, but how wrong he was.

One weekend Richard came down to Tanyards, looking very pleased with himself.

'Ok everyone, guess what new venture I've just started?' he gleefully asked at dinner. 'Let's do twenty questions.' He smiled, confident that we wouldn't come up with the right answer.

'Animal, mineral or vegetable?' I asked.

'Well, I suppose it's mineral,' he said.

We started guessing. 'T-shirts? Taxis? Hotels? Schools?'

'No, no, no, no,' he replied. He loved this game.

'Ok, you win,' we said, when the twenty questions were up.

'Well, we've done lots of studies about the condom business,' he said, enjoying our incredulous looks, ' and Durex has such a stuffy image. People are embarrassed to even say the name, let alone buy them – plus, they have a virtual monopoly and charge too much.' We caught each other's eyes, enjoying his enthusiasm. 'AIDS will be a thing of the past if everyone is happy to use condoms, so we've started Mates, a new condom company to undercut Durex and make condoms seem more, well, sexy.'

We all laughed as the simple brilliance of his plan sank in, and then Mum stepped in, cutting her son down a peg or two. 'Oh, Richard,' she sighed, 'When are you going to do something worthwhile with your life?'

The smile dropped from his face and he pleaded quietly, 'I'm trying, Mummy. I'm trying.'

Robert had started a film arm of Virgin called Virgin Vision. Their ambitious team included Stephen Navin, who was to so enrich my life. Their first project was *Electric Dreams*, a modern-day version of *Cyrano de Bergerac*, in which the love triangle was between a girl, a boy and a computer. Steve Barron was directing his feature debut and Giorgio Moroder produced its pulsating soundtrack; the theme song by the Human League has since become a classic.

Flying to join Robert, who'd been working on the film in LA, I experienced my first taste of film industry lunacy. MGM, the studio which had picked up the film, sent a stretch limo to collect me up from the airport and put us up in a suite at the Sunset Marquis hotel. The two days before the premiere were insane; we couldn't open the door to our room because of all the job offers and invitations that were jammed under it. 'We could get used to this lifestyle,' Robert and I thought as we lay in the March sun, sharing a chilled bottle of Californian sauvignon blanc and observing the shenanigans of an ageing rock star and his groupies by the pool.

MGM had enormous hopes for *Electric Dreams*, with the film set to open in over 1,200 cinemas nationwide. Robert and I met

Ileen Maisel, the executive in charge of the film, for lunch in The Ivy to raise a glass to the film's success during its premiere on the East Coast. We waited for the time when the viewing figures from the early screenings were collated. Eileen went to call her New York office from the restaurant phone, before all too quickly returning to our table, her eyes averted.

'I'm afraid the film has to be pulled,' she said. 'Not enough people went to the screenings to gather decent word-of-mouth. I'm so sorry.' And with that she walked out of the restaurant, leaving us to pick up the bill.

I swear the receptionist at the Sunset Marquis was reluctant to look us in the eye when we returned to the hotel. There were no notes pushed under our door and not one message on the answerphone. We had gone from gods of the universe to untouchables in one afternoon. Feeling rejected by Los Angeles itself, we hired a car and drove to Santa Barbara for the weekend, where to add insult to injury, it rained.

The film industry is as compelling as it is ruthless, and Virgin and Robert were seduced by its allure twice more. The first time was to finance a screen version of Orwell's *1984*; the director Michael Radford and producer Simon Perry, who in their eagerness to complete the film quickly, exceeded their budget with such abandon that Robert lost much of his hair. He attempted to persuade them to commission Eurythmics to write the soundtrack, knowing that they would do a stunning job while hoping to recoup some of the film's overspend through a record deal.

Talking to Annie Lennox about the project recently, I realise how appalled and let down they were by the experience. She and Dave Stewart were given three weeks to complete the soundtrack and worked around the clock to produce an extraordinary album; they delivered it at the eleventh hour, only to hear nothing back. Unbeknownst to them, the project had been hit by drama and they found themselves caught up in a battle between the vision of the director and the needs of the producers. When the film won the award for Best Film at the *Evening Standard* British Film Awards later that year, Mike Radford shattered us all by angrily denouncing Eurythmics and Virgin Vision in his acceptance speech. Knowing how much Robert had put into the film and lost in the process, it was devastating to hear Radford tearing into Virgin Vision in front of the entire British film industry. Trying to hide my distress, I turned to Rupert Everett, who was sitting to my right. In an attempt to console me he could only say, 'Well, darling, at least you won!' I suppose he had a point.

Virgin's last foray into film was financing *Absolute Beginners*, directed by Julien Temple and produced by Stephen Woolley and Nik Powell, our old neighbour and Richard's erstwhile partner. It was a decision that sadly sealed the fate of Virgin's involvement in the film business forever.

*   *   *

At that time I could just about justify going to New York for the odd 'business trip' by selling a few vintage posters. After my month tramping the city's streets as a teenager, I still thought of it as my town and felt at home in the crime-ridden, chaotic city. In 1984, I found myself on the only Virgin Atlantic Boeing 747 on the way to Newark with Yu-Chee Chong, an art dealer who specialised in historic images of Singapore and had a knockout sense of style and a devilish sense of humour. Night had fallen and the captain invited us into the cockpit, where we looked down at the network of red and orange glowing ribbons, as commuters returned to the suburbs from Manhattan, energy surging along every highway.

Then the captain radioed the control tower. 'Virgin 001, Virgin 001, are you receiving me? Over.'

The airline was still new enough for the air traffic controller to quip, 'Virgin? How can you prove it? Over.' The captain rolled his eyes as he banked the mighty plane to line up with the runway.

Once we were through customs, we wove our way through traffic into the centre of town to the Upper East Side, where we were staying in a grand apartment that belonged to a colleague of Yu-Chee's. We had all of Manhattan before us, but what to do? Yu-Chee suggested we visited her friend, Evelyn Samuels, who was studying history of art at the Warburg Institute. The daughter of John S. Samuels III, a coal magnate from Galveston in Texas, Evelyn had just married a Brit named Nick Welch, and adventure was in the air.

We headed downtown to the Samuels' loft on Prince Street in SoHo, took the elevator to the top floor and entered a cavernous room with exposed brick walls and a Harley Davidson artfully positioned as a centrepiece. John S. Samuels III was entertaining a few elegantly dressed friends. We quaffed a glass or two of champagne, pretending that we did this every day of our lives, before Evelyn suggested that we leave the oldies and walk around the corner to the newly opened Palladium club, the successor to Studio 54.

Our plan had one fatal flaw: the Amazonian bouncer, a Grace Jones-lookalike in a spray-on latex catsuit, took one look at Evelyn in her Laura Ashley floral print dress, Yu-Chee in her Chanel suit and me in my baggy Annie Hall trousers, and sent us to the back of the queue. A crowd was gathering, and Big Grace was clearly relishing her power. But then something remarkable happened: a white limo swept up, the crowd parted like the Red Sea and Andy Warhol got out, dressed in a white suit. To our embarrassment, Evelyn started shouting. 'Andy, Andy – over here!'

Andy looked over in our direction and beckoned to us. 'Over here, girls,' he drawled, and we cocked our heads and smiled at the open-mouthed bouncer as we followed Warhol into his inner sanctum at the back of the club. It transpired that he had not only been a guest at Evelyn's wedding but had given her a screenprint of a dollar sign as a present. A postscript to this story is that Evelyn went on to become Professor Evelyn Welch, a renowned expert on the Italian Renaissance and mother of Florence Welch, lead singer in the band Florence and the Machine.

The following night I met up with Fiona Whitney, who had come from LA to join us. We ventured back to SoHo, this time to a loft on Spring Street that belonged to the Jaffe family. Lee Jaffe took us to an unconverted industrial floor to meet his flatmate Shenge Ka Pharaoh and a strange evening followed. Fiona and

Lee connected over quantities of cocaine, while Shenge and I chatted and danced around. He never sat still and clutched a paintbrush that he'd continually dip into pots of paint before painting on every surface he could find, leaving wild heads with spiky Afro hair on hubcaps and strange toy cars and big cat-like faces on discarded objects in the abandoned loft. I bent down and snorted a line or two of coke; the evening confirmed my prejudice against coke, the ensuing conversations being frustratingly disconnected. However, hanging out with Shenge – who many say was the energy and brains behind Jean-Michel Basquiat – was a real privilege.

Back in London I began to curate – not that I would have used the term back then – exhibitions, first with Kate Flannery and then with Louise Hallett. We hit on the simple formula of showing an overview of artists from the twentieth century, decade by decade, and then focusing on six contemporary artists.

One hundred or so works were hung, from floor to ceiling, in the flat at Oxford Gardens. Looking back at our old catalogues now, I'm amazed at the range and quality of the shows. The works were loaned on consignment by the London galleries I'd once framed pictures for and who now generously opened up their storerooms to us. We had paintings by Howard Hodgkin, David Hockney, Patrick Procktor, Victor Pasmore, Henry Moore, Christopher Wood, Augustus John, Bridget Riley – an astonishing list of modern British masters. Between us we knew plenty of first-time collectors who wouldn't dream of walking into an intimidating West End gallery but were happy to come to our private views, with their drinks, nibbles and log fires.

We'd zip on a dress, slip into a pair of stilettos and, armed with a bottle of champagne, a blue duplicate book and a sheet of red dots, we'd sell paintings by the dozen. Our shows became so successful that galleries became reluctant to loan works to us as we were depleting their inventory, leaving us with no option but to take the plunge and open our own galleries.

I called Mum, proud to tell her that I had my eye on a space on Blenheim Crescent, just off Portobello Road. 'Portobello Road?'

she said, sounding rather disappointed. 'Oh Nessie, why aren't you opening on Cork Street?'

Regardless of Mum's disdain, I opened The Vanessa Devereux Gallery in 1986, a 200-square-foot shoe-box of a space next door to the Travel Book Shop, the very shop that Julia Roberts would stumble into a decade later.

How I loved my morning walk from Oxford Gardens down the Portobello Road, nodding to stallholders as they arranged their fruit and vegetables and saluting to shopkeepers as they raised their protective window grills. Reggae would be pulsating from basement flats, while rich smells of coffee and freshly baked bread wafted from the Moroccan cafes and the pungent aromas of hams and cheeses tempted me into Garcia's, the Spanish supermarket. The air rang with traders warming their voices up before singing out their bargains. As I neared Blenheim Crescent, the Salvation Army would be opening its doors to welcome in rough sleepers to take their breakfast and their morning pledge, while publicans arranged tables on pavements nearby to tempt them back to the devil.

Soon after opening the gallery, Dominique Taylor, Richard's former PA who had recently separated from Roger Taylor, the drummer in Queen, came to work for me. Dom relished doing all the admin I loathed. She was my saviour. Over the five years of the gallery's existence we were joined by a succession of three young directors, Sarah Howgate, Thomas Dane and Rose Lord, all of whom had different skills and confirmed my belief that you're only as good as the people you work with – they all went on to have meteoric careers in the art world.

The space was small but our rent was low, so we could afford to take risks, and nobody was dictating who or what we should show. Much of what I did in the gallery was instinctive: we would go to degree shows and other galleries, both commercial and public, and we talked to art-school tutors, collectors and artists, asking them who they rated.

We didn't take on a single artist who came to us without a recommendation. However, I always wanted artists to feel we were on their side, so I made sure I answered each request with a considered response – a decision I cursed when we became more successful and the requests mounted. However, this courtesy has paid off over the years, as time and again I've been approached by artists thanking me for encouraging them early in their careers.

There was one damaged soul who became incandescent with rage when we turned down his request for an exhibition. Dominique and I were out one morning and Sarah Howgate was on her own when he entered the gallery and starting screaming obscenities at her. Sarah did her best to calm him down but, instead of leaving through the door, he turned and ran at the shop window, hurling himself through the thick plate glass. Sarah called me half an hour later to tell me what had happened next. She was finding it hard to see the funny side of the story.

The artist had staggered back inside and then whipped off all his clothes before running upstairs and clambering onto the roof. There he stood, bloody and naked, shouting abuse and drawing a large crowd on the pavement below. The police were called and managed to wrestle him back into the gallery, before covering him with a grey packing blanket and bundling him into a waiting squad car. 'All in a day's work,' I explained to poor, traumatised Sarah.

It's hard now to imagine how provincial the London art scene was in the mid-1980s, a time when most people's idea of good art didn't extend beyond traditional sporting prints or Victorian watercolours. Showing contemporary artists, and especially those from abroad, was considered rather racy. I relished pushing the boundaries of good taste, and leapt at the opportunity to show artists from other cultures.

When the American writer Andrew Solomon introduced me to a group of unofficial Soviet artists, I couldn't resist the challenge of becoming the first UK gallery to show their work. Rather than struggle with complications around shipping and customs, we invited Sven Gundlach and Irina Nakhova to come to London and produce their work here. The freedom offered by the city was there to test their self-control, and to add to our woes, Sven's wild

Soviet sexual allure certainly didn't help them keep their eye on the job at hand. While researching this book, I emailed Andrew to ask him if he knew what had happened to Sven and Irina. He hadn't heard from them for years, and thought Sven had given up as an artist. I looked up Irina and it was rather gratifying to see that she had been selected to represent Russia at the 2015 Venice Biennale.

We also exhibited works by Lee Jaffe, whom I'd dismissed as too cool for school when we were in his New York loft. He'd painted a series of stunning studies of blind blues musicians on rough handmade paper. He had gone from New York to Jamaica, where he'd played harmonica with Bob Marley, the only white man to have ever played with the Wailers. OK, Lee, I admit it: you're pretty cool after all!

My gallery director Thomas Dane championed the Spanish sculptor Pep Duran Esteva, who worked in an old Barcelona shoe factory. We showed artists as diverse as Sonia Boyce, whose work investigated the theme of being a woman of colour, and Bridget McCrum, an elderly sculptor from Devon who carved birds from monumental blocks of stone and made them soar.

During our opening month, we held exhibitions by four emerging artists: Sunil Patel, Margaret Hunter, Emma McClure and Pete Nevin. Pete mentioned that he thought the girl who was working in the studio next door to him had 'something about her', so I decided to pay her a visit.

Just entering Tracey's studio was an experience in itself. Streams of tracing paper toilet roll were hanging from the ceiling to the floor and I had to weave my way through them to get to the back of the room, where Tracey was sitting cross-legged on a cushion, drawing. Each strand of paper had been covered in delicate pencil drawings of naked bodies or animals. We chatted for an hour or two, her tentative confidence slowly emerging through her crooked but electrifying smile. I knew then that she possessed some intangible quality, and I kick myself now that I didn't recognise her potential and invite her to join my stable of artists. I did, however, help to get her career going by writing a letter of guarantee so she could rent her first flat, and also by introducing her to the collector Stuart Evans, whom I took to her studio later that week. I'd convinced Stuart to stop buying art by dead modern British artists and have the courage to collect young emerging ones and he embraced the challenge with enthusiasm, buying an oil painting. It was Tracey Emin's first sale.

Witnessing the impact that a sale can have on an artist was one of the most rewarding aspects of running a gallery. As soon as the collector had committed to a work, I would call the artist with the good news, which meant, more often than not, that they could cover next month's rent. When you buy a work, you're playing a role in the creative process by both enabling an artist and encouraging them to continue.

In those days I'd spend hours in freezing studios as we selected works for shows, regretting that I hadn't remembered to wear gloves and thick-soled shoes. Trust between artist and dealer is paramount as you discuss which pieces to hang and which ones to set aside and possibly rework. This process takes time, and lifelong friendships can be formed in the process. I felt as if I was taking a little of the artist's soul away with me as I carried their works to my van.

In 1987 I found myself sitting at dinner next to a quietly spoken, modest man called Robert Loder, whom I could tell also took pleasure in the absurdity of life. Before long we realised we shared an interest in art and he told me that he'd just donated his collection of prints to the Ashmolean Museum in Oxford. In 1959 he'd spent a year in Johannesburg, working with Trevor Huddleston, the celebrated bishop who was involved in the fight against South African Apartheid. He had developed an interest in African art and formed the African Arts Trust. Later on, he and the sculptor Anthony Caro set up the Triangle Workshop, bringing artists from different countries together to explore new ideas.

'Blimey,' I thought, 'this man knows his onions.'

'Which do you think is more interesting, welded sculpture or moulded sculpture?' he asked. I should have confessed that

I hadn't a clue but instead launched into some spurious answer, gesticulating wildly with my hands and catching the tip of my nose with my little fingernail in the process. As I dabbed at the bleeding wound with my napkin, Robert smiled but not wanting to humiliate me said nothing, and I adored him from that moment on. We became firm friends, and when I later asked him if he would be director of my gallery, he said yes.

Robert and I would visit exhibitions together at least once a week, and I came to be profoundly influenced by his enthusiasm for the role that artists play in our lives. He recognised that visionaries are often outsiders and forgave their eccentricities, supporting them by offering spaces in which they could experiment, as well as with the occasional purchase. He not only encouraged disheartened artists to continue, helping them articulate their vision, but also connected them to collectors and galleries. It was thanks to him that I showed Fred Pollock, Beezy Bailey and Louis Maqhubela, all of whom are still respected artists.

Early on in our friendship, I confided in Robert that I had a phobia of some social interactions. One example was that I tended to freeze when asking the girls behind the front desk at Sotheby's and Christies for directions because they had an uncanny knack of making me feel unworthy. He smiled at me and said, 'I was taught a rule of thumb when I was your age and it hasn't failed me yet.'

'Tell me,' I laughed, expecting him to crack some joke, but in fact he gave me an astonishingly simple tip, which still helps me almost daily.

'Almost inevitably,' he said, 'people are the size they make you feel. If they make you feel funny, they usually have a good sense of humour themselves. If they make you feel boring, they're inevitably mind-numbingly dull. And if they make you feel smart, they're usually pretty clever.

Anyway, those posh auction house girls aren't interested in adding "MBA" to their names – they're just after their MRS.'

Robert had become acquainted with an extraordinary group of intellectuals who were trying to undermine the hideous South

African regime from within. These included the Nobel Prize-winning author Nadine Gordimer, her husband, the art dealer Reinhold Cassirer and their neighbours, Sydney and Felicia Kentridge. Sydney was a respected barrister who made his name representing the family of Steve Biko at the inquest following Biko's death in police custody. When Reinhold asked Robert if he could recommend a London gallery who would hold an exhibition for Sidney's son William, Robert suggested the Vanessa Devereux Gallery.

Born in 1955, William Kentridge studied politics and African studies at university and went on to study art at the Johannesburg Art Foundation, after which he studied at the Ecole Jacques Lecoq, a school in Paris that specialises in miming, movement, and physical theatre. Three years later, after two low-key shows at the Market Gallery in Johannesburg, this quietly spoken man walked into my tiny space wearing what I now know to be his uniform of black trousers and a white shirt and carrying a huge roll of drawings under his arm. He unfurled the roll and showed me his mesmerising charcoals.

'This one, *The Kiss,* is a metaphor for the relationship between F. W. de Klerk and President Pinochet of Chile,' he explained. 'And that's a self-portrait of me, as I fall from the picture in despair.'

I looked on in silence.

'And this image of a suburban swimming pool filled with the detritus of consumerism is pretty self-explanatory. Johannesburg is a strange place to be right now,' he went on. 'Every year we fortify our houses against the masses, with incremental precision – our walls a little higher here, some extra razor-wire there. Creeping fear is so insidious.'

His drawings were tough, lyrical and stunning, and I was desperate to show them. We had one small hurdle to overcome – the embargo on South African sports, goods and culture. I knew that this work was important and needed an international audience, so William and I decided to simply go ahead and have the exhibition – to hell with any backlash.

Working on the Marrakech Biennale twenty years later, I was confronted with a similar dilemma when I had to decide whether or not to show an Israeli-born artist after there had been some negative coverage in the Arab press around her inclusion. I referred then to the South African cultural embargo, an initiative that had proved that denying a country a cultural voice has no bearing on its political outcome – in fact, the opposite is true. Unless it is state-sponsored, art from even the most extreme regime should never be censored.

Over the next five years we held three exhibitions of work by William Kentridge. I went to visit him in South Africa and saw his technique for making stop-motion animated films first-hand. Robert and I spent a happy week in Italy with his family, helping with the harvest at the local vineyard. I learned about the role the arts play in politics and their importance in defining a nation's identity and introducing humour at the darkest moments. I also learned how art can better create impact through raising questions rather than preaching didactic messages.

In mid-1980s London, galleries tended to show established artists and were clustered in Mayfair, on or around Cork Street. The Young British Artists were just leaving art school and the East End hadn't yet become a gallery district. The Lisson Gallery was one of the few other galleries that dared to show young experimental artists. We wanted to celebrate young talent and give it a voice. We were perfectly positioned to do this in Portobello: it was not only inexpensive but it also had a somewhat anarchic atmosphere. To us, anything seemed possible.

Meanwhile, other interesting spaces were opening up in Portobello: Kitty and Joshua Bowler opened Crucial Gallery, Catherine Turner and Chris Kewbank at the Special Photographers Company, Anatol Orient's pioneering ceramics gallery and Prue O'Day's gallery, Anderson O'Day.

Understanding the power of a street gathering with performance art, live music and free wine, Anatol, Prue and I called a meeting with the other arts-interested people in the Portobello area, with a view to launching a festival. The idea of inviting all the galleries, bars and restaurants in the area to take part in a celebration of the arts was a popular one.

We launched the Portobello Arts Festival on a balmy April evening, opening with our first Kentridge exhibition. The response from the public was overwhelming. Halfway through the evening, I left Reinhold to deal with the crowds desperate to buy the works, and wandered out onto the street. As I walked down the busy road past countless animated faces, for a fleeting moment I felt as if I was at the centre of the universe.

* * *

London, July 2017

Beezy Bailey called me last month to tell me that Robert Loder had advanced colon cancer. I went to visit him that afternoon and we sat in his homely conservatory, surrounded by books, photographs and paintings.

'What a rich and varied life the art world has offered us, Robert,' I said, after a few minutes of contemplative silence.

'Yes, it has rather,' he said, his eyes lighting up.

'You have no idea how grateful I am for all your help in the early days of my gallery,' I said. 'I couldn't have done it without you.'

'Here, I've got something for you,' he said, cocking his head while writing something in a copy of his book *Making Art in Africa*.

I looked him in the eye as he handed me the book. 'Ah, Robert,' I said, 'you're still as beautiful as ever.' He smiled and we walked to the door. When he had closed the door, I sat on his front step and opened the book.

'For Vanessa,' he had written. 'We had a good time on the journey.'

Yes, I agreed, thinking over the cast of characters from my world back then. We certainly did.

2

NECKER ISLAND DREAMING

Richard bought Necker Island in 1978. He was twenty-eight, and the island was a barren rock, just under one hundred acres of scrubland. Its only vegetation was a thousand barrel cacti, their red-tipped phalluses saluting the sun, and one solitary palm tree – it was the very image of a cartoon desert island. Where others saw logistical problems, as well as clouds of mosquitoes, Richard saw the natural beauty of the island – its screeching terns, scuttling hermit crabs, and warm, pristine sea. Any problems were viewed as mere challenges to overcome. The island's Great House was built, ready for our first visit in the summer of 1985. This was the beginning of an annual pilgrimage, a tradition that continues to this day.

I remember the thrill of arriving on this remote island for the first time, nearly forty years ago. The journey to Necker was an endurance test back then, but it filled us with wonder. Were we really flying on a Virgin plane to Richard's private Caribbean island? First we flew to Newark and checked in to the crew hotel. Though we were jetlagged, we couldn't resist taking a car into Manhattan for a night out. We were up at the crack of dawn the next morning to catch a flight to Miami or Puerto Rico and on to Antigua, followed by a small onward plane to Beef Island in the British Virgin Islands and finally an hour-long RIB ride to Necker. The second day of travelling was interminable, but our excitement just about compensated for our lack of sleep and the stress having to make so many tight connections.

In the early days Necker had a natural simplicity, with two picture-postcard beaches in the south and a craggy shore dotted with turtle nests in the north. A sandy track led from the dock up to the Great House, which had been built from local stone and hardwood to blend into its environment. Necker was nestled within two semicircles of coral reef, as if the island was held in the hands of nature itself.

Our family was growing in 1985. Richard and Joan had had a daughter, Holly, and Lindy had two sons with Bertie, Ned and Jack, and had recently had a baby boy, Otto, with her new partner, Robin Brockway. Lindy, Robin, Otto, Robert and I – and Mum and Dad, of course – were about to set off to stay on Necker for the first time. Travelling with us was a rabble of friends, including Stephen Navin and his brilliant partner Shelagh Macleod, who both worked as lawyers for Virgin, and Simon Draper.

Simon was travelling with his young girlfriend Françoise, the sister of Dominique Taylor, who would later work with me in my gallery, and their six-month-old baby, Julian. Also boarding our flight was Steve Barron, the softly spoken film director who had founded Limelight, a production company that primarily made music videos. He had just finished directing 'Billie Jean' by Michael

Jackson, 'Don't You Want Me' by the Human League and 'Promised You a Miracle' by Simple Minds (for Virgin Records), and he would go on to direct the film *Electric Dreams*. Also joining us on Necker were Patrick Zelnik, who ran Virgin France, and his wife Carolyn, and Richard Griffiths, who ran Virgin Music Publishing, and his wife Olivia. The Branson family may have been small, but the Virgin family was vast. We were all young and enjoying the creative wave that was sweeping London in the 1980s.

The partnership of Richard and Simon helped Virgin grow at an astonishing rate; Simon's attention to detail and his knowledge of music combined with Richard's nose for promotion and his ability to make great deals. There was no fancy head office with a flashy marble reception desk; instead, Richard based himself on his houseboat, which was moored in Little Venice. Simon's office was in the Virgin Records headquarters in Vernon Yard, a cobbled mews just off Portobello Road. There were other Virgin offices dotted all over London, each run by a trusted director, and as the company became international it established a presence in many European cities, too.

To create a common culture and feeling of team spirit among these scattered companies, Richard organised an annual weekend away for all Virgin employees, regardless of status. Rod Vickery, the company's commercial manager, would contact the tourist board of the chosen destination and suggest that, if they were to profit from a group of 400 people spending a weekend in their country, Virgin would expect the local police and customs officers to turn a blind eye to the odd bit of recreational 'smoking'. These crazy trips did the trick. Everyone understood that 'what happened on away weekends, stayed on away weekends'. Throw in some dangerous activities and some bad behaviour from Richard, and hey presto, the Virgin spirit was born.

***

I remember us gathering in the Upper Class lounge at Gatwick Airport at 8 a.m. In our private area, cordoned off with red ropes, I couldn't help feeling somewhat fraudulent – as when Andy

Warhol had taken us into the Palladium, I knew I didn't belong to this rarefied world.

'A glass of champagne, maybe?' an attentive hostess suggested. We shook our heads, grinning at each other, but then my father piped up. 'Why not? Just a little one.' Then someone else said, 'I can't let you drink on your own, Ted.' 'Oh, happy days,' replied Dad, and we were off.

I look at Mum and Dad and wonder how they must be feeling. They're enjoying themselves immensely and talking to everyone in the lounge. My father is more relaxed, waiting for people to approach him before entering into discussion, while Mum is chatting away to the manicurist in the salon about how she juggles work with being a parent and asking the chef how he makes his eggs taste so good. Rather than finding all this effort exhausting, she's genuinely interested, and her energy seems to increase with each conversation.

I recall a recent study into the qualities needed to be a successful entrepreneur. We're all fascinated by why certain people rise and others don't and it seems that the common denominator of successful people is their ability to make decisions quickly and move forward. I wonder how many studies have focused on the role that parental love plays in success – not just on the character of the developing child, but on all those around them as adults. I watch as my parents work their magic.

Mum and Dad showed up for every Virgin shop opening and record launch, openly taking pleasure in their son and his success. Those who do business with Virgin as well as the company's employees have witnessed this family support. A loved person is trusted. It is an invaluable gift.

I glance up from a magazine every now and then and realise that Mum and Dad are becoming parents to the entire Virgin family. I'm going to have to share them yet again. My throat feels tight at the thought.

'Don't be a silly muggins,' I say to myself. 'There's plenty of love to go around – now's not the time for self-pity.'

Looking out the lounge window, I see the Boeing 747 waiting for us to board: a mighty beast with its tail emblazoned with the red tick of the Virgin logo. A 747 seems too big for any one person to own, let alone my brother. I look around the lounge and wonder if the other travellers are in awe of the plane too, but they all look nonchalant as they read their morning papers and tuck into lavish breakfasts, delivered by a team of eager hostesses in distinctive red pencil skirts, tight white shirts and high heels. Don't these people have any idea what went into launching the airline and what goes into keeping it going?

By contrast, our party was all too aware of what it took to launch Virgin Atlantic. Nearly everyone had cautioned against the idea, fearing that it might topple the rest of the company. But the more people tried to persuade Richard that the idea of creating a transatlantic airline from scratch was insane, the more stubborn he became. Launching an airline was certainly a risk, but he was convinced that if he could transform the passenger experience of flying, Virgin Atlantic could be profitable.

Everything that Richard owned was mortgaged to lease the plane. Staff then had to be recruited and trained to embed the Virgin culture into every aspect of the flying experience – from the check-in personnel to the pilots, every engagement with passengers had to be genuine and personable. The in-flight entertainment was cool and up-to-date, and food was a vital component – no more artificial-tasting mush, but real bread, apples and choc ices. This kind of service is standard nowadays, but in 1984 it felt revolutionary.

Regardless of the previous month's heated boardroom discussions, our party was spinning with excitement. None of us had been born into this life of luxury, and the nagging fear that it could disappear at the whim of the bank meant that we relished every second. Working for Virgin demanded ball-breakingly hard work and loyalty, but all this effort was amply compensated for.

This group of excited family and friends had all contributed to the foundations that made the airline possible, though in truth, we didn't think of it as an 'airline' at that point, its 'fleet' consisting of one, and then two, ageing planes. We knew Richard wanted to make long-haul travel a pleasure rather than a tiresome necessity, and there was certainly the potential to make Virgin Atlantic profitable, but we hadn't understood that one of his driving motivations was to disrupt the complacency of British Airways, which had a virtual monopoly on the transatlantic route.

As much as my big brother enjoyed teasing his little sisters at home, at school he was always willing to stick up for the underdog. He hated witnessing his classmates being bullied by unscrupulous masters and power-hungry prefects; unlike those who were afraid to put their heads above the parapet, Richard would happily leap to their rescue. Having good hand-eye coordination and a fearsome competitive spirit meant that he was quite the sporting hero. On the other hand, he was also dyslexic. The masters tried to teach him by rote, beating him in frustration as he failed exam after exam. These memories of his schooldays equipped Richard with the sensitivity to empathise with those being crushed by oppressive hierarchies, and the confidence to defend them.

So here he was, launching his own airline, the David to British Airways' Goliath, and loving every minute of the challenge. And here *we* were, giggling like schoolchildren and about to board a Virgin jumbo jet. It was all rather absurd.

'Another drink, Dad?'

'Why not!'

A willowy hostess bent down to hand him a gin and tonic, and with a cheeky glint in his eye, my father, now a judge, hoping no one else was in earshot, gleefully exclaimed, 'Ah, Nessie – thank goodness there's no justice in this world!'

We were to be guinea pigs preparing Necker for its first paying guests. That meant testing the menus, unpacking crates of paintings, board games, a library of books, surfboards, dinghies and tennis racquets. We were to experience the bar, as well as the spa. We embraced our task with enthusiasm and, in a moment of exuberance, Simon and Robin proposed to their girlfriends: Necker was to hold its first wedding, and a double one at that.

Oh the joy of dressing the dock for the nuptials. Palm fronds were tied to form an arch under which the two brides stood, dressed in their white nighties decorated with sprigs of bougainvillea. Simon arrived by dinghy and Robin on his windsurfer. The wedding rings were made that morning from slices of copper piping, and the four were blessed by a priest from the neighbouring island of Virgin Gorda. After the ceremony, our happiness was complete, as we danced barefoot in the sand by the light of the moon.

* * *

Summer 2017

Landing on the Red Dock at Necker this summer, everything is the same and yet also subtly different. There's Richard, welcoming us in his swimming trunks as he did when we first visited the island all those years ago, his mischievous grin as wide as ever. The blond mane that he sported back in 1985, though just as thick, is now silver-white and tousled by hours of kitesurfing. It's a pastime that not only keeps him as fit as a whippet but provides him with the solitude he needs to focus on his diverse and growing empire. My goodness, he looks good for a man rising seventy.

The island is also home to numerous different breeds of lemur, endangered in their native Madagascar due to deforestation. Groundsmen have draped nets over the palm and banana forests, allowing the lemurs the run of the tree canopy, though many of these gentle animals escape them and play fearlessly among us. To the left are the tennis courts, the sports pavilion, the beach pool and a thatched dining area. Further along the track is another wooden-thatched shack, which houses every toy that might conceivably be needed to enjoy the sea: Hobie Cats, kites, paddle boards, kayaks, flippers and snorkels.

Here, the track forks to the right and Otto, Ludo and Milo, three of Lindy's five sons, head off with their girlfriends towards Bali Lo, a group of huts nestled around a pool and shrouded in thick tropical foliage. The rest of us walk on up the hill past well-disguised offices, a plant house and a sign offering directions to the spa and the gym.

As the road nears the summit, it forks again. This time my kids – Noah with his wife Honor, and Louis, Flo and Ivo with their partners – peel off to Bali Hi, more Balinese buildings built at the end of Turtle Beach. I walk over the hill with the kids and watch the flamingos, some of which are nurturing tiny grey chicks on their strange mud mound nests. A giant tortoise plods by. He likes having his chin stroked and stretches out his neck in bliss.

By the time we reach the Great House, Mum, who has been driven up the hill in one of the island's golf buggies, is there to welcome us, along with Joan, her hair blowing in the warm breeze. A clutch of staff offers us an iced flannel, and one of them is holding a large tray of crystal glasses of chilled Moët. We have arrived.

Ned and Jack, Lindy's two older sons, are both married, Ned to the actor Kate Winslet and Jack to Alexandra Chong, a tech entrepreneur. Kate has two children, Mia and Joe, and Ned and Jack each have a child with their new wives: Bear for Ned and Kate, and Isla for Jack and Alexandra.

Also staying in the Great House are my niece Holly and her husband Freddie, with their two-year-old twins Artie and Etta, along with my nephew Sam, his wife Bellie and their two-year-old daughter Eva-Deia, and the youngest of the clutch, their baby boy Bluey. Lindy and I are single, and Mum has an imaginary friend.

Spending a week every year with my family on Necker Island has given me the opportunity to view forty years of life pass as if watching a stop-motion film, the passing of time so clearly illustrated as the images flip through. At the beginning I can see the small group from our first visit, then friends couple up and, tragically, one or two of them die; babies are born, before growing up, marrying and having babies of their own. The passing time is reflected in the trees multiplying, new buildings dotting the landscape.

There I am, young and newlywed, with no cares about what might lie ahead; then with babies, who are at first mere bundles, but then learn how to walk, swim, play tennis and before you know it are showing off to their partners, leaping in the air on their kiteboards. We reach a point in the film where my parents encourage each other as they struggle to climb the hill to the Great House, then of Dad – Pasha Grandaddy – being carried by his grandsons in a sedan chair. The next image is of us scattering his ashes underneath a cactus on the island's rugged north coast, as his beloved terns circle and screech overhead. The closing shot is of Richard teaching his grandchildren how to dive. They hurl themselves into the water and swim towards his open arms, with their heads underwater and their little bare bottoms bobbing across the pool.

* * *

Just three weeks after we left Necker, on 6 September 2017, Hurricane Irma devastated the island, with winds of over 200 miles per hour. The damage was extensive and most of the buildings were destroyed. Miraculously, two days later, the flamingos began to fly back to their destroyed nesting site. Most of the lemurs survived, although some are being treated in a makeshift field hospital set up by their keeper on the island. The giant tortoises have yet to be found.

3

GREAT STORMS, LIFE AND DEATH

On 24 October 1987, the London stock market collapsed. On 25 October the south of England was struck by a hurricane and at 2 a.m. on the twenty-sixth, our first child Noah was born. The midwife wrote in her notes that he had the complexion

of 'peaches and cream'. Love and pride flooded my being, but nothing prepares you for the sheer physicality of childbirth. Once you've experienced the torture of your womb reluctantly opening and have seen your enormous belly compressing as your baby slithers, flesh ripping, into the world, your relationship with yourself and with everything around you is forever transformed. You are MOTHER. If you can survive that pain, you can survive anything to protect your offspring, and you will.

The day before Noah's birth, a Swedish language student answered a card advertising for an au pair that I'd pinned on a notice board in the local church. I called her father for a reference. 'I don't know why you're thinking of employing Maria – she's never touched a baby in her life.' he said.

'Well that's good, because neither have I,' was my reply, and wishing us good luck he rang off.

Maria was wonderful and the perfect support. I'd seen many new mothers intimidated when people helping them would tut when the baby's routine was not strictly adhered to or when standards of sterilising were allowed to slip – I didn't want to travel down that road.

I would feed Noah first thing in the morning and then walk to the gallery, and Maria would wheel him back and forth to be nursed several times a day. Leaving Noah during the day felt OK at first, but as his needs became more demanding I felt ever more conflicted. During the school holidays, Robert's mother Barbara came down to London to help, and I loved the pleasure she took in holding our chubby baby in her arms, cooing stories into his ear about the adventures they would share together. Unlike my mother, who was always busy busy, Barbara was relaxed and could focus on helping us transition from being a couple to being a family.

Over endless teas while I nursed Noah, we discussed the trials my poor mother-in-law was experiencing during her marriage to Humphrey. She'd recently made a bid for freedom and had gone to live in a friend's cottage, but money was tight and she'd been forced to limp back home after breaking her leg. Barbara's good humour couldn't conceal the desperation she felt at her imminent retirement.

Barbara insisted that her three home births had provided her most treasured memories, and thanks to this enthusiasm and the fact that Noah's birth hadn't exactly been pleasurable, when I got pregnant again eighteen months later, I followed her lead. Planning a home birth was more engaging than the hospital experience – unlike depressing hospital appointments, where I would often wait an hour before seeing a random nurse, my own sensitive and supportive midwife, Katie, would visit me to monitor my baby's progress and check for potential problems. Meeting at such an poignant moment in my life and sharing my hopes and vulnerabilities created a bond with my midwife that transformed the birth experience.

Planning a home birth is a battle, though – at every turn we encountered people asking whether we'd considered the risks. We would answer with statistics from countries where home births were encouraged, saying that in cases where there are no complications during the pregnancy, giving birth is as safe at home as in any superbug-harbouring hospital. St Mary's in Paddington was only ten minutes' drive away, and the maternity unit there had all my notes in case I had to dash there in an emergency. However, I did know that we were taking a risk. If something was to go wrong, the responsibility was squarely on our shoulders.

The baby was due on 20 December. On the eleventh, Robert and I were having supper with friends. Two-year-old Noah was sound asleep, and the Christmas tree was decorated and surrounded by presents. I wallowed on the sofa, barely able to move as we chatted happily about the past year, with the fall of the Berlin Wall and the subsequent collapse of the Soviet Union, and wondered what the coming year held in store. Then the phone rang. As soon as Robert answered, I knew something ghastly had happened. He exploded in grief before the rest of us had any idea of what had been said, kicking furiously at the coffee table and sheering it in half in his pain. Barbara had suffered a catastrophic stroke while writing her Christmas cards.

Robert left immediately and drove through the night to Northumberland, but his mother died before he reached her side. She was sixty-four.

I was nervous about going to Barbara's funeral so close to my due date, but my midwife Katie assured me that babies have a sixth sense and know when to hang on. Not altogether convinced, Mum and I took the train north with an overnight bag containing some mini nappies and a couple of babygrows.

The ancient church in Mitford echoed with barely repressed sobs. Not only did Barbara's family and friends attend her funeral; so did a crowd of her former pupils. She had clearly been one of those teachers who would be remembered for life.

I returned home alone and crawled under the Christmas tree to remove the tags from Barbara's presents, before redistributing them among the rest of the family. I had loved that jewel of a woman completely but, when surrounded by such raw familial sorrow, I felt that I should keep my own grief private. Lying in bed I gave in to silent tears, biting on my knuckles in the vain attempt to protect my unborn child from my sobs.

Ashen-faced with exhaustion though stoic in his sadness, Robert returned to London on 22 December. Early in the morning of the twenty-third, I woke with the familiar gnawing lower-back pain of labour. I didn't want to wake Robert from his healing slumbers and pottered around the kitchen, leaning over the work surface when the contractions began to build and concentrating on decorating the Christmas cake while breathing out. At 7 a.m. I took him a cup of tea, at which point he took one look at me and quite rightly rang Katie, asking her to come around as quickly as possible.

'Don't worry, Rob,' I said calmly, 'Noah took hours to commmme...' But my voice caught and I emitted the low growl of second-stage labour, unable to stop myself from bearing down. 'Oh my God – the baby is coming now!'

Outside, a storm was in full swing, complete with flashes of lightning and claps of thunder. Electricity in the air set off a car alarm in the street below. Robert's sister Clare was in the bedroom next door, reassuring Noah that my moans were happy noises and that the storm was Granny Babar sending messages from heaven. Having battled across London in the storm, Katie rushed into our bedroom and found me hanging onto our iron bedstead, my teeth gritted, desperate not to let the baby arrive before she was there. The calm midwife, still wearing her raincoat, placed a reassuring hand on my back and told me to kneel and relax – and out plopped something that looked like a hard ball, completely encased in a slimy membrane. I looked down between my legs at whatever I'd given birth to, which resembled more alien than baby. Katie ripped the sac from its lifeless face and sucked liquid from its mouth. A few seconds later the silence was broken by a gentle mew and she laid the grease and blood-smeared baby on my tummy.

Clare tiptoed in, with Noah in her arms, and they sat on the side of the bed. Noah stared at the slithery creature, with its minuscule fingers and still black eyes, in silent wonderment, cocking his head to one side.

'This is your baby sister Florence,' we whispered. 'You have to take care of her – she's very little.' And with that, Noah lost interest and went off to play with his toys.

Rob was understandably shattered, so Clare looked after Noah while I bathed with Florence and wondered how on earth we were going to cope. Then the doorbell rang – I'd forgotten that we'd invited Granny Dock to come and stay for Christmas. Aged ninety-one, she'd flown out to Necker Island to be at Richard and Joan's wedding, stayed for the celebrations and then come straight back to London to be with us for Christmas. Still shaky-legged, I carried the one-hour-old baby to the front door to meet her great granny. I presumed the elderly lady would be keen for a rest having taken two transatlantic flights in three days and so offered to show her to her room. But she wouldn't hear of it.

'Let me look after the baby while you have a rest,' she said. A few years previously I'd overheard her saying to a friend, 'I'm not really interested in my great-grandchildren – their genes are too diluted.'

I chuckled as I left her sitting on the sofa, completely absorbed in the hour-old baby on her lap, while I went to bed and had a long sleep. When you have young children, sleep and time to yourself become elusive luxuries and you'd barter a diamond mine in exchange for a single night to catch up on either.

But it wasn't to be. Just eight months later, I realised I was pregnant once again. Another magical home birth produced another beautiful baby boy, Louis. He had been much wanted, of course – he simply arrived a year or two earlier than ordered! The demands of having three babies in three years stretched us to our limits. Apart from our London household, the new cottage needed our attention and Virgin was going public, putting Robert under untold pressure.

My gallery was also taking its toll. Balancing the needs of the artists, whose livelihoods depended on me, and those of Robert and the children was stretching me to the limit. I finally decided that it was time to call it a day when watching a TV interview with an educated Kurdish man who was fleeing Saddam's brutal purge. He was cold, penniless, terrified and hungry, and in the face of such oppression, the self-obsessed art of the eighties suddenly felt vacuous. The gallery had to go.

We bought two what only can be described as idyllic cottages, a hundred yards apart and surrounded by fifty acres of fields in Bepton, two miles from Midhurst in Sussex and overlooking the South Downs. One would be for Humphrey and one would be for us.

Our new and ever-present neighbour brought fresh challenges. I couldn't help thinking that Humphrey's irascible behaviour – his pedantry, volatility and chaotic lifestyle – may have contributed to the stress that caused Barbara's blood pressure to reach boiling point. He wasn't evil and had moments of charm, but these hardly compensated for his inability to control his emotions; I was most troubled by his insensitivity to our need for boundaries and his lack of respect for our privacy.

Rob was conflicted. He felt unable to protect us from Humphrey's omnipresence and the deadening effect he had on our relationship, and when he saw his father through my eyes, I sensed that he resented me for stirring up long buried feelings of shame.

I wasn't alone in finding my father-in-law hard to live with. One afternoon, when Humphrey was away for a couple of days, Robert's forthright Aunt Marion and I went to his cottage next door to pick up his telephone messages. We were inevitably talking about him as Marion sat by the phone and fiddled with the answer machine.

'Oh Lord, Marion,' I moaned. 'I'm not sure I can put up with Humphrey for much longer.'

'I don't blame you, Ness,' she replied. 'He's always been impossible and he seems to be getting worse as he gets older. Our mother was to blame – she was so unkind to him as a little boy, but you'd have thought he'd have grown out of it by now.'

'Just look at this place – it looks as if it's lived in by a tramp,' she said, as she stood up from the hall table and reset the machine.

Two days later, Clare called me with panic in her voice. 'Have you heard Dad's outgoing answer machine message?' she yelped.

'No,' I said.

'You're going to die when you do. Call me back.'

I dialled Humphrey's number with some trepidation. There was a whirr before the message started: 'Oh Lord, Marion, I'm not sure I can put up with Humphrey for much longer. I don't blame you, Ness – he's always been impossible. Just look at this place – it looks as if it's lived in by a tramp.'

Too late – Humphrey had already returned home. I walked up to his cottage, saw him sitting in his conservatory and rang his front doorbell, but he didn't answer. When he appeared two days later, I expressed a genuine apology; he smiled and we said no more. In that moment, my heart bled for this man who had spent his whole life drowning in a sea of emotions, unable to distinguish one from the other.

We found ourselves gravitating towards our friends with young children, who would come to stay at weekends or lived nearby. Shelagh and Navin, friends from our first trip to Necker, had separated and Shelagh was now married to Matthew Bannister, who worked for the BBC. When Virgin Records was sold to EMI in 1992, Shelagh became the company's head of business affairs, a role which at that time was almost unheard of for a woman. I found it hard to believe that someone as brilliant as her wanted to be my friend, and she became another guide and mentor whom I loved with all my heart.

Our old friends from before we were married – Hamish and Anna, Dr Tim Evans, who was yet to marry Annabel, Nico and Richard Stead, Joey and Richard Oulton, and my old friend Charlotte Hutley, who had married Rupert de Klee – were soon joined by wonderful fellow parents we met through school, as well as artists and work colleagues. Bodley and Sallie Ryle, who lived up in Yorkshire, would think nothing of making the eight-hour round trip to go to a party. Bodley worked in London and in 1984 asked if he could stay with us for a few days a week, just until he found his own flat. Much to everyone's amusement, Bodley never did find his own flat and has lived with us to this day.

As a group of friends, we embraced the saying that 'it takes a village to raise a child.' All our children were almost interchangeable as they rolled around us like puppies. It's as easy to bath two three-year-olds as one, and laughter made light of the work. Being godparents to each other's children further reinforced the web that secured us tightly together; the children were able to run free, making dens, inventing games, performing plays and cooking sausages on campfires.

In November 1992, while we were sitting watching Maggie Thatcher droning on about there being no such thing as society, Robert suddenly said, 'I don't think I can stand this any longer – let's go and live in Los Angeles. I've got more than enough work to do there. Just for a few months, before Noah has to go to school.'

'Brilliant idea,' I replied, rather to his surprise. And on 1 January 1993 we rented our flat and flew to California.

We landed on the first day of the second Rodney King trial, the first one having concluded with the exoneration of the police, which had precipitated the LA riots. Tension was in the air. Our good friend Steve Hendricks, a colleague of Robert's, welcomed our excited family to the massive white mansion that he and his wife Lisa had embarrassingly rented for us on Beverly Drive. Our other friends the Webbers were also hugely supportive, suggesting nursery schools and places to eat. And of course, this was also Fiona Whitney's hometown.

'We can play, Nessie,' said Fi, now a single mother with two young kids of her own. Memories of our days as a young family in London blur into each other, but taking three months out of our routine ensured that this period of our lives has stayed in my mind. I remember taking Louis as a two-year-old to 'Mom and Me' classes with six other tots and their immaculate mothers. In LA the moms talked only of their fears – of germs, of intruders, of wrinkles, of not getting their toddlers into the right schools, of losing their husbands – and their greatest fear of all, of becoming fat.

Years later I wrote a short play called *Mom and Me*, and our youngest son Ivo staged it at his school. Seeing a group of teenage boys sitting in a circle with dolls on their laps, imitating Californian mothers, highlighted the absurdity of the women's cares.

I can still see Flo, as clear as day, running naked with Fi's daughter Charlotte on a chilly, windswept beach in La Jolla, and I also recall receiving a ferocious ticking off from a passing walker, who said she'd report us for child abuse.

'We're English,' we replied.

'Well, that's OK then,' was her reply as she walked off, shaking her head.

Friends and family came to visit, and enjoyed the novelty of our Hollywood lifestyle. Noah proudly introduced his Granny to his class at Beverly Hills Kindergarten. As the children sat transfixed, she was invited to tell them a story. Mum was in her element and started by asking a question. 'As you can see, I'm a very old lady,' she said scanning the children's faces. 'Now, how do you think I got here?'

A hand shot up in the front and a little girl shouted, 'On *The Mayflower*, ma'am.'

'Not quite,' laughed Mum, not wanting to humiliate the child.

Another hand shot up before Mum had time to start her story. 'Can you tell us something else, ma'am?'

'Of course,' said Mum.

'How did you lose your fingers?'

That became the story she told, and the children loved every gory detail.

The day of our departure coincided with the closing verdict in the Rodney King trial, our three-month stay having been dominated by media reports of the case. The anticipation of rioting was reaching a climax, fuelled by the insatiable hunger for drama required by twenty-four-hour news channels. The silence of the empty streets was ominous but we witnessed no sign of unrest as we sped along the empty highway towards LAX.

* * *

Back in London, not working allowed me to devote my days to family and friends. I missed the gallery, but the insanity of our social life, buying and developing a new house in Notting Hill and weekending in Sussex left little time for much else. Virgin had gone public in 1986 and went private again two years later. Virgin Vision evolved into Virgin Communications, an umbrella company for the parts of the business under Robert's responsibility. As the government relaxed the broadcast rules and regulations, Virgin Communications started the TV Super Channel and Virgin Radio. Virgin Vision also became involved in post-production and the Internet, in addition to Robert's already expansive portfolio of businesses.

At this time, the Young British Artists were gaining recognition thanks to the support of a number of collectors, many of whom were encouraged by Charles Saatchi's high-profile patronage. Michael Craig-Martin was influential in giving the group focus: he tutored a number of the YBAs at Goldsmiths College and has been a loyal godfather to them ever since. Inspired by Damien Hirst's charismatic leadership, they held a number of exhibitions – their first was Freeze in 1988. London's cultural currency was rising, and international galleries were opening every week. The focus of auction sales had switched from 'modern', meaning post-war artists who were mostly dead, to 'contemporary', which meant work by artists who were not only alive, but also alarmingly young.

London was also becoming an international business hub, and it seemed that every high-achieving young couple were coming to live in Notting Hill. Every other stucco-fronted house seemed to be a building site, with the voices of Polish builders echoing within. Our once-rundown and untidy but culturally diverse neighbourhood was transforming before our eyes. Thankfully, despite the odd designer shop appearing on the Portobello Road, the market and the area's large stock of social housing ensured that it held on to much of its bohemian character.

Back in the 1990s, the social epicentre of our part of Notting Hill was the Acorn Nursery School, opposite St John's Church on Ladbroke Grove. It was the source of all gossip and intrigue; Ruby Wax, a fellow parent, commented that the Acorn toddler 'need never schmooze again'. All the connections they could possibly require in life were there at this nursery – for these kids were the offspring of captains of industry, film moguls, writers, models, rock stars, architects, bankers, artists, comedians, broadcasters and entrepreneurs of every description.

Jane Cameron was the school's founder and head, and we all adored her. The Acorn's notorious school productions were our social equaliser. It's impossible to be competitive when you go to watch your little Johnny lisping his way through 'Thistles, thistles, that's the meal for me.'

However, the men could *really* show their worth at the school's annual charity dinner, when the final lot, a patchwork quilt made of drawings by every child, was auctioned. The big hitters removed their jackets, puffed out their chests and went head to head.

'One thousand pounds, two thousand, three thousand pounds,' the auctioneer called out, pointing around the room at a fearsome rate, to gasps from the audience.

'Four thousand, five thousand, six thousand, *seven* thousand pounds.' Glasses were filled, and wives were getting nervous and subtly placing hands on their enthusiastic husbands' elbows. Bidders dropped out, leaving just two fathers, both determined to get the quilt. The auctioneer, a fellow parent, drew his breath: 'Eighteen thousand to my left, nineteen to my right and twenty thousand pounds to the bidder on my left.'

The room is silent, as we look from one man to the other. This battle surely must have come to an end? But no – up shoots the hand of the under-bidder and down comes the hammer. 'Twenty one thousand pounds to you, Paul on my right!' The room bursts into whoops of applause.

Madness was all around us as house prices rose at an absurd rate, giving us a level of security that we tried not to take for granted. The rises were so rapid where we lived that it felt like we were the one London neighbourhood that *didn't* talk about house prices during that decade – the rise was so obscene that to discuss it would have been embarrassing. As the millennium drew to a close, I felt a ghost walk across my grave and shivered as I witnessed the lunacy that was taking hold.

4

WANNABE

Months of writing have sharpened my focus and recall, during which the words have been flowing, but now I'm frozen. I've already walked the dog, hoovered the house, emptied the bins, chopped some kindling and laid the fire, so there's nothing now to do other than go upstairs to my desk and open my laptop. But how do I go about writing the next chapters? Can I bear to recall the coming years, minute by minute? I hop around, flapping my hands and trying not to hyperventilate as I force myself to climb the staircase and face my demons.

When I think how often two people remember the same events differently, I'm reminded of the work of David Hockney. In one of his series of photographic works, he attached six cameras at regular intervals to a scaffolding plank that was attached to the side of a Land Rover. The cameras were then driven though a landscape, each taking photos at the same time, capturing wildly varying images.

My memories of what happened to me come from my fixed position. I'll try to imagine images seen from other positions, but I won't always succeed.

* * *

Over the years, Robert and I had developed a way of making decisions that dodged any hint of confrontation. Having a positive, can-do mentality, I'd take the course of least resistance, either running with Robert's plans or, as I also liked to get my own way sometimes, running with my own. We rarely made plans together. He didn't share our financial situation and, in all honestly, I wasn't that curious. We were the very definition of two separate pillars supporting our temple of love. In a curious way, our family life seemed to work rather well. There were so many decisions to make, and we generally respected each other's judgment and shared similar values.

In planning to have babies, we followed the same pattern. Robert had never expressed any excitement about the idea of having children, but when Noah and Floey were conceived he seemed extremely pleased when he heard the news. I had a hunch that, by not getting involved with the decision-making, he was absolving himself from some of the responsibility. Both our mothers had bemoaned the fact that they had stopped at three children and, with their words egging me on, I thought I would dive in once again.

I'd turned a blind eye to the fact that my husband was struggling under the pressure of work and family life, but it was clear that he was becoming increasingly angry and never seemed to be satisfied. Nothing I did seemed right: I bought the wrong coffee, socks went missing, the Christmas tree was crooked…

'Please Rob,' I asked in desperation, looking for some encouragement, 'can't you occasionally give me some praise?'

'You know I don't give praise lightly,' he replied. 'It would become meaningless if I did. And besides, if I presume you'll always get things wrong, I'll get a pleasant surprise when you don't.'

I was able to cope by reassuring myself that the children were growing up and would soon become easier to manage, but Robert was finding the chaos infuriating and the noise levels uncontrollable. He felt frustrated at having to leave for work every morning and frustrated when he came home in the evening. He wanted to move to the country and live there full-time, a dream that I resisted, the words 'deepest darkest Devon' ringing in my ears. I'd witnessed the misery of girlfriends as they drove their offspring down country lanes to and from school, for hours each day. I could have coped with the driving and the dark winter evenings alone while Robert was working in London if I'd been happy, but the truth was that I too was miserable.

So why did I get pregnant again? I felt our family had someone missing. In the end we obviously agreed it was the right decision, but in taking the plunge unilaterally, boy did I go about it in the wrong way.

Facing forty often takes its toll on men. Women, their lives fulfilled with motherhood, neighbourhood and sisterhood, don't seem to react as drastically to this turning point, but by contrast, men feel their powers diminishing: menus have to be held at arm's length, historic rugby injuries begin to stiffen and many feel the need to clutch at straws in the hope of retaining their youthful vigour. Robert's first straw was a mansion set in 300 acres of Sussex farmland, and when this didn't do the trick he began saying it had always been his dream to own a Scottish island.

To my horror, I would find copies of *Country Life* hidden under the bed or in the car's glove compartment, pages turned down at the corners, depicting windswept rocks in the North Sea. Then, on the way to stay with Charlotte and Rupert de Klee on Mull, Robert announced that we were taking a four-hour detour to view an island that looked promising.

We didn't need another house and we certainly didn't need an island, so I sulked as we drove the car off the Fort William Motorail. My legs were twitching, the overnight train journey having tested my pregnant body. As we drove over the brow of a hill, I raised my eyebrows and nodded to Robert as the children started fussing on the back seat. Then I looked out of the window. A golden eagle was flying low over a mountain loch, its wings reflected in the still waters below. A calmness entered the car. Thirty minutes later, our bedraggled party tumbled out onto the slipway at Dorlin and I took in the view of the ruined Castle Tioram. Apart from the peeping calls of oystercatchers as they darted by, the silence was so complete that it rang in our ears. Highland cattle were chewing at wildflowers on the mudflats and, over the water, a mere ten-minute boat ride beyond, was Eilean Shona, the island that was to become our very own Neverland.

Buying Eilean Shona was an act of lunacy: over two thousand acres of land crying out for attention, with ten cottages in various states of disrepair, crumbling outbuildings and an eleven-bedroomed main house with a leaking roof and an ancient boiler. But there was magic there too, a magic J. M. Barrie had recognised when he wrote the screenplay for the 1924 film adaptation of *Peter Pan* during a summer holiday on the island. From the moment we stepped onto the island's mossy shore, we were bewitched.

And once again, extraordinary people came into our lives just when we needed them. Marie and Ian Lewis were only in their mid-twenties. She'd been brought up in the Highlands and studied sculpture at Glasgow School of Art. They'd been married under the ruins of Castle Tioram less than a year earlier and now bravely agreed to come and manage the island's redevelopment for us. With their no-nonsense practical spirit, enthusiastic approach and creative vision, they set a tone of quality for the island. We respected their approach and loved working with them. It's hard to imagine how many decisions we had to make to get the place up and running, but with this keen and capable young couple at the helm, everything seemed possible.

On the day we completed on the purchase, aware that time was of the essence, I'd waddled through John Lewis, flanked by two anxious sales assistants, and bought pretty much everything needed to make a large house work: forty-eight pillows, ninety-six pillowcases, vast quantities of towels, duvets, knives, forks, glasses, teapots, wastepaper baskets, and so on.

Ivo was born at home the following day, at 2.04 p.m. on 9 March 1995, weighing in at a robust 9 lbs 11 oz. When the other children returned from school an hour later, he was ready to join the gang and formed the final carriage of their train as they hauled him around the kitchen at speed by the handles of his carrycot, chuff-chuffing round the kitchen table. The kids painted a huge poster saying, 'It's a boy!' and pasted it to the front of the house, encouraging a steady stream of neighbours to come and pay homage to the little chap. The family was complete.

* * *

Dominique, Navin, Clare and I planned Robert's fortieth birthday party on Shona, on 11 April 1995. Navin and Clare crammed a van full of provisions and drove it up to the west coast of Scotland, while Marie and Ian prepared the island for the big party.

There has never been a party like it – forty of our precious friends, all discovering our wilderness island with us. As they arrived, the sun was setting. We chugged around Riska Island on our rusting barge, glasses in hand, revelling in the beauty of the moment. Ian cut the engine and in the golden light, the reedy sound of the opening bars of 'The Dark Island' floated across the still water as David, the local bus driver's son, played the bagpipes on the battlements of Castle Tioram. During the next two days, Marie spoiled us with sumptuous meals: we shucked fresh oysters on the fine white sands of Shoe Bay by day, and ate roasted haunches of venison in the dining room, lit by a hundred flickering candles by night, before dancing the night away in the village hall with local musician Fergie Macdonald setting the pace on his famous fiddle.

* * *

A year later, Comet Hale-Bopp was shining in the night sky, its phenomenal tail playing tricks on us mere mortals below. We were at the Sussex farm one weekend. The children were finally asleep and I settled down to stick photographs from the previous year into an album that the family still pore over, memory after memory laid down for eternity. The photographs are mostly of the children: their first days at nursery as they grin through missing front teeth, snow-ploughing down ski slopes, dancing naked in rainstorms and proudly holding up school trophies. There are photographs of Robert and our four naked babies running into the sea on Shona, hand in hand, whooping as they hit the freezing water, and of him throwing each laughing child high up in the sky.

I was feeling content for the first time in a while. Robert's spirit had been lighter lately. He'd even taken to smoking the odd cigarette. A fortnight earlier, he'd suggested we take a break without the kids for the first time in a few years, and he'd taken me to stay at La Gazelle D'or in Morocco. I felt happy and relaxed, believing that we'd begun to turn a corner at last.

Rob entered the kitchen. 'Would you like a glass of wine, Ness?'

'Lovely. Yes please.'

He came back in with two glasses and sat down opposite me, not speaking for a while. Then, quite out of the blue, he said, 'Ness, I've got something to tell you.' There followed a long pause. 'I've fallen in love with someone else.'

I carried on sticking photos in the album as my stomach turned to liquid, my heart raced and our future flashed before me as if I was drowning. From this moment on, rather than having the freedom of nurturing a family built on the foundations of love and loyalty, we would be condemned to a lifetime of damage limitation.

I couldn't speak. Sweat began streaming down my back, as if I'd been bitten by a rattlesnake. The phone rang in Robert's study next door, and he got up to answer it. I could hear his loud voice through the wall. 'I'm not sure, Becky,' he said. 'I'm afraid she hasn't taken it very well.'

At that moment, I realised that this was not something the two of us could work out on our own. There was someone else in the room, and that person was intent on invading our lives.

Robert hated the cliché of running off with a twenty-six-year-old from the office, and he hated the fact that Becky was also known to have made moves on her previous boss. In order to reconcile the misery their actions were causing, he had to prove that no one had ever experienced a love like this before.

Robert insisted I keep his affair secret. 'She's like heroin – I know I have to give her up,' he said, wringing his hands. 'I know it's difficult for you, but you have no idea how much I'm suffering.' I so wanted it to be true – the giving-up bit, not the suffering. At this point I felt nothing but sadness, for all of us.

Our friends in the Virgin Vision office had been put in an uncomfortable position: the affair had been going on under their noses, but they hadn't said a word to me in the hope that it was a passing fling. Even my mother knew – I wondered why she hadn't looked me in the eye recently.

'Just give us three months – then I'll know which direction to go in,' Robert said.

I can't believe that I had so little self-esteem that I agreed to his plan, but I've since found out that this is common practice with an affair. One friend of mine told me that the only power she had over her husband during this 'probation period' was peeing in his bathwater before he went on a date with his girlfriend, but I didn't even do that.

The word was out. Our once rock-solid family was being blown apart. During those three dreadful months, adrenalin kept me going. However much I ate, which wasn't much, I still lost weight. I could function on a few hours of sleep per night and I could drink for Britain, secure in the knowledge that I wouldn't get a hangover. To describe the pain as torture is no exaggeration, for this is a pain inflicted knowingly on you by a person you love deeply, whose steely cruelty is incomprehensible.

I hated lying to the kids when they asked me where Robert had gone. 'My darlings, he'll be home soon – he's just gone away for a few days on a business trip to Los Angeles,' I'd say, knowing full well that he was yomping around the Kenyan bush or languishing on a Mexican beach with his girlfriend.

One day between their travels, the phone rang. It was Becky, asking if she could speak to Robert. 'No, you can't,' I said, almost laughing at the girl's audacity. She remained silent.

'Do you have any idea of the damage you are causing our family?' I asked.

'But I love him,' she replied.

'So do we. All of us.'

She remained silent and then I lamely, but in retrospect rather poignantly, said, 'But you never knew his mother.' She put down the phone.

'How can she be doing this to us?' I asked Robert. 'How can she so brazenly set out to destroy our family?'

'You don't know what I tell her about you, Vanessa,' was his reply. That shut me up.

Doctor Tim thought counselling would help, but reader, *never* contemplate having couples therapy when your partner is high on the dopamine of furtive sex – it is, without doubt, the most humiliating experience I've had to endure. I could see Robert's eyes literally roll in boredom as the therapist greeted us with 'Now tell me, what seems to be the problem?'

Once three months had passed, he told me that his affair was over. I wanted to believe him – he was the father to our four children and I needed to respect him, to trust him and to have faith that he was going to be the father that the children deserved. And yet he couldn't stop deceiving us. The terrible realisation dawned on me that, as a wife, you become the enemy and are blamed for the shame that results from your husband's lying.

Each discovery of deception, whether a hotel receipt or some foreign change on a bedside table, was like a fresh snake bite. Knowing that the man you love is in the arms of another woman eats into your soul. Negative thoughts flooded my brain, as I lay awake in bed at night: you're not pretty enough, not young enough, not clever enough, not wise enough, not sexy enough, not witty enough, enough, enough, enough.

Robert describes that period as 'driving through life without a road map'. I'm not sure what role his co-pilot played in their direction of travel, but I know their moral compasses were skewed a long way from true north.

In retrospect I can see that I should have shown him the door the minute he told me that his heart was elsewhere and allowed him to find his own destination. There would have been fewer lies to bear, fewer stories of deception and more time to heal. Instead, our misery dragged on for years.

Robert and I had hoped to re-engage during a holiday on Eilean Shona that summer and were cautiously tip-toeing around each other. Not realising the extent of the damage that the previous six months had inflicted, I was naively optimistic, believing that we were on the right path once more.

Humphrey was staying with us, and the tension in the air was playing on his nerves, too. At dinner one night, Robert went to check on the sleeping children, but my stomach lurched as I heard the hall phone ping as the receiver was lifted from an extension upstairs.

'Humphrey,' I asked, 'Do you think you could give Robert and me some time alone together tonight?'

'No I will not,' came his reply. 'You don't need time alone together – what you need is to just get on with your lives, and in any case, you should have the sensitivity to realise that I'm part of the family, too.'

'I don't think you understand,' I whispered, trying to stay calm. 'We're really, really close to a precipice here.' With that Humphrey jumped up, pushed his plate away and knocking his chair over, ran chuntering from the room.

Robert returned. 'What on earth have you done to upset my father?' he demanded.

'I just asked him to give us some time on our own,' I said apologetically.

'You silly girl,' Robert hissed, his rage barely suppressed. I walked upstairs, climbed into a spare bed and lay wide awake all night, my pain too deep for tears.

Humphrey booked himself on the sleeper train the next day, but with the time of his departure approaching, he took himself off for a long walk. Panicked, Marie and Ian ran off to try and find him, while Robert and I desperately stuffed his scattered clothes into a suitcase. We felt a surge of relief when he returned in the nick of time and waved him off from the end of the pier. Maybe now we could relax, I thought, but the damage had been done.

The next day, Robert announced that he had an urgent business meeting in London. He took the boat over the loch and was gone. Later that night, I received a phone call telling me that he had taken Becky straight down to our farm in Sussex. I lay on the kitchen table and wailed. Marie, in an effort to find a silver lining, suggested that maybe I should view Becky as my guru.

'I don't want a fucking teacher like her,' I groaned. But looking back, it was the beginning of a learning curve – of sorts.

Charlotte, my loyal friend, drove across Scotland from Perth, climbed into my bed and held my hand all night, before taking the boat back across the water at the crack of dawn, in order to be at work in Edinburgh by 9 a.m.

Unlike many young children who start to behave badly when there's tension between their parents, ours were as good as gold. They'd do anything not to upset Robert, subconsciously not wanting to push him further away. Noah, aged nine, became the little man of the house and was always thinking of ways to help. He drove the boats and helped me make day-to-day decisions. Floey, seven, was our entertainer, there to make us laugh. Louis, aged six, was always good-humoured and kind, and Ivo, our chubby baby and the darling of us all, might have only been a toddler but he was keen to show that he was a tough guy, too.

Yet still I had to lie to them and learned to smile while my chest ached. I tried to concentrate on their needs but my mind was racing away. On the whole I managed to keep in control, but occasionally my guard slipped.

Mark and Amanda Tandy were bringing their boys to join us on the island. I popped the kids into a Canadian canoe, planning to cross the choppy waters to greet them, and we started paddling.

'One, two, three, four, one, two, three, four,' we chanted, battling against the out-rushing tide and the in-rushing River Shiel.

We passed the castle as a heron flew overhead. And then Noah said, 'I miss Daddy.'

'So do I,' I said. All five of us started crying uncontrollably. We just couldn't stop. Ivo tried to climb over Louis to sit on my lap and then Louis wanted to join him. The weight of the two boys knocked me backwards off my narrow seat, and my paddle slipped away. We were terrified, a family at the mercy of the elements as the unstable canoe swirled in the conflicting currents.

Ian pulled up beside us in the rib, and Mark scooped us up from our rocking canoe. 'I know what we'll do, chaps,' he said. 'We'll perform a play.' Thanks to him and days of rehearsals, the party was entertained and distracted for the rest of the week.

Shortly afterwards, we went to visit Mum and Dad on holiday in Menorca. The children were convinced that my parents had excluded Robert from the trip because they didn't approve of him – it was time to tell them the truth. The boys cried silently, while Flo became hysterical. 'Is Daddy's girlfriend prettier than me, Mummy?' she wailed, and then sobbed herself to sleep in my arms. I'll never forget the relief of holding each child's chin, looking them in the eye and telling them that I would never lie to them again. It was one step in the right direction, though the agony continued.

Brian Eno and Anthea Norman-Taylor knew of my plight and invited me to join them for a week in St Petersburg, where they were living for six months. I stayed in a tiny flat overlooking the imposing Hermitage Museum and saw Anthea and then Brian on alternative nights, as they didn't want to leave their girls alone with a babysitter. Their advice was considered, though from two very different perspectives; both were wise and insightful and I will always be grateful to them. Arriving back at Heathrow, I scanned the crowds, fantasising about

Robert being there to meet me, holding a big bunch of flowers and saying it had all been a terrible mistake. He wasn't.

I hung on the words of everyone I met, both wise friends and chance encounters. 'Attempt an elegant disengagement,' said my neighbour. 'With every step, think where you want to be in five years' time,' said another. Books and films suddenly seemed to hold the keys to the locked doors ahead, and every conversation resonated with insights into human behaviour. I was told to do what was best for me, but how on earth could I separate that from what was best for my children?'

I know Robert would have given anything to return to a time when we could have assessed our lives and worked out a way of living that made us all happy. I believe even now that we were essentially a good couple and had the wherewithal needed to address our issues, but this is not possible when a third party is involved. Robert had left for a simpler life with less responsibility and a partner who could devote all her attention to him, with no need to face the layers of complex family relationships and historical hurts. To him, the answer was obvious – simply leave all that behind and start afresh with a new girlfriend, one who you had met just a few months previously.

'Being separated isn't going to be so bad,' he said on one visit, and he went on to list the times he was going to see the children. 'I can have them every other weekend, for half the school holidays, and can take them out mid-week, too.' He smiled, oblivious to the fact that he was also listing the times he was going to take the children away from me, and them away from their mother.

* * *

Once again, Robert told me that he had ended his affair, and once again I found out that this wasn't the case. With no basis of trust, the situation became completely unstable.

'How dare you accuse me of lying,' he said, even though the evidence was right before my eyes. I was a wreck and found it hard to be civilised when we spoke, yet yearned for him to come home. We would be twitchy with his comings and goings, the kids getting anxious when he came to the house and disappointed when he didn't.

Then their father started climbing mountains. On the night before he went to Antarctica to climb Mount Vinson, Robert took Noah to see *Into Thin Air*, a film about the tragic 1996 Everest expedition when half the party froze to death. Noah became increasingly quiet as days passed without a word from his father, who had been holed up in a refuge after a snowstorm. I began to really resent him. Until then, I had been able to understand his conflict and could blame Becky, but now I wasn't so sure.

One day I asked him how he could pursue his own happiness while causing such lasting emotional damage to his children. 'It's strange, Ness,' he said, 'but I can't help thinking that having a broken childhood will make them into more interesting adults – more creative in some way.' What the fuck!

Rob moved out but still spoke in the singular when he talked of trips he'd taken, always saying 'I'm doing this' or 'I'm doing that,' even though I guessed that Becky was hovering somewhere in the background. He'd rented a flat but continued to say it was just temporary, while I still harboured the belief that he simply needed time on his own to 'sort himself out'.

Our friends were in a state of disarray, but still I felt the weight of history pulling us together. I felt programmed not to live apart from the person to whom I had committed my life and there was a large part of me that was still in love with Robert. Together we'd built an expansive life and one that was full of potential. And of course, the children's well-being was paramount.

That autumn, Hamish, ever the restorer, encouraged Robert to take me to Ravello in Italy for a romantic weekend. The autumn weather was soft. We were silent and, I thought, at ease. We walked down to the sea and climbed back up the steep cliffs, and then wandered the narrow streets. One night, we were joined for dinner by Gore Vidal. While his partner Howard Austen was talking to Robert, I turned to Gore and said, 'Tell me something, Gore. You're one of the most insightful men in the world. What do you do when your husband is having a midlife crisis?' The ageing writer took my hands in his and paused before sharing his wisdom. 'Why darling,' he said, as if it was obvious, 'you seduce his lover.'

In the taxi to the airport, Robert talked about how grateful he was to Hamish for persuading him to give our relationship another chance. 'I must give Hamish a painting as a thank you,' he said, as we boarded the plane.

When we arrived home, I caught Noah's eye and gave him a tentative thumbs-up. He clenched his fist and mouthed, 'Yes!'

The following morning, Robert got up, dressed, helped make breakfast for the children and did the school run while I went to play tennis. A sixth sense sent a chill through my bones as I re-entered the silent house and went upstairs to my desk. An index card stared up at me. On it, in Robert's usually illegible script, were two clear words: *I've gone.*

We'd taken advice about how to talk to children about our separation. Both parents must sit down and explain that Mummy and Daddy still love each other, even though they don't want to live together anymore. However, this calm approach clearly wasn't going to work in our case.

I was told that morning that asking children to write their feelings down is a good way to help them organise their thoughts. I dreaded hearing their voices as they come home from school. A number of kind friends, including Hamish, had come to the house to simply be there. First Noah came in; on seeing me, he also had a sixth sense and said nothing but opened his pencil case and started snapping his pencils in half, one by one. Next came Flo, then Louis, then Ivo. I told them one at a time. They were terrified and didn't know whether to cry, to rage, to blame or to dissolve.

'I know what we'll do,' I said, remembering what I'd heard that morning. 'Let's all go upstairs and write a letter.'

We went to the study and I gave each of them a sheet of paper and a pencil. Ivo started to draw a house.

'I'm going to write to Becky's mother,' said Noah. 'She must be able to stop her daughter from taking Daddy away from us. It's just not allowed.'

Flo chose to write a letter to her father, while Louis wanted to get straight to the point, and decided to write to Becky herself. 'Mum,' said our seven-year-old dyslexic son, chewing the end of his pencil as he grappled with his thoughts, 'how do you spell "fucking"?'

Without a beat I replied, 'f, u, curly c, kicking k, i, n, g.'

'Thanks, Mum,' he said, deep in concentration. 'Now, how do you spell "bitch"?'

5

MONUMENT TO THE MIDLIFE CRISIS

I've wasted years obsessing over that time of my life. Of course, there's no easy way to break free, but I have no idea what was going through Robert's mind when he chose to contaminate all the memories of our past. Was it a bridge-burning exercise? Or was it a subconscious attempt by Becky to obliterate Robert's last touch of intimacy with me? One day our cleaner Maria suddenly blurted out that she had a secret that she could no longer contain. One Saturday while I'd been down in Sussex with the kids, she'd been to the London house to sort the laundry and had heard Robert and another women cavorting in our bed.

It was not only the bed that we'd conceived all our babies in, but the bed on which they'd taken their first breaths. Surrounded by family photographs and trinkets made by the kids in school, it had been a place of sanctuary during nightmares and sickness, a place of rough and tumble, of pillow fights and pillow talk.

Knowing about this creepy betrayal made me flip me from borderline-coping to borderline-insane; this casual violation seemed to me a deliberate attempt to destroy everything that we'd once held dear. Becky only lived around the corner and they could afford to stay in any bed in any hotel in the world, yet by using that particular bed they'd laid waste to a family dream.

When I later asked Robert why he'd done it, he said that men don't think in the same way as women. I said OK, but pointed out that Becky was a woman. He shrugged his shoulders. What could he say?

There were times when I'd be thrown off balance by a wave of despair. How was I going to get through the next hour, let alone the next day? It was terrifying to realise that I was on a train that I had never intended to board and had no known destination. My head was filled with Rod Stewart singing, 'Knowing that you lied straight-faced, while I cried, still I look to find a reason to believe.' I was enraged at my inability to stop fixating on Robert and Becky, as if a lethal parasite was slowly devouring all the good within me, leaving only distrust, humiliation, paranoia, bitterness and shame. I rang our farm to arrange a time to pick up my things and the answering machine clicked on: 'Robert and Becky aren't in right now . . .'

I drove down there in a van with a friend and retrieved my clothes, the photo albums and some gifts the kids had made for me. On the kitchen windowsill, behind a pair of curtains that I'd made just months before, was a card that read, 'Darling Becky, Happy Birthday! What a year you've had – new job, new house and a new man. Congratulations! Love Mum x'

I hated myself for being unable to lift myself out of that muddy well, where negative emotions oozed into every cell of my body. They seeped down my throat, filling my chest and restricting my breath. While doing the seemingly endless tiresome jobs that go hand-in-hand with raising a young family – scooping up dog poo in the garden, queuing in supermarkets, packing and unpacking bags, reciting times tables and emptying the dishwasher – I would fight the urge to imagine what they were up to. I imagined them together in our bed, their sweat seeping into the mattress. To think of anything constructive was an effort too far. I could just about get the kids up, off to school, fed, bathed and put back to bed again, but nothing more.

Noah, always so brave and grown-up, broke down only once, when his new goldfish, one that he kept in his bedroom and happened to have named Robert, had flipped out of its bowl.

'Robert's died, Robert's died!' he screamed down the stairs.

I rushed up wondering what on earth was going on, and there on the floor was Robert, so covered with the coir matting that had stuck to his scales while he flopped around that he was unrecognisable as a fish at all. I picked up the inanimate Robert and plopped him back in his bowl, willing him to start swimming again, but the strange, hairy creature rolled over onto its back. 'Come on, Robert, live,' I said.

It didn't take Freud to know that Noah didn't need this tragedy.

'Live Robert, live,' added Noah.

We stared at the stiff, floating fish and gave it one more chant. 'Come on man! Come on Robert!'

And with that, first the tail and then a fin twitched, a gill pumped and the fish flipped over and swam free of its furry coat. Noah and I high-fived – all was going to be all right after all.

Louis's pet rabbit, on the other hand, had just disappeared. Night after night, the poor boy would silently climb into bed, until his lights were turned off, when tears would overwhelm him.

'I want Hoppy,' he would wail. 'I want Hoppppy.' Fully aware that Hoppy had probably become a fox's supper, I was unsure how to console the grieving boy. One day a kind neighbour told Louis that he'd seen Hoppy frolicking with Mrs Hoppy and a family of baby rabbits in Holland Park. Louis didn't cry for Hoppy after that, but he did cry. I should have asked him what was upsetting him but instead I made the error of just cuddling him and telling him that it would be all right. After weeks of anguish, he finally sat up and said, 'Mummy, I know why Daddy's gone and it's all my fault.'

'Oh my darling, Lou,' I replied. 'It's not your fault.' And then I finally asked a question. 'Why do you think it's because of you?'

'He left because I can't read and write,' he said, burying his head in my lap.

It is impossible for anyone to hold a weeping six-year-old boy who's blaming themselves for their parents' divorce and not feel a surge of anger towards the woman who has taken their father from them. At this point, it was far easier to blame her than their father. I would have rather have not blamed anyone at all, but my mind clung to a narrative that gave our predicament some reason. The easiest one to grasp was that an ambitious twenty-six-year-old trollop, who had previous form, had offered midlife-crisis man who was overburdened with responsibilities an exit route, with plenty of ego-massaging and red leather-skirted sex – lots of it.

My friends, family and neighbours understood how close the children and I were to breaking down and became the rocks we clung to. We would regularly stay with Lindy and Robin and their boys for the weekend, as well as with Mark and Amanda Tandy and Richard and Joan. Their order and routine provided a framework around which we could function. Coming home on Sunday nights was never easy: I would park the car and carry the sleeping children up to their beds one at a time, worried about leaving the others in the car on a London street at night, but fearful of waking them in case they couldn't get back to sleep.

Just as I was about to let self-pity overwhelm me, my neighbours Faith and Michael Gollner would ring. 'Just checking that you're all right, Ness,' they would say.

'I'm fine now that you've called,' I would answer, before wandering around the house, preparing for the week ahead and locking all the doors. In truth, I'd never experienced such loneliness.

It was then that Bodley, our house guest who had never moved out, really started to earn his keep, patiently listening to me going over different scenarios, again and again. I knew I could pick up the phone and call any number of friends – the Bannisters, the Dewars, the Oultons and of course the de Klees – and whatever they were doing they would let me rant on. I'd call Sallie Ryle with a glass of wine on the go, not wanting to drink alone and knowing that she'd happily pour herself one too and talk for hours. Sometimes I'd call Clare and ask her if she would mind if I just cried, because crying on my own felt impossibly bleak.

Walking out around the neighbourhood became a trial, because I couldn't bear to bump into anyone I knew. The humiliation of being left is all-encompassing, as is the gnawing agony of realising that you've failed as a wife and as a mother.

The previous year, Ronald and Sharon Cohen had invited Robert and me to a dinner with Tony and Cherie Blair; Tony's charisma had charmed us and we'd made a hefty donation to the Labour Party in the run-up to the May 1997 election. As a result, we were invited to the Royal Festival Hall to celebrate Labour's victory, and I went with Navin as my plus one. There was hysteria as Tony walked into the building at 2 a.m. – 'Things Can Only Get Better' was booming out over the PA as we all whooped and cheered. We walked back along the Embankment, the brilliant sun rising over the river. 'Things can only get better,' Navin said, laughing.

In August, I took the children to Kensington Palace to add flowers to the growing carpet spilling down the front lawn after the death of Princess Diana. We were approaching the end of the millennium, the end of an era, the end of one life and the beginning of a fresh one – but how should we regain some dignity, some humour, some energy and some love?

Tracey Emin, her then-partner Mat Collishaw and I ended up drinking in the Colony Room Club in Soho one night, and I told Tracey of my inability to stop playing that grubby, scratched, self-pitying record.

'Vanessa, first you've got to get rid of your bed,' she told me with utter conviction. 'I'm going to write you a poem for your new bed – promise me you'll use it.' As I rode the night bus home in the early hours of the morning, I chuckled at the wonderful contrasts that life throws up – 3 a.m., with four young children to get ready for school that morning, having had an inspiring evening and the hint of many more to come. Things *could* only get better.

Less than a week later, I opened an envelope from Tracey containing two poems written in her distinctive sloping hand. I asked the furniture design duo Precious McBane to make a new bed for me, and they embroidered Tracey's poems on the headboard:

Oh God you made me feel so beautiful
And then I wanted to feel it again and again.

And then the lines that expressed it all:

With myself, by myself
Never forgetting.

Next I visited Grayson Perry in his house in east London, thinking that a Grayson urn for my ashes on the mantelpiece would be a solid reminder of mortality.

'So Vanessa, tell me, what's going on in your life?'

'Well Grayson, I don't know really where to begin…'

A month later I picked up a giant pot of glorious playfulness. On the lid Grayson had crafted a ridiculous masturbating ape burnished in gold. Scratched into the pot were images of Prince Charles, his hat embossed with the word 'tampon', motor bikes, photos of alluring young women with pouting lips labelled 'marriage wrecker' and drawings of fat middle-aged men with drooping breasts and sagging scrotums. On the front of the pot was boldly written: 'Homage to the Midlife Crisis'. Oh joy.

Walking into the Sadie Coles Gallery, I was confronted with a huge photo of Sarah Lucas, her naked bottom barely covered by a T-shirt with 'COMPLETE ARSEHOLE' scrawled on the back. As my depression began to lift, art was taking on meaning again.

Lawyers had told me I would be within my rights to restrict Robert's access to the children to one night every other weekend, but I knew that would do no one any favours. Robert was a good father, and the kids needed him. Instead, he came to the house to take them to school on Tuesdays and Thursdays, put them to bed on Wednesdays and had them to stay in Sussex every other weekend. We agreed to share the holidays.

Previously, except for the weekends when we'd gone to Morocco and Italy, I'd rarely spent time apart from the children – my world was bound up in their rhythms. The first weekend they went to Sussex, I tried to sound excited for them as I strapped Ivo into the baby-seat in the back of Robert's Shogun, reassuring them that I was going to have a lovely weekend too, and waved enthusiastically until they were out of sight.

Then I walked back into the house, leaned against the front door and unable to deal with my misery, screamed so hard that I had a panic attack and collapsed on the floor. From then on, knowing that this was a faultline in my self-control, I set myself a routine: I'd wave them off, go back into the house, make myself a cup of tea and a plate of Marmite toast, take it up to my bedroom, light the fire, close the door and climb into bed to watch a DVD. Two hours later, I'd emerge, ready to face the weekend.

Generous friends offered me hospitality with open arms but, without my children I felt the urge to break free from family life – it was time for me to do things for myself. The problem was, I didn't know how. The idea of lighting a candle in a room with only me in it seemed ridiculous. Selecting a film to watch on my own became a conundrum of significant proportions, though Simon from Video

City on Notting Hill Gate patiently recommended film after film having witnessed me staring blankly at the brimming shelves. I'd never bought food with only myself in mind before and had never planned a weekend or gone to an exhibition without first consulting Robert, or family or friends. I'd barely ever slept in a house on my own, let alone spent a whole weekend alone.

On returning to London one weekend, I was appalled to see that a new neighbour had felled a magnificent, protected plane tree, which had screened out a block of flats and made our garden feel like an ancient wood. In London, if you cut a tree down without the permission of the borough council, you face a £20,000 fine – a drop in the ocean when you stand to make a couple of million pounds on the house you can build in its place. After the previous six months of deception, I'd become hypersensitive to anyone who wasn't straightforward with me. I walked around and rang the front door, and my new neighbour answered. 'Hello,' I said. 'My name is Vanessa and I'm your neighbour.'

He put out his hand, a smile on his face. 'I'm Igor,' he said. 'Pleased to meet you.'

'Would you mind telling me what happened to the tree behind your house,' I asked calmly.

'Oh, that tree,' Igor replied. 'I'm afraid the builders cut the roots by accident and it died.'

I put my hands on either side of Igor's face, grabbed his ears and shook his head with all my might. 'Don't you lie to me!' I shouted as his head bobbed up and down. Then, not knowing what to do, I just let go of his ears and walked away. For years afterwards, before we eventually became friends, he would cross to the other side of the road if he saw me coming. My new sensitivity to dishonesty became a twitching antenna and was to get me into trouble more than once.

One night, my friend from New York, David Teiger, invited me to the Savoy for a glass of champagne before we went on to a grand dinner. 'You look beautiful,' he said, and I smiled, knowing that this was always his opening line. 'Now, tell me, Vanessa, how have you been?'

I had plenty to tell him, but found it hard to know where to begin. Years earlier, he had taken Fiona Whitney and me out for dinner in New York. We'd chatted away all evening and told him our impressions of America, two naïve girls throwing around superficial opinions with little respect for our cultured host. During coffee, he had written something on his paper napkin and pushed it quietly towards me. '*Don't Tell, Ask*,' it said.

Now, remembering the napkin, I responded, 'David, you tell me your news first.'

'I've been buying Sarah Lucas over Tracey Emin – her work seems to have more substance. What do you think?'

'I find it hard to have a subjective opinion. I love Tracey's straightforward honesty – she speaks to the crazy, vulnerable, hormone-driven side of all of us.'

'Ah,' said David, 'so life's not exactly on an even keel.' He ordered a bottle of Krug and I filled him in on my latest sorry tales. As we stood up to leave for the dinner, I wobbled on my heels. 'Steady, Vanessa – maybe you should eat something,' he said.

Our taxi swept through the grand entrance gates to Number One, London, the Duke of Wellington's London residence, and David steadied me as I negotiated the steps. The dinner was to celebrate the achievements of the Tiger Fund, an investment vehicle that had made colossal returns for a few chosen investors, largely as a result of the CEO's relationships with world leaders and opinion-makers. David introduced me to our host, who then introduced us to Margaret Thatcher, who in turn simply ignored us. 'One sip of wine before dinner won't hurt,' I thought as I grabbed a glass from a passing waiter.

I don't remember much about dinner other than listening to the speech by Julian, the Tiger Fund CEO, as he detailed the fund's mind-boggling success; the contented murmurs of the diners laughing at his self-effacing quips and the applause as he assured them that their fortunes were going to grow exponentially and all they had to do was take pleasure in spending the money.

I looked around at the crowd's taut faces, sequins, perfect postures jutting clavicles and coiffed hair, and turned to the man sitting to my right. 'Are you absolutely loaded, too?' I asked. He looked a little surprised. 'I mean, I know you must be if you're here, but I just want to know – where does the growth come from? What makes all this money make 10–15 per cent per annum? The profits must be coming from somewhere – someone must be losing . . .'

The man still said nothing, but I couldn't stop myself. For some reason I thought continuing would give him something to latch onto and he could explain. Then David was at my side, his hand firmly taking my elbow and raising me up.

'Ladies and gentlemen, it has been a pleasure, but I fear we have to go.' He smiled and the table all nodded to him, bidding us a relieved goodbye.

'David, I'm so sorry,' I said. 'I tried the old "Don't tell, ask" routine, but I just don't get it. Something's wrong – I just can't stand half-truths or people who won't face up to the truth. I let you down, I'm so sorry.'

David said very little but seemed amused. 'Let's talk about this in the cold light of day,' he said, kissing me on the cheek and sending me towards the main door as he re-entered the banqueting room. My heels were far too high, my dress was too thin and it was raining.

'I'm afraid there aren't many taxis tonight, miss,' said the doorman. Two other men were also leaving early, and their car swooped into the courtyard. 'Please could you give this young lady a lift, sir?'

'Only if she doesn't mind going via Claridge's,' came a curt, American-accented reply.

The younger of the two men jumped into the front seat and I got into the back with the other as the doorman leant through the rear window. 'Goodnight, Vice President Gore,' he said.

I tried to pull my little red dress down towards my knees. 'What an incredible evening,' I said to break the ice.

'The food didn't agree with my stomach,' Al replied.

I thought I'd try to entertain him – and for some reason chose to share the story of my recent dinner with Gore Vidal. David's 'Don't tell, ask!' was screaming caution, but still I launched in. 'A few weeks ago I had dinner in Ravello with Gore Vidal...' The vice president didn't encourage me to continue. 'Sorry, the story only makes sense if I give you some background.'

I could see we were approaching our destination, so I talked even faster. 'The thing is, my husband had been seeing a young trollop and was agonising about whether to run off with her or stay with me and our four kids. We were in Ravello to rekindle some romance.' The young man on the front seat sat rigid and Al stared straight ahead as the limo stopped at a red light. Should I open the door now and quietly slip out? No, I had to finish the story.

'Anyway,' I pushed on, ending with Gore Vidal's advice that 'you seduce his lover', just as we pulled up to the hotel entrance. I looked towards him, waiting for a little vice presidential chuckle, but instead he and his preppy intern leapt from the car with a swift 'Good evening' and almost fell over each other as they pushed through the revolving door.

I wanted to call someone to gleefully share in my humiliation. 'It's a shame I can't call Robert,' I thought, as the limo swept away under the dripping Bayswater plane trees. 'He would have loved it.'

* * *

A major benefit of not having a partner was becoming apparent: a single person has so much more time to nurture old friendships and embark on new ones. I often went to stay with Shelagh and Matthew Bannister, and Shelagh and I tended to speak daily, either in person or on the phone.

In 1996 they experienced the agony of giving birth to a baby boy, Gabriel, who had died two weeks before he was due to take his first breath. I watched as they carried their son's tiny white coffin to his resting place in Redford Cemetery, while crows cawed plaintively overhead. On holiday a month later, we were on the beach and Shelagh mentioned that her breasts were bleeding. The doctors had said it was due to her milk drying up after the stillbirth, but she was clearly worried.

She had every right to be – on our return she was diagnosed with breast cancer and underwent a double mastectomy, but

271

unfortunately the cancer had spread to her lymph system. The doctors were cautiously optimistic but recommended chemotherapy. Shelagh never complained or panicked. She was disciplined with her diet, exercise routines, cold caps and alternative therapies. She didn't want her illness to define her – she was determined to keep it on a parallel track and not take over her life.

My God, she was brave. Her silent suffering made me love her completely. She'd call me with the results of her three-monthly check-ups; when they became six-monthly, it seemed that her disciplined approach was working. However, a dark cloud still hovered and we began to mark every occasion as if it was our last. Shelagh's heightened state of being gave us permission to buy not just any old plonk but good-quality wine and treat ourselves to the odd fancy frock, and when it came to booking holidays, she didn't want to waste time going anywhere less than perfect.

A year after Robert left us, I was still struggling, and I defy anyone else not to. The children were so young – Ivo was just two – and it made my heart ache to see them making such an effort to control their sadness. I was facing the first summer holiday without them – two full weeks. We flew from Necker to Miami; Mum and Dad were taking the children back to the UK to meet up with Robert, and I was going on to LA to meet up with Fiona. At Miami Airport, as I was waving them all off at the international departure gate, Louis took fright and refused to leave me. He lay on the floor, clinging onto my ankle and wailing uncontrollably. My parents tried to pry him off. Then the other children began to cry, while Mum bit her bottom lip.

'Come on, little chap,' said Dad. 'We'll take care of you. Come on, little chap.' Then, finding the emotion too much, my usually restrained father stood up and said under his breath, 'That fucking man – how could he do this to his children?'

Eventually the exhausted party left hand in hand, and I made it to my flight just in time.

Fiona picked me up from the airport. 'My God, Ness, you look absolutely dreadful!' she said as I walked into Arrivals. 'Brown, but skinny as anything.' Driving along the highway she continued. 'What you need is a nice little boob job!'

'Fiona, don't be so ridiculous,' I replied. 'It's the last thing I need.'

'Don't be such a prude, Ness. Everyone does it here.'

'That might be so,' I said, 'but I'm completely against plastic surgery. It's superficial and everything I don't believe in about the consumerist society. And anyway, I'm rather fond of my boobs – they're just a bit deflated because I'm so thin.'

Fi was focused on her goal. 'I know this brilliant surgeon in Beverly Hills. He does all the stars. Honestly, Ness, he's brilliant.'

'Fi,' I replied, already feeling somewhat worn down, 'I'm honestly not interested.'

The next day we were sat in Dr No's office. I was slightly taken aback by the fact that he was wearing cowboy boots, and before I knew what was happening, he was drawing dotted lines around my bosoms with a Magic Marker.

'Vanessa is more interested in the Meg Ryan than the Dolly Parton', I heard Fi saying.

'Please, I'm really not sure,' I said lamely.

He took us past a number of curtained cubicles where ladies lay on their backs after Botox treatments, dabbing bloody tissues at their foreheads.

'Lydia,' said Dr No to one of the women, 'would you mind showing your breasts to these two prospective patients please?'

Still lying down, Lydia raised her T-shirt with one hand, exposing two of the most perfect, soft, nut-brown mounds of flesh I'd ever seen.

'See how great these little puppies look?' the doctor said gleefully. 'I use this special technique and go in under the muscle. You see? There's no line, and the breasts feel completely natural.'

With that, he walked up to Lydia and began to knead her exposed breasts. 'Come and have a feel,' he barked. I put out a rather tentative hand and felt a bosom while trying to look serious. Only in LA.

In the car on the way back to Hancock Park, Fiona banged on. 'Come on Ness. He said he would give us a two-for-the-price-of-one offer, or four for the price of two. That way, I sneak in free!' Now I felt under pressure. 'What's more,' she said, 'he has a cancellation tomorrow morning.'

I took my tapestry into the clinic, thinking that when I came around from the procedure I could do some sewing. I went in first. After an hour or two in the theatre, the doctor went to check with Fiona what size implants I'd asked for. 'Ness asked for Meg Ryans,' she told him. Apparently he went ashen and rushed out. It appeared he had made an error and implanted some Monroes in there. The pain I felt on regaining consciousness was indescribable. My chest was in spasm, my blood pressure began to drop alarmingly and I was losing the ability to speak. 'I think I'm going to die, Fi,' I whispered.

Dr No didn't want to lose a patient, and nor did he want to be seen to be having an emergency. Paramedics jammed me in the service elevator and wheeled me out of a back entrance to the ambulance. All I can remember is the pain.

In intensive care in Cedars-Sinai Medical Center, I blew up to such an extent that a nurse had to cut off my rings and my plastic hospital wristband. My liver was struggling, along with my kidneys. Dr No came to visit and defensively explained that my post-op collapse was my fault for not telling him how much I'd been drinking. A few years later he would lose his licence to practise medicine. Fiona visited me somewhat sheepishly and I couldn't stop looking at her breasts. She hadn't intended to go for the full Dolly but due to some miscommunication, the full Dolly she had. Her magnificent new appendages were going to get her into all sorts of trouble over the years – once a little too close to home for comfort – but what are friends for if not to challenge us?

Do I regret the episode? Well, it would have been a bloody silly way to die. Apart from that minor detail, to regret anything, for too long, is a mistake. There is no going back and I also learned a great deal. It's true that, if I hadn't been in that vulnerable emotional state, I would never have elected to do something so invasive, but I have to admit just one thing.

My new little puppies knock Lydia's into a cocked hat.

6

AND ALL THE MEN AND WOMEN
MERELY PLAYERS

Morocco, November 2017

'Oh, you little devil,' would be Mum's response if I told her someone had caught my eye, before adding, 'But what fun!'

She and I are sharing a room at Kasbah Tamadot, Richard's hotel in the Atlas Mountains. Richard, his kids Holly and Sam and my son Noah are hosting a hiking and biking expedition up Mount Toubkal to raise funds for the family's 'Big Change' youth empowerment organisation. There are thirty-five go-getting entrepreneurs in the party, while Mum, at ninety-three years old, is in her element and happily flirting with them all.

Having peaked a little early, she is helped back to her room by one of the hotel's gentle Berber waiters. When I go and check on her before dinner, she's curled up under the duvet, fully dressed, with the light on. As I tiptoe in and bend down to turn off her bedside light, she sits bolt upright.

'Oh, Nessie,' she says, 'why have I always been so, now what was it? P and P?'

'Sorry, Mum – what's P and P?'

'Oh, I remember,' she says. 'Why have I always been so prim and proper?'

We both giggle before she burrows under the duvet again and instantly falls back to sleep.

***

This takes me back to our story, and a point where one miserable chapter ends and an altogether more optimistic one begins.

My life was gaining some traction once again. You won't be surprised to learn that this had more to do with my decision to stop drinking after my near-death experience, rather than my new boobs. Embarking on a period of sobriety provided a foundation for more positive behaviour: less lamenting and remorse, and more energy, confidence, self-esteem and fun.

I made an unexpected connection with a Nigerian prince on the Virgin Atlantic flight back from LA, a powerfully built, smooth-talking giant of a man. I flew on to join the Ryles and the Bannisters at a rented villa in Tuscany for the weekend. Shelagh was livid with me for actually electing to have breast surgery, but she forgave me and she and Sallie were soon helping me choose delicate new lingerie from La Perla and Prada, while singing 'Some Day My Prince Will Come'.

I wasn't exactly the 'catch of the century' with my little 'gang of four' all under the age of ten, but I could live in hope. They say that to get over an old partner you've got to get under a new one, and it's true. I realise now that it was not so much that I yearned to be loved but that I was missing having someone to love.

I needed to dip my toe in the water again, so to speak – get back on the horse, more like. The prince was the perfect person to get started on and provided me with enough stories to entertain my girlfriends for months. This being a family-friendly book prevents me from going into all the details of my years of dating, but here are one or two brief insights into the complications of finding love again.

Prince M. asked me out for dinner on a night when Robert's redoubtable Aunt Marion was visiting, so I invited him to join us for supper at home instead of going to a restaurant. The three of us had a surprisingly relaxed meal and then Marion decided that we should watch Bill Clinton's live confession following his affair with Monica Lewinsky. Watching it with these two was surreal, to say the least. Marion took herself off to bed. I was seeing Prince M. out, when he thrust me against the front door, pushed my feet apart with his and held my hands above my head with one hand while simultaneously frisking me with the other, LAPD-style. He ran a hand down my arms and my back and over my buttocks, feeling his way first down the outside of my leg and then, more slowly this time, up one calf and inner thigh and down the other.

'How do I know you're not bugged?' he whispered in my ear, before scooping me up, my legs locking around his waist, and kissing me on the lips. After he left, I rushed upstairs into Bodley's room and woke him up with, 'Bod, Bod, I've just kissed the prince!' The poor chap rolled over and managed a thumbs up before going back to sleep.

Lindy invited me around to supper to introduce me to a softly spoken windsurfing champion who'd recently split up from his girlfriend. He was a complete Adonis and in a moment of madness I slipped my phone number into the breast pocket of his shirt. He rang to arrange a date. Before we met, I joined a friend in the pub and told her about the impending liaison.

'Be warned, Vanessa,' she cautioned. 'The first time I went to bed with a man after my divorce, I was overwhelmed with emotion. I just couldn't stop crying.'

I met the surfer at a bar, determined to feel strong and confident. We had no foundation for a relationship, having barely spoken, but rather hastily found ourselves back at Lindy's house, kissing and losing ourselves in each other's chemistry.

'I can deal with this,' I thought, as I ran my hands up and down his delightful muscular arms. 'I'm not going to cry.' I looked into his dreamy blue eyes. 'Hey up, what's that?' I thought, a little confused. 'Is that a tear I can see?' I could feel his body emit a barely disguised sob.

'I'm so sorry, Vanessa,' he said. 'It's just too soon for me. I miss my girlfriend.' I felt instant relief as we blew out the candle beside the bed and snuggled down, spooning like two children on a sleepover.

Those who haven't been rejected for someone else, especially someone eleven years younger than them, will have no idea how much courage it takes to open up your heart again and expose your vulnerability to another. There's also the real fear that you might fall in love again. The brittleness that comes from self-protection is not attractive. It's all too easy for heartbroken girls, nursing glasses of white wine, to get into the habit of telling endless stories against men – I did this myself, but without the drink I could fight against the urge to pick the low-hanging fruit from the lemon tree of bitter jokes.

Three months later, however, I slipped off the wagon. Sallie had taken me to one side at a wake after a funeral.

'It's not that you're not good fun when you're not drinking,' she said, taking two glasses from a passing tray and handing me one. 'It's just that I can't stand the idea of you never drinking again.'

She had a point. I'd begun drinking with enthusiasm after Robert had left. For the first six months, my system was flooded with adrenalin, which cushioned the negative effects of the booze, but as the months passed, although I was rarely drunk, being continuously topped up drained me of self-esteem and, sometimes, of self-control.

After I stepped over that 'going sober' line and called it a day, with no particular period in mind, I became calmer, more focused and energised. I drank a glass at the funeral, but by this time my frame of mind was stronger and I could stop after one or two. Chilled Chablis has always been my weakness, but now, when I'm pulling the cork on a fresh bottle, I hear Shelagh's Scottish wisdom ringing in my ears: 'Ness, without a little self-denial, nothing has a value.' She had a point.

My confidence was beginning to return, if somewhat slowly. Having reluctantly accepted an invitation to a wedding in Kent, I found myself seated next to the groom's brother. The groom's very handsome brother. 'He's bound to be married,' I said to myself as we tucked into the first course. Talking came easily while candles flickered in the marquee. His seven-year-old daughter came and sat on her father's knee, wrapping her arms around his neck and staking out a claim to his attention.

'Of course he's bloody married,' I thought, my heart sinking. But then he told me his wife had recently left him. An hour later we were kissing behind the marquee alongside a gaggle of snogging teenagers. The following week, he called and suggested we meet at Claridge's for a drink.

My girlfriends were all aligned in their advice. 'Play it cool, Vanessa. Don't let him know how much you like him!'

'I promise I won't blow it this time,' I replied.

I walked into the bar, sat down opposite him and he ordered us a drink. We stopped to look at each other. Without thinking, I said, 'My God, you're beautiful.'

He suggested we take a room upstairs immediately – this wasn't quite going to plan. Luckily, I was able to report back to my friends that I'd had to fulfil a previous commitment and go to another dinner.

We did meet up subsequently though, without telling a soul. I'd go to his flat, where we would talk and make love under the stern gaze of his ancestral portraits. Then we'd lie together, our heads propped up at each end of the bed with our legs entangled, and talk some more, both of us grieving the loss of our previous partners, our innocence and our family expectations. When we made love, he would flare his nostrils like a thoroughbred stallion.

Rich and joyous memories were beginning to obscure the wretched ones – it was time to gather the reins a little tighter.

The millennium was drawing to a close. I felt the weight of its significance and was excited by the zeros in 2000 and losing the '19'. The potential new leaf to turn over was massive, with the slate wiped clean and the canvas primed. With the children all at school or nursery, I had time to work for the first time in years. I cut out a headline from the *Guardian* and stuck it on my fridge: 'GIVE UP MEN AND TAKE UP THINKING INSTEAD.'

I first had an inkling of the importance of the looming millennium in 1990, when I was invited by John Whitney to take part in a brainstorm at the Royal Society, investigating how the UK should celebrate this monumental moment in history. About thirty of us, mostly from the arts, spent a day dreaming up big ideas. The Millennium Commission, funded by the National Lottery, was going to hand out enormous grants, but how should they be spent?

Nearly a decade later, we were seeing the fruits of all that creative thinking. Rather than squandering the money, much of it was allocated to capital projects. Every museum and sports organisation in the country had applied for grants to build or refurbish galleries and stadiums. Much of the country was encased in scaffolding, ready for the big unveiling in 2000.

Nick Serota, the director of the Tate Gallery, had asked if I would help fundraise for Tate Modern, the vast new gallery planned for the redundant power station on the South Bank. As soon as he showed me the hanger-like space of the old turbine hall, the thrum of engines still pulsating through the building,

I sensed the excitement that this project could bring to London. To gather support for the gallery was as easy as falling off a log and I'd soon introduced Michael Bloomberg and Peter Simon to the project, both of whom went on to become major supporters.

Another project I became involved with was the Tabernacle, a community centre in the heart of Notting Hill. This quirky Victorian temple had recently been taken over by a charismatic, energetic former teacher called Gill Fitzhugh, who asked me to be a board member during their lottery application and refurbishment. The Tab was essentially a police no-go area – drug dealing was rife and the risk of violence ever present. Gill, standing all of five feet tall, set about cleaning the place up. She told me that the first dealer she'd approached had thrown her off balance somewhat. 'From now on,' she'd told him in her most teacherly manner, 'the Tabernacle is going to be a drug-free zone. Would you leave now, please?'

The man dug his heels in. 'No, I will not leave,' he yelled. 'Because I'm not a fucking drug dealer – I'm a fucking burglar!'

The transformation of the Tab into the thriving community centre it is today was largely due to Gill's courage and tenacity, as well as her ability to love and smile. Once the building work was finished, I interviewed a number of candidates for the post of running the gallery space. Peter Simon, who had made his fortune from the fashion chain Monsoon, generously sponsored the director's salary. Kate MacGarry was the clear choice and went on to hold some remarkable exhibitions, including the then-unknown Yinka Shonibare. Kate's eye was second to none. I loved her energy, and her enthusiasm reminded me of when I first started my gallery fifteen years previously. After a couple of years running the gallery at the Tabernacle, Kate told me she had found an East End space of her own, and I was happy to help put together a consortium of like-minded people to support her. Her gallery, with its close-knit stable of artists, has continued to thrive to this day.

I also joined the board of the North Kensington Amenity Trust, an organisation set up to manage the twenty-five acres of land

and buildings underneath what is known as 'the Westway' to those living under it and 'the M40' to those driving over it. The trust managed community centres, skate parks, offices of not-for-profit organisations, nightclubs, cafes, a riding stables, a travellers' caravan site, gyms, workshops, shops and parks. The meetings, though long and sometimes contentious, were never dull. My parents' conviction that engaging in civic life was an obligation and not an option enriched my life, as well as providing me the satisfaction that I was doing the right thing.

Prue O'Day and I have remained firm friends ever since our Portobello Arts Festival days. On 1 May 1999, while on an early-morning walk together, we had the idea of inviting sixteen people to pool some money over a five-year period, which we would use to put together an art collection on their behalf. Having owned galleries ourselves, we understood how difficult it was to engage new collectors and thought that choosing people with no previous interest in art would make the challenge especially rewarding. It was a dazzling May day, and everyone we invited to join, whether strangers at a lunch party or friends on the school run, said yes.

The Wonderful Fund was a joy. Aware of our responsibility to our collectors, Prue, who was by now a respected art adviser, and I scoured the art fairs in New York, Basel and London. We also visited as many exhibitions as we could and held talks with our group to discuss their purchases. In contemporary art terms, our resources, at just over £50,000 per year, were meagre; the thrill was in the challenge of buying work before the artists became internationally recognised. Tracey Emin, Antony Gormley, Wolfgang Tillmans and Michael Craig-Martin graciously came to give talks at dinners for the group at my London home. The collectors didn't know their luck and nor did our children – by sitting in on the talks, our daughter Florence soaked up extraordinary insights into the artist's mind as if she was being read a bedtime story.

The Wonderful Fund was, however, misnamed – though it was indeed wonderful, it was never intended to be a fund but was rather an exercise to provide a snapshot of the emerging artists of the millennium. After the collection had been shown, first at the Marrakech Biennale and then at the opening exhibition of the newly refurbished Pallant House Gallery in Chichester, the 120 works were distributed among those involved through a combination of a silent auction and pulling straws. Everyone received their initial investment back, as well as a number of works of their choice.

My friends continued to be endlessly welcoming in the two years after Robert left home. I was aware that it was quite an ask to have all five of us to stay for weekends, but I had no intention of buying a house in the country myself. Then, one Saturday in the spring of 1999, I saw a photo of a Sussex farmhouse, surrounded with fields stretching down to the sea, that was coming onto the market. The Bannisters encouraged me to go and view the house immediately. Then I made the mistake of calling Mum and Dad, who'd moved into an old manor house in West Wittering to be near Lindy and her gang, a mere mile or two from this property.

We all met up. It was a ridiculously pretty day, with blue skies, skiddy clouds and a gentle breeze. The birds were singing and the daffodils were dancing. The house itself was perfect, modest in scale but with plenty of bedrooms, rambling outbuildings and room for improvement so I could make it my own. There was absolutely nothing that I could find fault with. I had no excuses to give.

Mum and Dad turned on me as the agent drove back down the long drive. 'Ness, you've got to put in an offer today,' said Mum, while Dad chuckled but said nothing. He too was desperate for us to move close by, but Mum's pressure was enough. I was but a lamb to the slaughter in the face of her enthusiasm and resistance was futile.

'I'm not sure I could cope with the responsibility of such a large piece of land.'

'Don't be so namby-pamby – of course you can cope,' Mum replied exasperatedly, as if worrying about borrowing a shedload of money and taking on a working farm was ridiculous.

'Let's think this through,' she said, barely containing her panic. 'It's going to go, Ness. It's going to go, unless you buy it today.

Call the agent now, saying you'll offer the asking price if they take it off the market immediately.'

I looked at Dad who gave a devilish grin, shrugged his shoulders and said nothing.

'Mummy, I can't do that.' I smiled at her, hoping she would understand.

'Oh yes you can – just have courage, Nessie, courage.'

* * *

The children and I all camped in the one-bedroomed farm office while the building works on the main house were completed. The novelty of one-room living was heaven; they'd run around on the open rafters while I'd sit nervously below, wondering if I could catch them if they fell. We were a gang and the farm was to become our place of play and creativity. Inspired by Charleston Farmhouse, the cottage rented and decorated by Vanessa Bell and Duncan Grant, the kids chose bright colours for the walls, which we decorated with wild patterns. Beezy Bailey, one of the South African artists I'd shown in my gallery, came to stay for a week and, helped by Caragh Thuring and Luke Gottelier, constructed outlandish sculptures on the rooftops.

My fortieth birthday was fast approaching, and I was planning to plant a wood to mark the new millennium, our fresh start, my new decade and above all, to celebrate friendship. Anyone coming to the party was asked to buy a sapling or two from my list, and the eccentric garden designer Ivan Hicks had come up with a planting plan that was part-wood, part-maze. It featured avenues of trees spiralling out from a central pond, a question mark of hazel, circles of yew, towering Lombardy poplars, a spiral of heritage apple trees, entwined aspens, hedges of field maple and copses of evergreen oak.

A decade later, when I was planning another wood for my fiftieth birthday, the issues of food shortages and climate change had come to the fore and this time it felt imperative to plant an orchard, of fruit and nut-producing trees. What a difference a decade makes.

Overwhelming sadness would still catch me unawares, a sickening, all-encompassing grief that I couldn't throw off, however much as I battled against it. I latched on to simple platitudes such as, 'accept and be free', 'concentrate on the positive' and 'think of others, not yourself', and would repeat them to myself in the hope of keeping depression at bay. Each night before turning in, I would creep into the children's rooms and kiss each sleeping beauty and remind myself not only of my responsibility but of my good fortune.

Until Robert returned from climbing mountains and gallivanting around Africa, the children were with me most of the time. As every parent knows, your days are full of the judgments of Solomon: when to crack down on bad behaviour and when to turn a blind eye, when to set boundaries, when to be charmed and when to stand firm. I fell back on my own upbringing again and again, and realised that I'd often use exactly the same language as Mum had.

The children were stricter with themselves than I was. Rather than enforce a curfew, I would say, 'What time do you think you should come back from playing with Freddie?' They would inevitably set a reasonable hour and stick to it.

On one occasion, after some misunderstanding or another, I sat them in a row on the sofa and hesitated, not having a clue what to say. They nervously waited for a ticking off, their feet dangling and hands on laps. 'OK,' I said, 'what would you do if you were a mummy in this situation?' They worked it out between themselves there and then. When it felt like I was losing control, rather than start raising my voice if they didn't do as I asked, I'd threaten to sing outside the gates when I came to pick them up from school. And there was one occasion when one of my sons had a friend to stay and things became rowdy after lights out. I stormed into their bedroom, wearing just a pair of knickers. I've never seen boys dive under the covers so quickly. Gold-standard parenting!

Pidge Freud invited me to dinner on one of my feeling-sorry-for-myself days. I'd been tempted to cry off. Pidge is a notoriously good cook who takes pleasure in putting people together, as well as feeding them. It was all very 'Notting Hill' – Harry and Lucy Enfield, Caroline and Paul Weiland and an unfamiliar face, a man called Howell James. Pidge had recently been left by her husband Matthew Freud and Howell's partner had run off with Peter Mandelson; the three of us sat at one end of the table, licking our wounds.

I adored Howell from that day on – it was as if this extraordinary man had dropped into my life from heaven. I was dreading another summer holiday without the children, and when I told him about my plans to go to the Hamptons in the US and visit various high-maintenance acquaintances from the art world, he intervened. 'Oh darling,' he said, 'You don't want to do that! Come to Italy with me and my friends – we'll look after you.'

So I did, spending two weeks with Howell, four other gay men and a lesbian couple. The group was a revelation, with their heightened sensitivity and respect of each other's feelings, their grace in listening to stories right to the end and their appreciation of clothes, culture and style. In their company I was not a childless mother or a divorcee – I was just me. Their humour was glorious, too. On the beach one day I nudged one of the boys and pointed out a topless young goddess gracefully oiling her limbs while standing in a brightly painted fishing boat.

'Look at that beauty,' I said, mesmerised.

'I know,' he said, turning back to his book. 'I noticed that boat yesterday.'

Howell was enjoying an illustrious career. He had started at Capital Radio and then worked as John Major's private secretary before becoming head of communications at the BBC. At this time, he was a partner in a PR company called Brown Lloyd James, and as with Shelagh, I marvelled that someone like him would want to be my friend. His take on life lifted my spirits and his faith in me gave me confidence.

The summer of 1999 was coming to an end – Robert and I had survived our first two years of separation. James and Annabel Dearden invited me to their house in Chipping Norton for the christening of their daughter, and at the end of the day Annabel came to wave me off.

'Who was that beautiful godfather?' I inquired as I climbed into my Mini. 'The guy with the blond hair and serene manner.'

'Oh, silly me,' she wailed, brushing her unruly hair from her face. 'That's H. He's single, and I didn't introduce you – he's the sweetest, and I mean the *sweetest*, man on the planet.' She called me the next day. 'OK darling, I've organised a dinner so you two can meet. He's only in the UK until Friday, so it's this Wednesday at the Ledbury – 8'o clock.'

While I was getting dressed for the dinner, Flo came up to my bedroom. 'Please don't go out Mummy,' she said quietly. 'I'm starting at my new school tomorrow and I'm scared – I need you here tonight.'

My heart sank. 'Come on, Flo – I promise you'll be ok. I'm only going around the corner for supper, and I've got a mobile phone now, so you can call me if you really, really need me.' Not the gold-standard parent now, but I was keen.

Six of us were gathered around the table. Annabel subtly sat H. beside me. I took a quick glance and confirmed that he was just as gorgeous as I'd thought at the christening. We began talking, and as he stretched across me to reach for a menu I swear I felt him run his index finger down my naked arm. Wow.

Diddle de do, diddle de do, my mobile rang in my bag. I answered it with a sinking heart. 'Ok, Floey, I'm on my way home now.'

I rang Annabel the next morning and came straight to the point, knowing H. was leaving town the next day. 'I really like him,' I told her.

'Ness, he's quite famous – I can't just give you his number.'

'Balls to that, but I suppose you're right. Could you call him and give him my number?'

She laughed. 'OK – just for you.'

H. rang me later, and we had a drink that night, I looked across the table into his eyes and wanted to dive into them there and then. When he next rang from LA, to say that he was returning to the UK the following week, I suggested he came down to the farm. The kids were with Robert and I gave strict instructions to Lindy, Mum and Dad to stay away. He was the epitome of West Coast cool. He'd been a guitarist in a rock band and, like many artists, seemed to have a layer of skin missing, leaving him sensitive to every detail. The late-September light gave the weekend a golden glow as we walked along the beach, ate in cafés and, come the evening, lay on the sofa and stared into the crackling fire.

We drove up to London and I dropped him off at his flat on the Chelsea Embankment without so much as a goodbye peck on the cheek. He didn't suggest a drink that night, leaving me with an intense yearning to see him again. He called the following day and invited me for a drink in the Surprise, his local pub. We sat looking at each other and barely talking – I wanted to touch him so badly. As the barman rang the bell for last orders, H. noticed a copy of the *Evening Standard* on the table next to ours. 'MILLENNIUM WHEEL STANDS PROUD' read a headline. 'Shall we go and see it?' he said.

We drove to the South Bank. I cut the car engine and we walked arm in arm, both in awe of the wheel looming above us. Then he kissed me, and I kissed him and we kissed each other, and then he said, 'Have you seen the new Globe theatre?'

'No,' I replied.

'Let's go,' he said.

We drove east along the river, parked behind the ghostly power station that would soon become Tate Modern and walked down towards the water. It was very late. A light breeze was rippling off the river. H. held me tight under his arm as we neared the imposing wrought iron gates of the Globe. We peered in. I could feel H.'s hand run down my back and test the texture of my short silk skirt between his fingers. I turned around and he smiled. I smiled back, as his hands drifted down to touch my naked thighs and yes, right there, out in the open, overlooked by the glowing dome of St Paul's, with my back against the gates, we made slow, sweet love.

PART FOUR

1999–2018

1

THE ROSE CITY

The last days of the twentieth century and the first days of the twenty-first were certainly memorable. I was finally coming to terms with being separated and in the days leading up to Christmas, I'd gone to stay with H. in LA. We'd driven up Route 101 to see friends in Carmel and then spent a couple of dreamy nights at the Post Ranch Inn, before saying a sad farewell on Christmas Eve. On hearing that I was going to be spending Christmas Day alone, Peter Gabriel and his wife Meabh invited me to join them, along with Peter's daughters and charming father, for lunch at the Hempel Hotel. By the end of the meal, half the restaurant had gathered around our table and was having an animated discussion about what the next millennium held in store. I hadn't realised how much fun you can have when you stray away from the traditional path.

That night I drove to the Dewars before going on for a Boxing Day lunch with the Deardens and their eclectic group of guests and catching a flight to Johannesburg where I met up with the children – they'd spent Christmas with Robert in Kenya. We then flew north to join Mum and Dad at Richard's safari lodge, Ulusaba. The only other guests were a family from Hamburg and we toasted the New Year together, our elderly parents arm-in-arm, all of us aware that less than sixty years earlier they were expected to be mortal enemies.

There was time for reflection, and time to talk, as we sat around campfires: the nights were alive with singing frogs and growling cats, and with crickets rasping out their African rhythm.

'Oh Dad, I feel so fortunate,' I said, giving the fire a poke. 'I'm so grateful to you for having me. I just don't know what I've done to deserve this ridiculous life.'

Dad purred beside me, taking another sip of his gin.

'I feel I should be doing more, giving back in some way,' I continued, 'but I'm not sure how to go about it.'

'Ah, darling,' Dad said, touching my cheek with his now-shaky finger, 'don't worry too much about it – every stage in life has its decade.' He paused, considering his words carefully. 'Right now, your priority is to make a nest for your children and provide them with the security to launch themselves off when they grow up. Then you can set about making a difference in the world.'

Dad was right, as ever, but I hadn't realised just how soon my time to make a difference would arrive.

Navin and the Bannisters also felt the weight of the millennium's importance, and initiated the idea of an annual Easter Pilgrimage. Our three families, plus Howell, gathered in Petersfield on Good Friday morning. We walked in torrential rain along the South Downs Way, resting over a pub lunch and then stopping in the late afternoon to re-enact Christ's passion under the dripping branches of an ancient oak. Exhausted and soaked to the skin, we arrived at Winchester Cathedral just in time for evensong. The priest welcomed our bedraggled band of pilgrims, including our golden retriever Millie, who, overwhelmed by the moment, couldn't stop herself from howling along with the angelic choir.

The following day we trudged on from Winchester towards Salisbury, keeping the cathedral's majestic spire in sight for the entire afternoon. Then came a Saturday evening feast and, the following morning we went to the Easter Sunday cathedral service. Thus began an annual gathering and since 2000 we've hiked along many of the great pilgrimage routes in England and Wales, mostly in spring sunshine. As with our annual Necker holidays, the group photographs taken every year outside a cathedral, and often with a beaming bishop at our centre, give us the opportunity to view the past as if watching a stop-motion film: the children, at first so young, grow taller; us adults, once strong, increasingly showing signs of age, with the odd knee brace or hiking stick creeping in.

* * *

I'd been dreading receiving this phone call from Shelagh and when I did, it winded me like a kick in the stomach. 'Don't you dare cry, Ness,' she said.

'I won't, I promise,' I said, as I crouched in the pantry behind the kitchen, away from the children, trying to compose myself. 'Where has it come back?'

'It's in my lungs this time,' said Shelagh. 'I start chemo tomorrow.'

'Oh fucking fuck shit wank,' I said, instead of crying.

We were already marking every moment as if it was imbued with a special significance, but now that Shelagh's cancer was on the march, we upped the ante on every front. Voyage, conveniently located next to the Royal Marsden Hospital, was one of our favourite clothes shops, and as proof that she was going to beat her disease, Shelagh would buy a new dress before every chemo session. The Bannister family bought Great Orchard near Petworth, an Arts and Crafts house complete with sunken garden and rolling views. Shelagh set about decorating it with her usual style, balancing optimism about her future with a desire to leave a fitting legacy. Every walk we took, every picnic we planned and every meal we ate was undertaken with awareness and gratitude.

In the summer of 2001, we rented a floor of a palazzo overlooking the Accademia Bridge in Venice. Shelagh, then in the middle of chemo, was determined not to let the children feel any hint of her suffering and her bravery made her plight all the more painful to witness. The Bannisters and I were joined by all our children, Howell, a new friend called Stefan van Raay, the delightful Dutch director of the Pallant House Gallery, and Robert.

Writing this now, I can't recall discussing Robert joining us on a holiday, and nor do I remember talking about the fact that there weren't enough bedrooms and that we would have to share. However, I do remember the holiday. The early-morning walks, with Stefan guiding us around notable churches and their masterpieces. Robert hiring a Riva and a driver, and taking the glamorous boat to Murano, where Shelagh and I bought eye-wateringly expensive sets of wine glasses, and to the Lido, where the film festival was taking place. I remember going to the Frette linen shop, where Shelagh bought a set of fine linens to adorn her new bed. She had begun to plan her end as she had lived – beautifully.

Over the years, I've grappled with the question of why I allowed Robert to re-enter our lives. To justify his destruction of our family life, he'd had to focus only on the negatives of my character, viewing everything I said through a dark prism. Seeing myself through his eyes had taken its toll on my confidence; choosing to step back into his gaze was verging on the suicidal.

His departure five years earlier had profoundly unsettled our family. We were just beginning to thrive again, the children accepting their dual lives and enjoying undivided attention from each of us, and I'd managed to use my time away from them positively, reading, working, enriching friendships, travelling and pursuing ideas.

I'd always accepted that outside forces had played a major role in our separation, while also acknowledging that we hadn't made each other really happy for years. I liked to remember the good times – Robert's brilliant mind and the fun of being with someone who gave his energy to everything. As a family, we Bransons tend to forget anything bad that's happened to us, and my father's Quaker philosophy – 'believe in the goodness of others' – echoed in my subconscious.

I relished my trips to LA to visit H., and it thrilled me to know he came to London regularly. Our relationship could hardly be described as having a future – our focus was on our own growing families – but the time we spent together was fulfilling and, at that time, suited us both brilliantly.

Deep down in my heart I knew that the children would be better off if Robert and I were united as parents during their teenage years, and it's impossible to separate your own well-being from your children's. Robert missed home, the family and the comfort of knowing he was doing the right thing. I missed all these things too, but I also missed Robert, the Robert I still believed in and loved. On returning home from Venice, he sort of just moved in. I'm not sure how it happened, but one explanation that I can muster is that our family complications paled into insignificance in the face of Shelagh's suffering. I also held onto the belief that our family was built with strong enough foundations to give us a chance of rebuilding a meaningful life together.

We briefly discussed this as representing a new beginning. I so wanted to feel love from him again and so wanted to feel part of a committed couple. To draw a line under our old marriage, we took the Central Line from Notting Hill to the City for an appointment with our divorce lawyers. After Robert had left in 1996, we got as far as signing a decree nisi; now, five years later, we both signed the decree absolute, the final piece of paperwork that ended our old, contaminated marriage.

'I wish all our divorcing couples came in looking so happy and in love,' said the young lawyer, as Robert and I hugged each other when the paperwork was complete.

Two days after Robert moved back in, we drove thirteen-year-old Noah down the M4 to begin his first term at Marlborough College in Wiltshire. Both Robert and Humphrey had gone there, and Noah was looking forward to starting his new chapter. Robert and I were still in a state of shock at finding ourselves back living together, and delivering our firstborn to boarding school make things feel even stranger. On finding Noah's dorm, it became apparent that I hadn't read the equipment list properly and had failed to pack any linen. Noah's roommate was Jack Whitehall, who would later entertain us all with his stand-up and acting career. His mother Hilary, who was efficient and incredibly kind, told us what we needed and Robert went into town to buy it. Then, having made up Noah's bed, we said our strained goodbyes, memories of our own first days at boarding school catching in our throats. Walking away down the corridor, we could hear the sound of Noah and his new friend Jack's hysterical giggling. He was going to be fine.

On the way back to London we stopped for fuel and Robert filled our diesel car up with petrol. A truck towed us to a garage and we sat in a dimly lit Indian restaurant next door for two silent hours, waiting for them to pump out the tank before we could set off for home again.

Three days later, the planes struck the Twin Towers. Along with the rest of the world, I watched the towers collapse over and over again, mesmerised by the visual power of the attack and realising that the world was never going to be the same again.

From the day of Robert's return, we were clearly living on parallel tracks. I was yearning to rebuild trust, security and love, while he was agitated and looking for any reason not to spend time at home. If I had been wiser back then, I would have responded differently, but he still felt the need to justify leaving his young family five years previously, which began to chip away at my confidence. Looking back now, the answer to our conflict was right in front of our eyes. Since 1990 and Nelson Mandela's release from prison, we'd witnessed the power of the Truth and Reconciliation Committee to relieve the suffering of perpetrators and victims, enabling them to live in harmony after the most dreadful atrocities. Clearly our impasse was on a different scale altogether, but Archbishop Desmond Tutu understood that compassion, apology and forgiveness are required to heal and free the soul.

Robert seemed unable to acknowledge the suffering that his actions had inflicted on us, and I in turn was too scared to ask him how he felt. He seemed to translate all the emotions that had been thrown up over the previous five years – shame, disappointment, entrapment and frustration – into resentment. At times it felt like he'd returned home to torture me with his unhappiness, for to live with someone you are unable to love is an act of indescribable cruelty.

And of course, the elephant in the room was Becky. The mere thought of her would make my head swim and adrenalin would pump through my veins, the lioness in me protecting my cubs from outside predators. I feared that by mentioning her name I would be making her real and inviting her to enter our lives once more. But the truth was that by not addressing that elephant, it grew larger by the day.

I believed that I could tough it out, but instead of confronting our misery I stuck to my mantra, 'accept and be free.' Robert was unable to hold me close and offer any intimate kindness or say anything that would boost my self-esteem. He knew in his heart why he'd left home, and seeing myself reflected in those cold eyes dragged me even lower. He kept asking me to give him time, but as the weeks passed, I became even more hurt, depressed and insecure.

The boys seemed to be in their own worlds and were able to take it in their stride; but Flo was angry. 'Daddy can't just leave home when I'm seven and return when I'm eleven without saying a word!' she said.

'Just give him time, Flo,' I replied weakly. Our friends and family were overjoyed to see us living as a family, so we had little option but to play along.

* * *

In the mid-nineties, Richard had attempted to circumnavigate the globe in a hot air balloon – an audacious plan requiring a vast technical team and optimal weather conditions. The experts selected Marrakech as the perfect launch site because it had still air at ground level and a powerful jet stream in the atmosphere above. For three years running, Richard, his two co-pilots, technical team and an entourage of about two hundred friends, family and press went there for a launch. These were the days before mass tourism arrived in Morocco, and the government saw to it that we were all treated like gods. The heady mix of the mystery of Marrakech and the excitement around the project was intoxicating, and I formed lasting friendships with people who opened up their incredible city to me. Richard's balloon failed to make it around the globe in the end, but I'd been introduced to a world of new opportunities.

The city that had so captivated my heart back in 1983 was about to take over my soul. In 2002, while Robert was running the Marathon des Sables through the Sahara Desert, Howell and I organised a riding expedition to the Atlas Mountains with the de Klees and the Bannisters. Mum and Dad joined us in the evenings as we sat around our campfires.

'Oh my goodness, I feel good in this country,' I said, quaffing a glass of surprisingly good Saharan rose as we lay on the rug-strewn ground after a long day in the saddle.

'We should buy a riad together,' suggested Howell, out of the blue. 'Just a little two-bedroomed lock up somewhere in the medina,' he added hastily, managing my expectations. I said nothing, but the following day, while riding over the grassy plains, I began dreaming about Howell's idea. I wanted to reinforce our friendship, but there was another, deeper reason for investing in Morocco: since 9/11 and the subsequent invasion of Afghanistan, there had been a small but noticeable change in Western attitudes towards the Arab world and I felt an urge to swim against that ugly tide.

The following day, we were having lunch with our Moroccan friend Abel Damoussi when Howell asked him if he knew of any small riads that might be available to buy. Abel's eyes lit up – of *course* he did. With our fantasy suddenly becoming a possibility, I began to get cold feet, while Mum poured me another glass of wine. 'Nessie, how many times have I told you? Don't be such a spoilsport!' And with that, we traipsed off to check out what Abel had up his sleeve.

None of the riads we saw felt quite right. A month later, Howell returned to Marrakech for a friend's birthday party and spent a happy afternoon speeding down alleys on a scooter with his arms around the waist of a young estate agent, and we both returned a few weeks later to view his shortlist. But again, none of the riads felt quite right. The light was dimming and. Adil Inti, the agent, was looking nervous; we'd only flown out for the day and were due to leave the next morning.

'There is one more,' he said. 'It's a little beyond your budget, I'm afraid, but it may be worth a look.'

'Nothing ventured,' said Howell, as he dodged an ageing donkey plodding its way home.

Crouching through a battered door-within-a-door, we groped our way down a long, dark corridor, through arches and over numerous thresholds to a dimly lit courtyard. There, before us, was a sight to behold: an orange tree surrounded by elegant colonnades and original mashrabiya windows. The ancient building was dissolving into dust. I shot a hand to my mouth to stop myself screaming in excitement.

'I love it, Howell,' I whispered, grabbing him by the arm. 'It's the one.'

Adil took us up a crumbling staircase to the terrace. Lit only by his cigarette lighter, there were sheer drops where steps were missing, but the scene once we reached the top was worth risking our lives for. The sun had dropped behind the Atlas Mountains, throwing them into silhouette and there, just a hundred metres away, was the Koutoubia, the thirteenth-century minaret and symbol of Moroccan spirituality, lit up in all its glory. The muezzin's call to prayer was echoing over the rooftops and the moon was rising.

It was now too dark to see the size of the riad and the proportions of the rooms we could see indicated that it was considerably larger than what we'd set out to buy. But buying it was not a rational decision – this was love. We offered the owners the asking price there and then; they agreed and we shook hands.

We asked Adil if he thought refurbishment was feasible. 'It is important to remember one thing about Morocco,' he said, his eyes twinkling. 'In Morocco, anything is possible.' He paused for a while, as we sighed in relief before adding, 'But nothing is certain.' This was a sentiment that has made us laugh and grind our teeth in frustration in equal measure over the last two decades.

On 25 July 2002, we found ourselves in the office of a *notaire* and surrounded by three professional men and their weeping wives, illiterate women who signed the papers with their thumbprints. It was while we were signing the papers that the *notaire* read from the deeds: 'Here we have the clean title deeds for number five, Derb Moulay Ben Hessian Cinq.' Howell and I nodded. The *notaire* then took a deep breath and went on, 'and numbers six, seven and eight.'

Only then did we learn that, rather than just buying the one house, we had also bought a fair proportion of the street. That night we celebrated our folly at Le Comptoir with fellow Marrakech adventurers Sarah and Christopher Hodsoll, drinking freely while we watched belly dancers, their hips trembling and fleshy tummies rolling. Before weaving our way back through the medina, we stopped outside our new front door and took a mound of wonky photos of ourselves, looking a little surprised.

There's magic in the air in Marrakech and if the energy is right, everything you need is dropped before you. Before we left the following day, nursing thumping heads and asking ourselves

'What on earth have we done?', 'How on earth are we going to restore this old palace?' and 'Are we insane?', Abel told us to go to the La Renaissance cafe in Gueliz, the city's new town, to meet Said Jabaoui, the former driver of the mayor of Marrakech, who agreed to become our caretaker while we pondered our predicament. An hour later we were on a flight back to London.

* * *

That Marrakech magic followed me everywhere I went – exceptional people appeared in my life, regardless of what country I was in. I was grumpy with Robert for agreeing to fly us all to Kenya for the October half-term, feeling that we needed some time at home to try and knit our family back into shape. To compound my irritation, Eric, a parent from school who had organised the trip, cried off at the last minute and we ended up staying on our own in Hippo Point, a grand mock-Tudor mansion on the banks of Lake Naivasha. But joy of joys, it turned out that the elegant and talented couple who ran the estate were looking for a new challenge.

'Do you fancy a year in Marrakech?' I asked, on hearing that they had just handed in their notice.

'Yes,' they said, without skipping a beat. Frederic and Viviana never asked what their salary would be, and we never checked their references – we simply trusted the gods of the project, and they smiled down on us.

Frederic, with his Gallic shrug and athletic presence, arrived in Marrakech in February 2003, three weeks before the Anglo-American invasion of Iraq. He set to work immediately and hired a team of builders to strip the building down before we started on the rebuild. At every opportunity, Howell and I would fly out to see what was happening.

And thus began the most rewarding creative partnership I have ever experienced. Howell, Frederic and I, often joined by Viviana, complemented each other's strengths, encouraged each other's more outlandish design ideas and trusted each other's instincts entirely. During the first part of the restoration,

I learned an enormous amount about design and, this being Morocco, about decoration too. We trusted Frederic implicitly as he set to work, bracing the thick exterior walls, digging an underground water catchment chamber, insulating, wiring and plumbing. We sent out money on a monthly basis, never doubting that it was being well spent. By the end of 2003, just ten months later, it was time to decorate the six bedrooms and buy furniture for the dining room, sofas for the mini cinema and books for the library. Compensating for my loveless existence at home, I poured my heart and soul into El Fenn and, as an act of faith in the project, shipped out seven paintings from my collection, including a sensual, two-metre-high masterpiece by William Kentridge, a large Terry Frost canvas of rich oranges and reds and a geometric painting by Bridget Riley that Robert had given me many Valentine's Days ago.

Moroccan artisans are famous for the quality of their work. Plaster was chiselled into decorative friezes and tiny ceramic briquettes known as zellige formed intricate patterns around doorways and over fireplaces. The walls were finished in tadelakt, a lime plaster mixed with pigments and then polished with stones, and the ceilings were made of stucco or hand-carved wood. Frederic inlaid camel bone in the walls in one room and brass-coloured balls in another. We designed the suites with romance in mind, with a bath next to a fireplace, rough-stitched leather floors, double showers, candles and incense.

Over our years of travelling together, we'd stayed in a number of hotels and loved playing the 'imagine this was your hotel' game. 'Deary me,' Howell would say, 'just *look* at that wallpaper.'

'What would you do if this was your hotel?' I'd reply. And then we'd be off.

At every stage of the refurbishment, when we came to decide whether we should we get the best-quality showers, kitchen or whatever else, our decision was always 'yes'. It was only as the expenses began ratcheting up that we realised that rather than offering the entire riad as a holiday let, we would have to rent the rooms out individually. Howell and I had become accidental hoteliers.

During El Fenn's refurbishment, we pored over books, taking inspiration from St Paul's Cathedral, Hagia Sophia in Istanbul, and closer to home, from the Jardin Majorelle in Marrakech and the Berber dwellings in the Atlas Mountains. In principle, we only used natural materials and, to support the local economy, employed local craftsmen.

Frederic was also a genius, and the excitement of waiting for his weekly crop of photos to appear on my computer screen – agonisingly slowly, in the days of dial-up Internet – was intoxicating.

On 15 March 2003, we welcomed guests to Howell's fiftieth birthday party at El Fenn just as our builders were sweeping the rubble out through the tradesman's entrance. His ninety expectant friends, in blissful ignorance of the previous twenty-four-hour panic, were entertained by fire eaters, snake charmers and Nor, a transgender belly dancer, on our terrace under the Katoubia. I raised a glass to Howell and he raised a glass to us. We'd done it, though we had no idea how ambitious the project was yet to become.

We were indebted to the many people who made El Fenn come to life: to Frederic, but also to our architect Amine Kabbaj, who was to play a key role in the next chapter of my life; to Abel Damoussi, who encouraged us to go for it in the first place; and to the open-hearted Moroccans who welcomed us at every turn.

Our expat friends were always there for us with words of caution and encouragement: the filmmakers Danny Moynihan and Katrine Boorman, and Trevor Hopkins, Kate Fenwick and her partner, the charismatic gangster-turned-sculptor Jimmy Boyle, the Hodsoll family, Stephen Skinner and Carinthia West, who wrote an article on El Fenn for *Harpers & Queen* soon after we opened.

A few months later, while cooking the kids' supper in London, I received a call from Mum, who was staying at El Fenn. 'Nessie, the king is coming to visit,' she said. 'There are security men everywhere!'

'Mum, slow down for a second,' I said. 'Which king are you talking about?'

'The King of Pakistan,' she replied.

'Goodness – is Frederic around?'

It transpired that President Musharraf had flown from Karachi to Marrakech via London for a state meeting, and having read the issue of *Harpers* that featured El Fenn on the way, he had asked the King of Morocco to organise a visit. When he toured El Fenn, Frederic said he took an interest in every detail. 'One day Lahore will become a world-class tourist destination,' he told Frederic, 'and I want El Fenn to be our inspiration.'

Condé Nast Traveller soon picked up on the *Harpers* story and put us on their list of the ten best new hotels in the world. El Fenn was launched.

* * *

In mid-December 2004, I received a call from one of our old neighbours in Midhurst, who had found Humphrey slumped in his favourite armchair. It transpired that he had called his girlfriend Karen to wish her goodnight, taken a sip of tea and then had a heart attack. Along with the immediate family, Karen and a couple of neighbours, a few of our good friends came to the funeral to support Robert and Clare; they included Shelagh and Matthew. I noticed Shelagh staring at Humphrey's coffin. Her fight was continuing, but her hideous disease was gaining on her. Robert's Uncle Tim gave a remarkably honest address, which allowed each of Humphrey's children to mourn him, knowing that their father's demons and their own struggles had been acknowledged.

A fortnight later, Matthew called us at 3 a.m. Shelagh had died, after an agonising ten days of semi-consciousness. I sat up for the rest of the night, relieved that her suffering was over but unable to believe that such a life force could come to an end. Matthew had made sure she died at home, surrounded by scented candles and with her children nearby, her emaciated figure dressed in a starched white nightie and lying between her soft Frette sheets.

My one contribution to Shelagh's funeral was to organise the flowers adorning her coffin. The florists I chose, Wild at Heart, understood exactly what she would have wanted – a cascading mass of creamy blossoms, as if nature had sprinkled them over her. Ken Berry flew in from Los Angeles, Simon Draper from South Africa and Richard and Joan from Necker, and St Luke's Church on Sydney Street in Chelsea was packed with her friends and colleagues. I watched in horror as the coffin was carried up the aisle: no one had thought to remove the cellophane wrapping from the flowers, giving it the look of a roadside car crash memorial. I fixated on those wretched flowers and to this day feel that I let her down. Navin gave a deeply felt, touching address and after the service we all walked across the King's Road to Chelsea Old Town Hall, where we drank a glass or two of Cloudy Bay wine, Shelagh's favourite tipple.

As the day drew to a close, we laid Shelagh to rest in the heart of her beloved South Downs. The children had picked snowdrops on the way into the graveyard at Bignor. I noticed that Florence, not having time to gather her own posy, had picked up a terracotta flowerpot of snowdrops from the back of the hearse. Shelagh's stoic Scottish mother, who was burying the second of her three daughters – for her eldest daughter Mog had also succumbed to this hideous disease – stood silent and tearless beside me. The vicar said a final prayer, wiped his hands on his cassock and nodded to the children, who threw their little posies into the grave.

'Please don't, Flo,' I thought to myself, and I watched as the pot flew in slow motion from her hands, before hitting the wood six feet below with a resounding clunk. Shelagh's sister Lorna and I remained behind to free the flowers of their cellophane at last, before joining the others for a cup of tea at Great Orchard.

2

My Arab Spring

'All my life I've felt on the side of good,' said Dad, as we watched our country slide towards war with Iraq. 'Now I'm not so sure.'

Ever since his posting to Palestine as a young man, he'd had a heartfelt respect for the Arab world and his genuine love for Islamic culture meant that he was thrilled by my investment in Morocco. After watching the horrific images of the bombing of Baghdad in March 2003 and lamenting the likelihood of a successful outcome, he rarely mentioned the war again.

One year later, in early 2004, after hearing George W. Bush saying, 'You're either with us or against us' on Radio 4's *Today* programme, I became agitated and took myself off for a walk around Hyde Park to work through my thoughts. How dare that man invite me to take sides in such a nuanced situation?

While we were rebuilding El Fenn, we'd experienced a country where Muslim spirituality shone through in all aspects of life: charity, acceptance, respect and love. For the American President to insinuate that Islam was the root of all evil was disingenuous, to put it mildly. The US, along with the UK, Poland and Australia, had invaded Iraq in 2003, despite millions of people taking to the streets to protest. Prior to the invasion, Colin Powell had created a plan to rebuild Iraq after the removal of the staunchly secular Saddam Hussein, but the rest of the world watched in disbelief as Donald Rumsfeld instead chose to expunge all Ba'th party officials. Rather than the country transitioning into a civil society, the Americans found themselves presiding over a rapidly disintegrating situation. More horrific images appeared on the news: Daniel Pearl beheaded in his imitation Guantanamo orange jumpsuit, Al-Qaeda filling the power vacuum and years later, the rise of a far more sinister group, ISIS.

Howell had been approached by Alastair Campbell, Tony Blair's communications chief, about joining a group called the Phillis Review that had been formed to review government communications in the wake of the scandal when Jo Moore, a Labour Party special adviser, was caught emailing her department, on the day of the 9/11 attacks, that it was 'a very good day to bury bad news'. The review recommended greater separation between the roles of politically appointed special advisers and civil servants, and Howell was appointed the permanent secretary of government communications. My friend and business partner being at the centre of the governmental decision-making process during such a turbulent period of history was fascinating, if not a little alarming.

Now back to the park. I was stomping along, terrified by the injustices being perpetrated in our name and almost pinging off the tree trunks in my agitation. There must be something I could do to instil confidence in the people I had grown to admire so much. Then it dawned on me: someone should start an arts festival. A festival of quality that would serve a number of purposes, but would primarily provide a platform for debate. The arts have always been a safe place in which to discuss contentious ideas. A contemporary arts festival would also stimulate curiosity by introducing a Moroccan audience to international artists. I began racking my brains as to who should get the festival off the ground – someone with experience, an international voice and a vested interest in the country. Then it struck me – oh lord, that was me! I called my old friend Abel right away. He embraced the idea of a festival immediately and agreed to be my partner. Arts in Marrakech, or AIM, was born.

In November 2005, with the help of Abel's flamboyant assistant Pablo Ganguli and Frederic, we held the first festival. Literary events were held at El Fenn, with writers including Esther Freud, Hanif Kureishi, Hari Kunzru, Mahi Binebine, Rabi Mubarak and Ahmed al-Madini. Anatol Orient did a stunning job of installing the Wonderful Fund Collection in the Musée du Marrakech and the eminent painter from the Casablanca Art School, Mohamed Melehi curated an exhibition of Moroccan art in the Bahia Palace. We held panel discussions, film screenings and candlelit poetry readings in Agafay, Abel's jewel-like riad. I'll never forget the joy of walking through the Jemaa el-Fna alongside Dad who was sitting in the back of a builder's donkey cart lined with Moroccan rugs and cushions, grinning with pride. The rest of the family joined us, as well as friends and artists, including Annie Lennox, Antony Gormley and Vicken Parsons, all full of good ideas of how we should develop the festival further.

And of course, we partied as if tomorrow would never come. The joyous fact about the art world is that socialising is thought to be part of the creative process. Well, over the years we've done a very good job of convincing ourselves that this is the case!

309

* * *

Back in London, we were only just managing to hold our family together. Robert, rather like a schoolboy trying to stop his neighbour copying his homework, seemed to be hiding chunks of his life from me, developing a business in Africa and spending an increasing amount of time away from home. Every time he boarded a plane I harboured the same sense of abandonment I'd felt when he left me five years earlier.

After a particularly hurtful verbal assault from Robert one Sunday morning, I stopped kidding myself that I could tough it out and gave in to a really good weep. A couple of days later I began to feel excessively tired, and by Wednesday I was so exhausted I wasn't able to walk up Portobello Road to Notting Hill. I sat on a doorstep and called my doctor.

'I have no symptoms, no fever and no headache – I can't explain it. I'm knackered to my core,' I said. 'I actually think I'm going to die.'

'Come and see me right away,' he said.

The doctor took one look at me and realised that I wasn't exaggerating. 'Don't you have any pain at all?' he said.

'Well, I do have a stabbing pain under my left clavicle.' Even before I had the X-ray, he told me I had a pneumothorax. My left lung had collapsed.

The lung specialist told me the collapse had probably been precipitated by my heavy weeping, causing a scar from a historic injury to burst the pleural membrane – the memory of the kick from Snowy when I was a teenager came to mind. The operation to fix it, a pleurodesis, was excruciating, and afterward the surgeon said that my lungs were riddled with pleural plaques, 'as if your lungs have been opened up and had candle wax dripped through them'. There was concern that I'd developed mesothelioma, a type of lung cancer caused by inhaling asbestos fibres; again, memories of sawing asbestos to hide the boiler in the Tanyards cellar came flooding back. Between bouts of terror while I waited for the test results, I had some surprisingly sanguine moments. Exhaustion after the operation meant that dying didn't seem like such a bad option; it simply meant no more pain. I also remembered Shelagh and rather than thinking 'why me?' thought 'why not me?'

After learning that I didn't have cancer after all, we planned a family expedition to climb Mont Blanc, which in retrospect was insane. Just seven months later, I found myself bent double trying to climb back up to the Aiguille du Midi, after turning back a few hours earlier without getting to the summit. Robert and I, plus the children, had set off from the Cosmique Hut at 3 a.m., inching our way up the mountain in a trail of head torch beams bouncing off the snow. I was the weak link and was in no way fit enough to make it. After turning back at noon, I was keen to enjoy the day and couldn't understand why our mountain guides kept hurrying us along. The sun was very hot and the snow was slushy underfoot, the hush of the thin mountain air disturbed by nothing more than the occasional electrical cry of a hooded crow.

The following dawn, tucked up under my duvet after the rigors of the previous forty-eight hours, I was woken by the clatter of rescue helicopters delivering stretcher after stretcher to Chamonix Hospital. A sheet of ice had sheered off the mountain and slithered silently down the slope. Twenty-eight climbers were caught on the same torchlit path we'd taken the morning before, killing nine of them.

* * *

Nothing was standing still in Marrakech and El Fenn threw up new challenges every day. One week I received a call from a friendly-sounding Englishman. 'Is that Vanessa?' he asked. 'I had the pleasure of meeting you a few years ago when I was doing a deal with Virgin Books.' He seemed to be attempting to reassure me I could trust him before he dropped his bombshell. 'I've just bought the riad next to you and I'm afraid to say that it transpires that I own the terraces directly above it.'

I let him continue while his words slowly sank in. 'As you know, El Fenn was once part of a massive riad that's been divided up over the years, but I'm afraid the law dictates that the property owner has possession of the terrace directly above their rooms.' I visualised the areas he was talking about – our terraces with the magnificent views of the Koutoubia.

'Oh no you don't,' I said, surprising myself with my conviction. 'Those are our terraces and we'll fight you at every turn to prove it.'

'I see,' he said, somewhat taken aback, before he said a hasty goodbye. Sensing he was about to enter a fight he couldn't win, he withdrew his offer for the riad, but Howell and I had the feeling that the only way to prevent endless legal battles in the future would be to buy the contentious building ourselves.

The very next week, Frederic told me that Mum had taken a shine to the riad on the other side of El Fenn. Now, I love my mother very much, but the prospect of her using El Fenn, with its adoring staff and endless whisky supply, as a glamorous old people's home was going to push our relationship to its limit. My wonderful business partner understood my anxiety. 'Ah well, darling,' laughed Howell. 'We'll just have to buy that riad too!'

Before the collapse of Lehman Brothers in 2008, the world felt awash with money and, with the encouragement of Richard, who explained that a hotel can't be financially viable without at least thirty bedrooms, we borrowed almost two million euros against our London homes and bought the two adjoining properties. Both had at one time been part of the original grand palace, so El Fenn would be complete once more. Frederic began drawing up plans for the development in earnest.

We had a working formula by this time: don't fight the building. We followed the generous spaces already available, which meant twin showers, plunge pools on private terraces, intricate stucco ceilings and elegant colonnades. To finish, we decorated with brightly coloured tadelakt walls, feature fireplaces and retro light fittings. Hand luggage restrictions were less strict back then, so we took out 1950s Sputnik desk lamps and more paintings on each trip: works by David Shrigley, Robin Rhode and Dr Lakra. Each room was different, and each room offered a surprise.

Alan Yentob, the creative director of the BBC and a fellow Notting Hill parent, had become a key supporter of AIM; he generously advised us and introduced us to people for each edition. He was staying at El Fenn while we were embarking on the new refurbishment, part of which had previously been a cavernous mattress workshop. 'You have to put a stage there,' he said, and so the Alan Yentob Stage was built, along with an integral cinema screen.

Years later I was often asked how on earth you start a biennale. The truth is that there was no initial master plan, but by trusting the energy of those with a similar vision, projects tend to take on a life of their own. After two editions of AIM, I spoke to Abdellah Karroum, who was then the only curator of note in Morocco. He had an artists' space called Apartment 22 in Rabat and had also contributed a remarkable show for AIM 2. Abdellah was happy to become the curator for the next festival on two conditions: that we raised the ambition of the event by calling it the Marrakech Biennale and, to prevent Moroccan artists becoming ghettoised, that we show Moroccan artists alongside international greats. I agreed.

Abel was justifiably anxious about fundraising for an arts event of such vision and stepped down. I wonder now if I would have continued had I known about the challenges involved in running a not-for-profit event of this ambition, and particularly one without core funding from the state, but ever the optimist, I pushed on.

The Biennale was evolving; it was still acting as a cultural bridge, but we wanted the content to be world-class. I was supported by a dedicated board who made the event possible with their collective wisdom and fundraising. Whenever I became overwhelmed or demoralised, Curt Marcus, an American board member, would remind me of the vital role the Biennale played in Morocco's development; there was no way I could give up. The king was happy to give us his royal patronage, which opened doors to the mayor's office, who granted us permission to use the city's public spaces and historic buildings. The tourist board welcomed us with open arms, providing airline tickets and helping with hotel rooms. Given time, there was no reason why the Marrakech Biennale shouldn't be judged alongside Venice, Sidney or Sao Paulo. We had a number of unique things going for us: stunning spaces in which to show works, a curious local audience, a workforce of artisans keen to support visiting artists, hundreds of students willing to volunteer and an international arts-savvy public who loved visiting the glorious town. There was nothing to stop us from being ambitious.

For decades Morocco had discouraged independent thinking – young people were bought up not to question their parents, their teachers, their mosque, their king or their god. The nature of good art is that it makes you see the world through different eyes. The current king's father, Hassan II, made artists and writers feel distinctly uncomfortable; King Mohammed VI, on the other hand, is an art enthusiast but has a difficult job bringing the rest of the ruling elite along with him. Communicating the role that the arts play in stimulating innovative thinking and driving the economy forward has been hard enough in the west; in an emerging North African economy, it was always going take time.

Being an outsider has been an advantage, meaning that I don't get bogged down in the local politics that have a tendency to divert people from the goal at hand. The Biennale's artists and curators were sensitive to the environment, and we experienced virtually no censorship. On one occasion, though, I did receive a panicked call from Abel, saying that officials wanted to close the main show down because the artist Faouzi Bensaidi was using a naked, androgynous shop mannequin in his installation; I simply slept on the request, and the problem disappeared.

The next curators we selected, Nadim Samman, a Lebanese–Australian living in London, and Carson Chan, a Chinese–Canadian living in Berlin – life in the art world has no national borders – introduced a rigorous set of core principles and environmental guidelines. To engage a local audience and encourage lasting relationships, we invited artists to come and stay in Marrakech

314

and saw our role as enabling their visions to become a reality. The town's incredible range of craft and engineering capabilities was thrilling for artists – as we know, 'In Morocco anything is possible.'

One of our most magical installations was Alexander Ponomarev's upside-down helicopter and he later constructed a thirty-metre reproduction of the Costa Concordia, the Italian ferry whose captain famously said that he'd accidentally fallen into a life raft rather than stay behind and search for survivors when the vessel ran aground. Ponomarev's boat, stranded like Noah's ark on the top of a hill in the dessert, was the very image of the folly of man. Another much-loved work, by Eric van Hove, was an exact facsimile of a Mercedes car engine, made by forty-two medina-based master craftsmen using bone, leather, metal and silk.

With the help of the British Council, we initiated an internship programme and worked with language students from the desperately underfunded Cadi Ayyad University, formally awarding them certificates at an official ceremony. I still get a thrill whenever I'm stopped in the street by one of these kids and hear how the Biennale gave them the experience and confidence to take interesting jobs.

I scoured my address book and called on old friends and acquaintances to help. We invited Oscar-winning producers, directors and screenwriters including Julian Schnabel, Kevin Macdonald, Eric Fellner and Christopher Hampton to work with students from ESAV, the school of visual arts. Provided they were available, no one on our wish list could resist an invitation to join us.

Over the years, I worked with dozens of driven young people, and their knowledge and technical and language skills, along with their tact, energy and humour, was contagious. It struck me once again that the tougher a challenge is, the deeper the resulting friendships. We relied on help from young volunteers who were grateful for the experience. While most artists were sympathetic to our meagre budgets, two high-profile authors pushed us to our limits.

We received almost daily emails from the PA of one of them. 'A.S. only stays in five-star accommodation,' she insisted. The next day we received an email saying 'A.S. always travels first class, and would you see to it that she flies in the front of the plane?'

I happened to see the author's publisher that night and mentioned her PA's attempt to bankrupt us. 'Don't be taken in by that old trick,' Alexandra replied. 'A.S. hasn't got a PA!'

Jess Bannister, Matthew's daughter who had grown up alongside my children, was that year's co-director. We were taken aback when Jess received a grumpy email from a writer for making the understandable error of booking her flights to and from London, when in fact she lived in Rome. Seconds later, Jess received a second email from the author intended for a friend and detailing an embarrassing medical complaint. As quick as a flash, her computer pinged as a third email came through, pleading to delete the last one and apologising for her grumpy and demanding first message. Of course we deleted the missent email, but we've relished that glorious moment of *schadenfreude* ever since.

The 2014 Biennale was directed by Alya Sebti and curated by Hicham Khalidi and went on to be ranked in the top twenty biennales in the world. The photographer Leila Alaoui had worked with us for three editions, taking my portraits for various articles and generously introduced me to her generation of young Moroccan creatives. She was a hard-working free spirit who lived in Beirut and worked all over the world.

On 15 January 2016, I received a phone call from Leila's cousin Yalda. 'A ghastly thing has happened,' she whispered.

Yalda told me Leila had been caught up in gunfire during a terrorist attack on the Hotel Splendid in Ouagadougou, the capital of Burkina Faso. 'She's a fighter, Ness,' said Yalda. 'Someone so beautiful can't die.'

Burkina Faso is one of the poorest countries in the world but sadly the medics there are all too experienced at treating gun wounds, so there was real hope. Leila had been shot by a young Al-Qaeda follower who had been just one metre away from her and must have looked her in her terrified kind eyes, before her driver heroically threw himself in front of her, attempting to shield her from her attacker.

Two days later, Yalda called again. 'She didn't make it,' she said. For a while her words didn't sink in and were scrambled in my head: 'Sorry, Yalda, but what are you talking about?' And then I sat on the stairs, and Yalda and I wept silently into our phones.

Responsibility for the Biennale was squarely on my shoulders, but knowing that it's always best to leave when people still want you to stay, I stepped down as president and handed the baton over to Amine Kabbaj – it was time for Morocco to own the event. In truth, I was exhausted and it was bankrupting me. As an organisation without state funding, we'd always been on the financial back foot. Key sponsors are always nervous about backing a major event unless it will definitely be ongoing, which we couldn't guarantee. Still, Amine was optimistic.

In 2016, twelve years after its inception, the Biennale was overseen by Reem Fadda, a Palestinian curator seconded from the Guggenheim in New York. The town was hopping with events in fifty-two venues, including an energetic programme of street performance, and all the exhibits were free. The Biennale had come of age. That year it was dedicated to Leila.

* * *

The story of El Fenn has been just as eventful and no less challenging. Jess Bannister was working in Marrakech for the Biennale in December 2009, when she called me from the hotel. 'Ness, I don't want to be the bearer of bad news,' she said, 'but the staff here haven't been paid for two months.'

'What do you mean? Frederic hasn't told us of any problems.'

'Ness, listen to me – Frederic is the problem.'

Howell and I kick ourselves now – we'd had so much faith in Frederic, but we'd underestimated the pressure he'd been under and should have recognised the stress of designing, building and running El Fenn. We'd been given the odd indication that things were amiss – there were recurring issues with the plumbing that weren't being addressed, and he'd forgotten to arrange a pick-up for us from the airport – but instead of facing up to the impending meltdown, we chose to ignore the clues and hope they would disappear.

Gushing compliments are far easier to relay than negative reports, and even though many people had noticed a slippage at El Fenn, no one apart from Jess had had the courage to inform us. Howell and I flew out to encounter chaos: Frederic, having been overwhelmed by addiction, had had an almighty breakdown.

It was the week leading up to Christmas and the hotel was fully booked with high-profile guests including Kristin Scott Thomas. On the flight from London, we wondered what we were facing. After a tragic showdown with Frederic, Howell had to return to work in London, leaving me to assess the damage, reassign signatories for the bank accounts, change the locks and generally clean up the mess. To compound our difficulties, a member of the kitchen staff was agitating to start a union; instead of working together as a team, I was facing the nightmare of having the staff turn against us. Our haven of peace was sinking into a vision of hell and I had no one to turn to. I was the grown-up now.

I called a staff meeting, and all fifty of the team turned up. A semi-circle of expectant faces were looking up at me as I sat up on a bar stool in front of them. I noticed the four or five agitators standing at the back. I had no idea what I was going to say, but before I knew it, I realised that I was falling back on the mantras I had been brought up with. Mum's words pumped me up. 'Nessie, stop thinking about yourself. To be a good leader, you can't be popular with everyone.'

And with that I looked them in the eye and told them exactly what was going on. Thanking them all for holding El Fenn together under such difficult circumstances, I stated as clearly as I could that unless we hung together the future wouldn't be bright.

'I hear that a few of you have been gathering support for a union,' I said. 'But as you can imagine, a union would mean that every aspect of your working life would be regulated – no flexibility of rotas, no unexpected bonuses, no unofficial compassionate leave and threats rather than discussion.'

No one replied and then I said, 'Now, if you were the owner of El Fenn, what would you do in this situation?' The atmosphere in the room immediately became more relaxed and trust returned.

Two days before the holiday season began, we promoted Ahmed to head waiter, Housain to head of food and beverages, our receptionist Rushdi to temporary hotel manager and Fatima, one of the cleaners, to head of housekeeping. Jess and the other Biennale director, Clare Azzougarh and her rapper husband Tarik, a member of the Wu-Tang Clan, agreed to become temporary managers.

Howell and I had to find huge sums to cover the missing wages and had no choice but to borrow more money against our London homes. And then, just as we were beginning to think we could start breathing again, the gods threw another spanner in the works.

It was April 2010 and Jess and I were working on the Biennale in London. An item popped up on her Facebook news feed. 'Ness, there's been an explosion in the Argana café on Jemaa el-Fna.'

My phone rang. It was our new manager, Adrian Campbell-Howard. 'They think it's just some gas bottles exploding,' he said somewhat optimistically.

I went to Hyde Park, where a crowd of half a million people were watching Prince William's wedding to Kate Middleton. The little girls were all up dressed as fairy-tale princesses, while the older ones chorused, 'Over here, Harry!' whenever he appeared on the screen.

I returned home to the shocking news that twenty-six people had been killed by a bomb planted in the iconic Argana café. The impact this would have on El Fenn was instantly clear, a feeling confirmed when Handelsbanken, who had lent us the money to buy the properties next to El Fenn, got cold feet about investing in Morocco and refused to refinance our loan. The one positive of Frederic leaving and the collapse in visitor numbers after the bomb, was the realisation that Howell and I could no longer consider ourselves accidental hoteliers: we needed to up our game. First we arranged for Julia Spence, Navin's partner and my good friend, to handle our PR and then we hired Peter Chittick, who had previously worked for the Soho House, as our finance director. Peter was clear that 'if you can't measure it, you can't manage it' – we finally had goals and budgets and knew the size of the beast we had to tame.

Then came the Arab Spring. Although the countries concerned were thousands of miles away from Morocco, it was easy for the tourists to confuse Morocco with the embattled places they'd seen on their television screens. One after another North African regimes were toppled: the Tunisian revolution began in 17 December 2010, followed by Egypt in January, Libya in October and Syria soon after that. There were protests in Morocco but they were peaceful affairs that were quickly brought to an end by constitutional reform instituted by the king. All was going to be OK, *insha'Allah*.

* * *

In the following few years I was going to have to draw on the inner strength I'd first needed when I called the knacker's yard all those years before, a resilience that had grown when I walked into that Brighton clinic, when I faced Robert's betrayal and upon Shelagh's courageous death. I was attempting not to slip into toughness though – it protects emotional vulnerability but also closes your heart to the joy of birdsong.

Life was flashing by at a fearsome pace, and the four children were fast becoming adults. I was not only living my own life but theirs too, sending them off on gap years and to university, organising endless birthday parties and driving up and down the M4 to school and back. The house in Notting Hill had become 'Youth Central' and I took pleasure in cooking mounds of spaghetti and chicken casseroles for ever-hungry teenagers.

The pressure was beginning to take its toll, but I was incapable of saying no to new requests and ideas. Was I fearful of having time to think, or did I feel too unworthy to take the time to look after myself? So many people were depending on me for their livelihoods at El Fenn and the Biennale, and I was also running TEDx Marrakech and managing The Farm and Eilean Shona. My parents and children also needed more of my time, while my relationship with Robert was less than supportive. There was a risk that I would sink, but I doggedly sailed on, right into the eye of the storm.

3

NEVERLAND FOUND

It was March 2011 when Lindy, Mum, Dad, Matthew, Joe and
Jess Bannister, Navin and Julia, Robert, Mark and Amanda Tandy
and Clare and I gathered in the theatre at Marlborough College to

watch Ivo play John Proctor in *The Crucible* by Arthur Miller. He lit up the stage and the audience was enthralled. Knowing how much it meant to his youngest grandchild, Dad had drawn on all his remaining strength, determined to be there. Aged ninety-three, he found it an effort to get dressed, let alone drive in a car for two hours and sit through a long play. After the show he shook hands with Ivo, who bent down and kissed his grandfather's cheek. Feeling overwhelmed by the number of people swarming around, I gave Dad a cursory kiss and waved him off.

The following weekend I flew to Marrakech to take part in a panel that was selecting artists for a residency programme. Before dashing out to work, I called home for a quick chat with Dad. Unusually, his housekeeper Beverly answered.

'They're just carrying the body downstairs now Vanessa,' she said softly. I let the phone flop away from my ear. My mind struggled to make sense of her words.

'Thank you, Beverly. Sorry, could I call you back in a minute? There's someone at the door?' I lied, unable to continue talking.

I sat on the side of the bed, trying to clear my head. 'OK, Ness,' I said under my breath, 'pull yourself together.'

I rang the hotel reception. 'Fatima, please could you get me on the first flight to London?' My words sounded strange. 'I think my father may have died.'

I sank back on the bed, grateful for the sanctuary of my cool room. A discordant cacophony of voices swirled around as holy men tuned their voices for morning prayers before the imam at the Katoubia began his loud incantation, releasing a city-wide crescendo of song: 'Allahu Akbar.'

And then there was a knock on the door, and the El Fenn staff filed in to pay their respects, quietly holding my hands in theirs and looking me in the eye, as they each said, 'Madam, I am so sorry to hear of your loss.' And with these words the fact is gently driven home: it is true. My father is dead.

That afternoon I joined the artist Yto Barrada, who was also on the selection panel. She didn't raise her voice above a whisper as we wallowed in a shaded pool, the quiet hours provided a soothing balm as I took my first steps in the foothills of grief.

A car arrived to take me to the airport. 'Yto, thank you so much for understanding my need for quiet this afternoon,' I said. 'I'm really touched by your thoughtfulness.'

'Actually Vanessa,' she whispered, 'it's just that I've lost my voice.' I gave her a hearty hug before getting in the car to begin my journey home. How that would have made Dad chuckle.

* * *

We organised a simple funeral service at Chichester Crematorium. I drove there with Navin and Julia via the funeral director's, where we adorned my father's wicker coffin with the spring flowers we'd picked that morning. I found the notion of his lifeless body being only two inches from my hands almost impossible to fathom.

Driving to the funeral, Navin broke the silence. 'Did you know that Chichester Crematorium is one of the best in the country?' he asked.

'No,' I replied, somewhat surprised.

'Yes, it's the crème de la crème,' he said. We were still giggling as we got out of the car, ready to give Dad a fitting send-off.

Following the service and gathering at Cakeham, a few of us walked down to the beach. I sat detached in grief but surrounded by kindness as we all watched Navin, Richard and Theo Oulton walk tentatively over the shingle before plunging into the sea, their whoops mingling with the sound of crashing waves for a mere two minutes before they hobbled back towards us, clutching their freezing balls.

Dad would have been horrified to think of his death causing us misery. I wanted to respect his spirit and not allow the numbness to last too long, but I didn't realise then that his death would trigger a sequence of trials that would test my health and sanity. It would be another five years before I began writing this book, and it would take me until I finished this final chapter to acknowledge the powerful forces that had been both my undoing and my redemption.

The following year, the blows that rained down on me were almost biblical in their ferocity. One of our boys became unwell, the Great House on Necker burnt down and my car was written off by someone running a traffic light. I'd steadily borrowed eye-watering sums against my house over the years, and the banks began putting pressure on me to pay off my debts. Climate change was also wreaking havoc: after three months of drought, the tinder-dry undergrowth on Eilean Shona caught fire, and two-thirds of the island was engulfed in flames, before a hurricane felled swathes of ancient woodland. To compound the stress, the finances of the Biennale were out of control, and I felt responsible for the debts. The onslaught felt comical in its relentlessness so, when I received the call that The Farm had suffered a serious flood, I could do nothing but laugh.

The following summer we were holidaying on Eilean Shona. After a picnic on Gortchen Sands, my mind set upon an epic swim. 'I'm not sure this is a good idea, Ness,' Robert said, cutting the engine and bringing the rib to a shuddering stop. Shoe Bay was deserted, with not a footprint in the fine sand.

Wine from our lunch on the mainland had lightened the mood among our landing party. The dogs leapt ashore and chased each other in circles. Ivo carried the anchor onto higher ground while we rolled out of the boat.

'Come on, let's give it a go,' I said. 'If we don't do it today, we never will.' The familiar sensation of changing gear from random idea to stubborn plan took over, as Robert shook his head.

Three of our party silently paddled up beside us in kayaks as a dozen seagulls fussed over a scrap of fish, their whiteness catching a ray of sun, brilliant against the grey sky. Matthew became agitated, his visceral fear of the sea caught in his throat as he tried to intervene. 'Chaps, let's just go home on the boat – I really don't like this at all.'

'The tide is with us,' I persisted. 'That'll give us a sporting chance.'

'I know, Ness,' Robert replied, 'but the wind is whipping the waves in this direction – it's going to be a horrible swim.'

By now it was late afternoon and there was no time to dither. 'Come on, Rob. Don't be such a spoilsport,' I said. The idea of wading into the choppy water and swimming the two miles home made me feel sick with apprehension, but something was driving me on. Something buried deep inside me wanted to prove that I was worthy of Robert, that I was unbreakable – even if it killed me.

We were no strangers to swimming in Scottish waters, which are a maximum twelve degrees Celsius even at the height of the summer. We understood that once you're in the water it takes a minute to calm your panicked breathing, two minutes for the pain to disappear and then a further five minutes before the sensation of well-being washes over you. But we'd never embarked on a swim this ambitious before.

'Jesus, Mary and Joseph,' Navin cursed, removing his sweater. Florence joined in the chorus of nervous laughter as she stripped down too. 'Yikes, Mum – this is insane.'

Navin, Robert, Flo and I tiptoed into the water and hopped from one foot to the other before running, whooping and diving in. We emerged, punching the air, and then put our heads down and set off.

Being a strong swimmer I knew that the cold, rather than exhaustion, was going to be my enemy and that I'd have to dig deep to overcome its effects. Bloody hell, it was cold. A turbo-charge of adrenalin shot into my system, my vision narrowed and I found my rhythm. Kick, kick, crawl, breathe.

I lost sight of the others. Pete, my designated minder, paddled beside me, though we didn't talk. I focused on the jetty. Kick, kick, crawl, breathe. A curious seal bobbed up in front of me. I ploughed on.

After about half an hour I noticed my fingers begin to curl, forming a fist rather than a paddle, as every spare drop of blood retreated to my core. This was clearly not good, but I told myself to keep calm. Panic at your peril.

'Are you ok, Ness?'

I attempted a cheery thumbs up and pushed on, but it crossed my mind that even if I needed rescuing, the air temperature wasn't going to warm me up and we hadn't thought to bring any extra clothes. In any case, the likelihood of me toppling Pete into the water while clambering onto his kayak was high. There was always the RIB, I reassured myself. Kick, kick, crawl, breathe.

'Robert has given up,' Pete said, encouraging me on. 'Ivo has taken him back to the house. The others are a little behind but still going strong. You're well over halfway.'

I tried to answer Pete, but my tongue wouldn't work and I gurgled like a stroke victim. There was no rescue boat now, but no fear. I had no thought but to reach the jetty, and no idea how far I had left to go. And then the effort was just too great. I stopped swimming and felt a peace flood my being. I just wanted to sleep. No more struggle.

They say that your entire life flashes before you just before you drown. Not so with me. I just remembered the Tanyards pool, with Lindy wrapping me in a warm towel, and as I closed my eyes I saw the smiling faces of each of my children.

Pete yelling from the jetty, fifty metres away, woke me. 'Come on Ness, you're nearly there. You're going to do it – don't stop swimming.' I kicked on, doing what I was told, strength arriving from nowhere. Pete hauled me onto the jetty and I sat for a second on the concrete before passing out. Then Flo swam in, youth on her side. Her quick thinking saved my life, I'm sure of it now. She ran up to the house, shouting to Robert to run a hot bath while Pete carried me close behind, my head slumped and limbs floppy.

I lay in the bath, aware of Flo on top of me shouting, 'Come back Mummy – don't leave us. Wake up.' I was floating down through a dark green, velvet-lined tunnel.

Robert was adding more hot water to the bath, as our frozen bodies rapidly cooled the water down. He made me some porridge and tea, in order to get some heat into my core. My blood surged, and my heart pounded once again. I was as sick as a dog and then fell asleep, waking a little stunned but very much alive. I'd managed the swim unbroken.

When stress mounts incrementally, many of us don't act to lessen the load until it's too late. Everything had been crumbling around me, but after the swim I realised I had to turn my life around. The way to do this was not only to stop battling upstream, but to get out of the water altogether.

To achieve this would take all the effort I could muster, but once I was committed to a change of direction, nothing could get in my path. There was no room for emotion to distract me from my course – I simply had to get from this breaking point to a place of peace.

Robert and I were 'talked out' – there was nothing more to say and we were unable to reconcile our conflicting narratives: I was still hurt, smarting with a sense of injustice, and he was still angry at my inability to understand. My blood pressure became dangerously high after Mum broke her hip and the replacement hip became infected with a superbug. I could literally hear my surging blood pressure, the whooshing pulses resembling a washing machine churning in my ear.

My first job was to sell the London house and pay off my debts. Robert felt the family house had been the glue that held us together. It was time to let him go free. Oh, how we both struggled, but I could allow no empathy for Robert's plight without tearing my own heart out in the process. When we moved out, I drove in one direction while he drove off in another. Within months he had a new girlfriend in South Africa. An era had come to an end.

Before the new owner's demolition cranes moved in, Florence formed the Ladbroke Terrace Collective, and for a fortnight in September our rambling family home of twenty years was turned into a gloriously chaotic stage for artists, musicians, writers and poets. The madness of creativity exorcised dark memories from the grand Georgian terrace and momentarily returned the now genteel area of bankerdom to the vibrant and creative Notting Hill of my youth.

But still the demons hovered, their ugly chants asking 'Where did you go wrong?', 'How could you have failed your children like that?' and 'If only you'd done that differently...' Cruel words from the past played out over and over again.

Moving into a new house with the children, along with Bodley, of course, continued the healing process. You can choose the memories you carry with you, and I dumped a skip's worth in the recycling bins, but still those damned voices chanted on – I just couldn't throw them off: 'You've failed, Vanessa. Without a man by your side you are nothing. If you'd done things differently, just imagine how your family would be today...'

The children and I talked about the past and how we were all dealing with our new situation. No one would have realised how much effort we were making to come to terms with where we found ourselves and how to move forward.

* * *

A fitting memorial for Dad was in order, and my friend and colleague Lauren and I did him proud by organising a gathering at the Royal Geographical Society. Navin yet again stepped up to the challenge, throwing himself into presenting a kind of 'This Is Your Life' that would capture Dad's joyous twinkle and entertain the audience. The grandchildren contributed by showing films or giving readings. Richard spoke about how he had telephoned Dad almost every day for advice and how much pleasure he took in every minute he spent with him. And of course, we all celebrated his easy, deep, contagious laugh. Then Peter Gabriel sat down at the piano and moved us all to tears with the song that he had written after his own father's death, 'Father, Son'.

And then we partied, raising glass after glass of gin and tonic to that extraordinary man and toasting his oft-quoted catchphrase: 'Isn't life wonderful.'

* * *

After taking over the presidency of the Marrakech Biennale, Amine Kabbaj called me to say that something remarkable had happened but I was to keep it a secret. He'd received a call from Mohammed VI's palace – we were to receive the king's medal for our services to the arts. I was to be made an Officer of the Order of Ouissam Alaouite. Clive Alderton, the British Ambassador, called to congratulate me.

'Thank you, Clive,' I replied, 'but I'm sure it's no big deal.'

'Come now, Vanessa,' he said. 'This is a very big honour indeed, the equivalent of receiving a knighthood in the UK. It's a sign of real respect and gratitude from the nation.'

I flew to Rabat the following day. Amine and I had lunch and then walked to the new Museum of Contemporary Art, where we were greeted by Clive. While we were waiting in the gallery, I looked around and noticed how many of the works in the collection had been commissioned by me, during the Biennale. Then trumpets sounded and the king's guard entered, chanting a mesmeric incantation before reaching an astonishing whooshing climax, and then in walked the man himself. I almost fainted as I walked up the red carpet, filmed for national TV as members of the Moroccan government and the museum staff looked on.

I caught Clive's eye and he nodded, encouraging me to step before the king.

'Miss Branson,' the king said. 'May I take this opportunity to thank you for all you have done for this country?'

'Thank you, Your Highness. I am most honoured.'

'I am afraid I may rip your shirt as I pin on this heavy medal,' he said as he picked up the gold star from its velvet box, which was held by an assistant.

'Your Highness, it would give me great pleasure to have my shirt ripped by you,' I replied, before realising what I'd said. He caught my eye and smiled.

To lighten my burden, more unexpected help landed in front of Howell and me just when we needed it, when Willem Smit agreed to take over the role of manager at El Fenn. I was a little wary of how his Dutch tell-it-as-it-is personality would play out with the spiritual Moroccans. However, after a succession of notes had been slipped under my door by disgruntled staff, Willem transformed El Fenn into the elegant hotel it is today, thanks to his enduring humour, his attention to detail and his understanding of how a hotel should be run.

The final weight was lifted from my shoulders when Graham Head and Madeline Weinrib bought into El Fenn, giving Howell and me the opportunity to recoup our initial investment and give Willem some equity in the business. I hadn't realised how rewarding it would be to build an entity strong enough to interest others in investing in it. El Fenn now has the necessary thirty suites and over one hundred attentive staff to manage them. The restaurant, bar and terraces are the best place in town to hang out and our store is a retail sensation; maybe all our work has been worth it after all.

***

Eilean Shona, January 2018

Bebe, my little black cocker spaniel, sat between Navin and myself as we sprinted up the length of the country to Eilean Shona in our rattling rental van. With my proceeds from the sale of our El Fenn shares, I'm buying Robert out of his half of the island. Navin is cataloguing and removing Robert's library while I'm finishing writing this book. Poetry is being carried on the breeze and infiltrating our thoughts.

We're staying in Tioram Cottage overlooking Loch Moidart, the tides ebbing and flowing as the blue moon exerts its powerful will. The weather rolls in over the Atlantic, a gale one day and snow the next, followed by periods of still, bright cold or blustery rain.

Robert predicted that our children, having experienced such trauma during their childhood, would grow up to become artists. He was correct, although I'm not sure he imagined their work would tackle their conflicted lives so directly. Louis has spent the last two years making a film initially called *The Great Rift Walk*, that set out to follow Robert on a heroic 5,500-kilometre walk along the Rift Valley, but soon evolved into *The Rift*, the story of a father and son confronting their relationship. By addressing the past, he has transformed his unhappiness into something quite beautiful, a film of courage and honesty.

The day is clear, blue and cold. I crunch my way up the snowy woodland path to the village hall, the island's very own version of an internet café, and settle down to read my emails.

Dear Ness,

I want to try to keep this short and clear. I accept sole and complete responsibility for ending our marriage.

For over twenty years I have allowed my attempts to explain and understand what happened to obscure the truth. Which is that whatever the circumstances of our relationship and whatever my state of mind it was me that jumped ship, shattered my marriage vows and reneged on my commitments to those that I love most. It was my actions for which I take sole responsibility that caused such a mountain of pain and suffering to you and to our children.

Sorry is a completely inadequate word in the circumstances but sorry I am – deeply, deeply. You have every right to be angry and to want me to be entirely absent from your life. It is pathetic that it has taken me this time, and watching myself in Louis's film, to come to this realisation. If I could wind back the clock and behave differently I would. I would pay more attention, be more caring of our relationship, be more aware of mine and of your feelings and not enter into an extra-marital affair.

But these words amount to nothing. I don't know what I can do apart from leave you in peace and respect whatever boundaries you care to set.

Rx

I shut the computer and close my eyes. We have been released.

* * *

The story is drawing to a close. The last year I've spent writing this book has been magical. Friends and family have taken on a new significance as I've mapped out how their lives interwove through mine. Some potent spells have been at play, as locked doors concealing unexplored mysteries have opened as I've approached each chapter.

When I began writing, I had no idea where this book was going to lead me. I simply clawed my fingers through the sediment of the river of my past, disrupting deep-buried air pockets of memories and catching the bubbles as they wobbled their way to the surface. But a year of reflection is enough; it's time to get on with living.

This story started with the birth of my father in 1918 and ends with the joyous news of the impending birth of our first grandchild – for Noah and his wife Honor are expecting a baby boy in June 2018, almost exactly one hundred years later.

In the evenings, Navin and I sit by the fire and listen to music, drink wine and talk of love and loyalty, history and adventure. We also talk of the next generation – of how capable they are and how happy we are to be handing the baton over to them. We discuss the influences of past generations and the forces that have taken us along the roads we travel on today and we speculate about the adventures that the coming years hold in store. We are grateful for our experiences, taking pleasure in the simple memories of walks, nature and friends.

'Do you think you're any wiser, one year on?' asked Navin, referring to our anxious day spent sitting by the Buddha.

'I don't know about wiser, but one thing's for sure – I've certainly learned a lot. It's wonderful to realise that almost every person you meet will have some significance later on in your life.'

Navin nods.

The truth is, I think to myself, absentmindedly stroking Bebe behind her ear, I do still kick myself for past mistakes, but with acceptance now. I'm beginning to understand that the secret to living in harmony comes from knowing when to battle against the elements and when to sail with the wind.

I top up our wine glasses, while Navin empties the last of the coal onto the dwindling fire. 'So what do you reckon are the ingredients needed for a life well lived?'

My clever friend then pauses before summing up our conversation. 'I think the Beatles had the answer,' he says. 'Amor est omnia quibus cares. All You Need is Love.'

'Och, you're a cunning linguist, Navin.' We chuckle. The old jokes are the best.

Flo, who has embraced the myth that those born in the caul possess witchy powers, tells me that when you reach fifty-eight, your Saturn returns. I believe her: change in the air.

I can already feel another chapter beginning, for, as Mum is often heard to say, and I'm never sure if it's a threat or a promise: 'You live for an awfully long time!'

LIST OF ILLUSTRATIONS

Front cover photograph
Me, Menorca, 1967.

'Sloe Gin', p. 3.
Ted Branson, Eilean Shona, *c* 2006.

'Mysteries Solved', p. 9.
Mona Branson, Invergloy House, Loch Lochy, *c* 1905.

'Museum of Curiosities', p. 19.
The Branson family, *c* 1900: my grandfather George (*third from left*) with his brothers, holding their sister Olive aloft.

'Ted's War', p. 35.
My father, Ted Branson, 1939.

'Deepest Darkest Devon', p. 47.
My mother, Eve Huntley-Flindt, *c* 1930.

'Mother Courage', p. 61.
My mother in her ENSA uniform, *c* 1946.

'Love Is the Devil', p. 73.
My parents, Eve and Ted Branson, 1949.

'Pear Drops, Robots and Budgerigars', p. 85.
With Mum, Richard and Lindy, Guildford, 1959.

'Peafucks and Roebucks', p. 97.
With Richard and Lindy, 1966.

'For Better, For Worse', p. 111.
With Mum, 1967.

'Trunks, Kicks and Shoplifting', p. 127.
With Lindy, Menorca, 1966.

'Dusk Over Fields', p. 143.
With Nabeel Ali, 1974.

'Aunt Clare's Story', p. 159.
My aunt, Clare Hoare, with Douglas Bader, *c* 1946.

'Two Slightly Distorted Guitars', p. 167.
'Froggy Went A-Courting' by Mike Oldfield, Virgin Records, 1974.

'Finding Beauty', p. 179.
The Annunication by Simone Martini and Lippo Memmi, 1333.

'Working Girl', p. 193.
Me at my pre-wedding lunch, 1983.

'Portobello', p. 205.
Responsible Hedonism by William Kentridge, 1986.

'Necker Island Dreaming', p. 223.
With Robert, 1988.

'Great Storms, Life and Death', p. 233.
Robert and Louis, 1991.

'Wannabe', p. 245.
The Devereux Family, 1995. © Catherine Yass and courtesy of Alison Jacques Gallery, London.

'Monument to the Midlife Crisis', p. 261.
Monument to the Midlife Crisis by Grayson Perry, 1999.

'And All the Men and Women Merely Players', p. 275.
With Shelagh Macleod, 2000.

'The Rose City', p. 291.
Noah, Florence, Louis and Ivo for our family Christmas card (with apologies to Gillian Wearing), 1999.

'My Arab Spring', p. 307.
With Dad in Marrakech, 2006.

MY LITTLE DEVILS

To my wonderful friends and family, who have led me into temptation, thank you.

Jack Abel Smith, Ned Abel Smith, Louis Adamakoh, Ucef Adel, Joe Addison, Michael Addison, Wendy Addison, Ajaz Ahmed, Meryl Ainslie, Lhoussaine Ait Oufkir, Sultan bin Salman Al Saud, Basma Al Sulaiman, Christine Alaoui, Faycal Alaoui, Leila Alaoui, Yalda Alaoui, Morten Albeck, Catriona Alderton, Clive Alderton, Alia Ali, Nabeel Ali, France Aline, Sarah Allan, Josh Allot, Renato Arruda, Chris Ayling, André Azoulay, Ahmed Azzeroi, Clare Azzougarh, Tarik Azzougarh, Angie Bailey, Beezy Bailey, Jessica Bannister, Joseph Bannister, Matthew Bannister, Raffaella Barker, Carolyn Barker-Mill, Yto Barrada, Steve Barron, Kate Barton, Niall Barton, Taïs Bean, Patrick Benjaminsson, Zizou Bennis,

Elaine Bentley, Omar Berrada, Ken Berry, Jane Birt, Neil Blake, Sandra Blake, Milly Boath, Anne Bonavero, Yves Bonavero, Katrine Boorman, John Booth, Kitty Bowler, Don Boyd, Hilary Boyd, Jimmy Boyle, Alice Bragg, Eve Branson, Holly Branson, Joan Branson, Lindy Branson, Mona Branson, Richard Branson, Sam Branson, Ted Branson, Ludo Brockway, Milo Brockway, Otto Brockway, Annabel Brooks, Elizabeth Brooks, Rory Brooks, Louisa Buck, Andrea Bury, Mohamed Bzizi, Nanette Capapas, Carson Chan, Paul-Gordon Chandler, India Chaplin, Richard Charkin, Consuelo Child-Villiers, Penelope Chilvers, Peter Chittick, Alexandra Chong, Yu-Chee Chong, Jonathan Church, Ulrik Christensen, Helen Clarke, Benedicte Clarkson, Carol Cocks, Michelle Cohen, Brenda Coleman, Mat Collishaw, Brendan Cox, Geraldine Cox, Peter Crawford, Ed Cross, Suhaila Cross, Abel Damoussi, Thomas Dane, Sally Davey, Janie Davis, Charlotte de Klee, Lara de Klee, Rupert de Klee, James Dearden, Gaby Dellal, Hamish Dewar, Barbara Devereux, Clare Devereux, Florence Devereux, Honor Devereux, Ivo Devereux, Louis Devereux, Noah Devereux, Robert Devereux, Lauren Dorman, Simon Draper, Mags Dyce, Pep Duran Esteva, Patrick Eakin Young, Jim Edmondson, Touria El Glaoui, Louise Elms, Jeremiah Emmanuel, Tracey Emin, Brian Eno, Delfina Entrecanales, Garth Evans, Kos Evans, Annabel Evans, Poppy Evans, Tim Evans, Reem Fadda, Catherine Faulks, Veronica Faulks, Charmaine Faulker, Eric Fellner, Juliet Fellows, Portia Fellows, Sarah Fenwick, Ed Fidoe, Christiana Figures, Wendy Fisher, Gill Fitzhugh, Matthew Flowers, Peter Gabriel, Carmen Galofre, Frances Galloway, Pablo Ganguli, Adrienne Garrard, Michael Gentle, Gini Godwin, Brenda Goldblatt, Michael Gollner, Mary Gordon Lennox, Antony Gormley, Jill Gosney, Luke Gottelier, Gail Gower, Taymour Grahne, Linda Grant, Jill Green, Viv Guinness, Hassan Hajjaj, Sue Hale, Louise Hallett, Niall Hamilton, Belinda Hancock, Laura Harris, Orlando Harris, Charlotte Harrison, Cynthia Harrison, Simon Hawksley, Graham Head, Lisa Hendricks, Steve Hendricks, Juliet Hill, Clare Hoare, David Hoare, Gerard Hoare, Jammy Hoare, Ro Hoare, Robert Hoare, Marion Hollis, Tim

Hollis, Trevor Hopkins, Anthony Horowitz, Colin Hosking, Jill Hosking, Sarah Howgate, Nick Humphrey, Margaret Hunter, Doc Huntley Flindt, Rupert Huntley Flindt, Said Jabaoui, Lee Jaffe, Howell James, Khurram Jamil, Dede Johnston, Sasha Jones, Amine Kabbaj, Abdellah Karroum, Dillie Keane, William Kentridge, Tarka Kings, Paul Kindersley, Sigrid Kirk, Clare Kirkman, Joe Knatchbull, Philip Knatchbull, Kevin Krausert, Meja Kullersten, Fiona L'Estrange, Eddie Lawrence, Othman Lazraq, Kate Lee, Wolfe Lenkiewicz, Annie Lennox, Ian Lewis, Marie Lewis, Hal Lindes, Amy Liptrot, Jonathan Lloyd, Robert Loder, Cas Lokko, Karl Lokko, Megan Lloyd Davies, Jenni Lomax, Rose Lord, Meryanne Loum-Martin, Eric Lundgren, Kate MacGarry, Lorna Macleod, Tala Madani, Sue Manning, Kenza Melehi, Curt Marcus, Peggy Markel, Amanda Marmot, Gary Martin, Sandra Masur, Dan May, Mourad Mazouz, Bridget McCrum, Hugo Macdonald, Lorna Macleod, Shelagh Macleod, Kate MccGwire, Joann McPike, Mouna Mekouar, Kenza Melehi, Vincent Melehi, Nachson Mimran, Miles Moreland, Natasha Moreland, Polly Morgan, Lucy Morris, Michael Morris, Paul Moss, Kate Mosse, Danny Moynihan, Carlos Moysie, Nuria Moysie, Valeria Napoleone, Jon Nash, Stephen Navin, Alice Neel, Hartley Neel, Phil Nevin, Annie Newell, Chris Newell, Hilary Newiss-Bazalgette, Jerona Noonan, Anthea Norman-Taylor, Peter Norris, Essic North, Freya North, Prue O'Day, Andrew O'Hagan, Emma O'Hea, Hermione O'Hea, Angie O'Rourke, Jean Oelwang, Deedy Ogden, David Ogilvy, Ben Okri, Colleen Olianti, Anatol Orient, Joanna Oulton, Richard Oulton, Romey Oulton, Theo Oulton, Kirsten Ovstaas, Vicken Parsons, Priti Paul, Nina Pawlowsky, Holly Peppe, Grayson Perry, Philippa Perry, Jacquie Perryman, Phoebe Pershouse, Fred Pollock, Madeleine Ponsonby, Nik Powell, Alexandra Pringle, Simon Prosser, Richard Reed, Pascale Revert, Anneka Rice, Bels Rice, Fatima Rim, Penny Robinson, James Rodrigues, Sukie Roessel, Tara Rowse, Sarah Rugheimer, Bodley Ryle, Sallie Ryle, Nadim Samman, Catherine Samy, Zina Saro-Wiwa, Faith Savage Gollner, Frederic Scholl,

Alya Sebti, Czaee Shah, Elizabeth Sheinkman, Alex Smilansky, Willem Smit, Penny Smith, Ginny Snape, Andrew Soloman, Scott Spector, Camilla Spence, Julia Spence, Pidge Spencer, Roman St Clair, Guy Staight, Katie Staight, Susannah Stapleton, Nico Stead, Octavia Stead, Richard Stead, Charlie Stebbings, Anna Steiger, Caro Stewart, James Stevens, Charles Sturridge, Monika Sulakova, Mark Tandy, Napper Tandy, Paddy Tandy, Dominique Taylor, Pennie Taylor, David Teiger, Yvonne Thomson, Caragh Thuring, Guy Tillim, Kristen Tomassi, Hans Ulrich Obrist, Francis Upritchard, Eric Van Hove, Stefan Van Raay, Hughena Waddington, Paul Waddington, Mats Wahlstrom, Philippa Walker, John Walsh, Ruby Wax, Eilean Webber, Georgie Weedon, Madeline Weinrib, Suzy Wells, Carinthia West, Louise Wheeler, Peter Wheeler, Clare Whitaker, Hilary Whitehall, Jack Whitehall, Fiona Whitney, John Whitney, Roma Whitney, Andrew Williams, Kate Winslet, Alan Yentob, Louisa Young, Osman Yousefzada, Jochen Zeitz, Robin Zendell, Fatima Zour.

NOTE ON THE TYPE

The text of this book is set in Linotype Sabon, a typeface named after the type founder, Jacques Sabon. It was designed by Jan Tschichold and jointly developed by Linotype, Monotype and Stempel in response to a need for a typeface to be available in identical form for mechanical hot metal composition and hand composition using foundry type.

Tschichold based his design for Sabon roman on a font engraved by Garamond, and Sabon italic on a font by Granjon. It was first used in 1966 and has proved an enduring modern classic.

NOTE ON THE AUTHOR

Vanessa Branson is an entrepreneur and the founder of the Marrakech Biennale. Between 1986 and 1991 she founded and ran the Vanessa Devereux Gallery on London's Portobello Road.

She owns and runs Eilean Shona, an island on the west coast of Scotland, as well as co-owning El Fenn, a landmark hotel in Marrakech. In October 2014 she was awarded the royal distinction of Officer of the Order of Ouissam Alaouite for her contributions to Moroccan arts and culture.

She is a trustee of the British Moroccan Society, the Leila Alaoui Foundation, Virgin Unite and the Global Diversity Foundation, and is on the board of Area9 Lyceum.